Solutions for Human Resource Managers

SHRM Information Center

SOCIETY FOR
HUMAN
RESOURCE
MANAGEMENT

ISBN 1-58644-003-9

DEDICATED TO OUR MENTOR AND FRIEND
MICHAEL R. LOSEY, SPHR, CAE, PRESIDENT AND CEO
OF THE SOCIETY FOR HUMAN RESOURCE MANAGEMENT, 1990–2000.

PREFACE

Solutions for Human Resource Managers reflects the questions typically received by the SHRM Information Center. The Information Specialists who wrote this book responded to more than 60,000 questions in 1999 alone on all aspects of Human Resources. We expect to answer 70,000 in the year 2000. The Information Center is currently staffed by 10 Information Specialists (9 full-time and 1 part-time), who respond to member's inquiries. The typical Information Specialist handles about 40 requests each day.

As we rank the top five areas of most frequently asked questions, the list begins with the Fair Labor Standards Act and discusses exempt/nonexempt issues. The Family Medical Leave Act is almost tied for first place with questions on all aspects of its administration. In third place are calls concerning the Americans with Disabilities Act and reasonable accommodation. Fourth is innovative ways of recruiting in the tight labor market. In fifth place are questions on performance management of employees and termination scenarios.

We hope that you will use this book to answer the many questions that you tackle in your day-to-day activities as an HR professional. As a member of SHRM, feel free to contact the Information Center to obtain answers about any additional questions that are not covered in this book. If you are not a member, you might consider joining so you can experience the services that SHRM has to offer. To learn more about SHRM, please see our web site at <www.shrm.org>. If you have questions or comments about the book, please direct them to our e-mail address at <infocen@ shrm.org>.

I would like to acknowledge the Information Specialists' hard work and dedication thoughout the year to complete this project: Lisa Clayborne, PHR; Bob Dix, CCP; Amy Maingault, PHR; Tim O'Reilly, SPHR; Anne St. Martin, PHR, CEBS; Coleen Shrout; Naomi Svendsen; Chris Tyler, SPHR; and Monica Waropaj.

I would also like to thank Deb Keary, Director of the Information Center, for her contribution and support throughout the project. Finally, I must mention the editorial services of Publications Professionals LLC for all the time and hard work that group committed to producing this book.

Elizabeth D. Bahnsen, SPHR, CCP
Senior Information Specialist
Society for Human Resource Management

Contents

Chapter 1   Human Resource Management.................................1

Background 1

Selection for Downsizing...................................12

Chapter 2   General Employment Practices.........................23

Laws...23

Affirmative Action Plans 26

Americans with Disabilities Act.............................29

Performance Reviews 32

Age Discrimination in Employment Act 37

Employee Terminations 39

Employee Survey..45

Employee Handbook Versus Policy Manual 46

Sexual Harassment..49

Employee Conduct..50

Chapter 3   Staffing 63

Pre-employment...63

Staffing changes 73

Adverse Staffing Practices 74

Equal Employment Opportunity.............................76

Recruitment..80

Questions for Employment Applications.....................87

Chapter 4   Human Resource Development.........................101

Training Program Cost-Benefit Analysis 115

Chapter 5   Compensation 119

General 119

Fair Labor Standards Act 133

Chapter 6   Benefits 151

General 151

Consolidated Omnibus Budget Reconciliation
Act (COBRA)..161

        Family and Medical Leave Act (FMLA) 165

        Retirement...172

    CHAPTER 7   EMPLOYEE AND LABOR RELATIONS..........................177

    CHAPTER 8   HEALTH, SAFETY, AND SECURITY.............................193

    CHAPTER 9   INTERNATIONAL HUMAN RESOURCES......................211

TABLE 1–1   SAMPLE AUDIT...6

TABLE 3–1   APPLICANT FLOW LOG: NUMBER OF HIRES 69

TABLE 3–2   APPLICANT FLOW LOG: RECORD OF HIRES 69

TABLE 3–3   SAMPLE EMPLOYMENT REQUISITION.................................75

TABLE 4–1   WHEN SELECTING TRAINERS FOR THE ROLE OF ANALYZER 103

TABLE 4–2   WHEN SELECTING TRAINERS FOR THE ROLE OF DESIGNER 103

TABLE 4–3   WHEN SELECTING TRAINERS FOR THE ROLE OF DEVELOPER...........104

TABLE 4–4   WHEN SELECTING TRAINERS FOR THE ROLE OF DELIVERER.............104

TABLE 4–5   WHEN SELECTING TRAINERS FOR THE ROLE OF EVALUATOR...........104

TABLE 4–6   COST BREAKDOWN 116

TABLE 5–1   SALARY GRADE—PERFORMANCE LEVEL RELATIONSHIP 129

TABLE 5–2   EXAMPLE OF A MATRIX BASED ON EVALUATION RATING...................132

TABLE 6–1   UNIFORM PREMIUM TABLE EFFECTIVE JULY 1, 1999 160

TABLE 6–2   2000 LIMITS ON BENEFITS...172

TABLE 8–1   SAMPLE ACCIDENT REPORT..198

HUMAN RESOURCE MANAGEMENT

Background

Q 1:   Is it Human Resources Department or Human Resource Department?

> **A:** The simple answer is that it's Human Resource Department. The phrase *human resource* (singular) is used as an adjective. It comes before a noun, for example, the subject of a sentence such as "A human resource professional is the best source of benefits data." The adjective *human resource* modifies the noun *professional*. However, the plural form of the phrase *human resources* is used as a noun. It can be the subject or object of a sentence. For example, one would say, "Ask Human Resources about the benefit plan." *Human resources* in the plural form is the subject of that sentence. The abbreviation HR can be used as either the noun or the adjective.

Q 2:   What is the typical HR reporting structure?

> **A:** The reporting structure really depends on HR's role in the company. Companies that view HR as strategic partners normally have the most senior HR person report directly to the President, Chief Executive Officer (CEO), or Chief Operating Officer (COO). An HR Department that plays more of a traditional role may not report to the President but rather to the Chief Financial Officer (CFO) or Vice President (VP) of Administration.

Q 3:   What should we include in an HR budget?

> **A:** The objectives of an HR budget should be to maintain departmental or organizational controls and to provide performance measurements. Predicting costs for HR can be difficult, but they can be simplified by doing your homework. You should collect as much information initially as possible. Good sources of information include the previous year's budget, the organizational goals, the current operating and capital expenditure budget, an analysis of major contracts, any new sales or contract bids, activity reports, the meeting minutes and reports of internal and external auditors, and the discussions with various staff members. Additional sources would

be anything that would indicate the need to spend money in the coming year.

From this information, the budget can be compiled for the upcoming year. Using the information collected, an HR professional will be able to make decisions such as knowing when to increase or decrease allocated amounts, when to create new categories, or when to delete them. Some of the categories that may be included in the budget:

- Compensation
  - Salaries and wages
  - Incentives and bonuses
  - Overtime
- Benefits
  - Social security
  - Retirement
  - Long-term disability
  - Medical
  - Dental
  - Vision
  - Life insurance
- Training
  - Tuition assistance
  - Seminars
  - Outside trainers
  - Training materials
- Travel
  - Conferences
  - On-site visits
- Employee Services
  - Wellness programs
  - Recreational activities
  - Social events
- Communications
  - Newsletters
  - Attitude surveys
  - Suggestion programs
  - Brochures
- Recruitment
  - Advertising
  - Travel
  - External recruiters
  - Orientation

Q 4:   What is HR's role in strategic planning?

A: There are many ways in which HR can assist the organization in its strategic planning process. But first it is imperative for the organization to have individuals with the required competencies and skills to meet organizational business goals. Because the role of HR has been viewed as ancillary over the years, HR must now attempt to present itself as a more critical success factor to the business and must lessen the perception of being a creator and enforcer of corporate policies. Because changing perceptions is never easy, HR will have to "walk the talk" so to speak and must try to earn the respect of management and employees. In some organizations this change may mean reengineering or reshaping the HR function so it can be perceived as valuable to the organization.

Once HR has established its value within the organization, the next step should be to learn the business. HR should look at the business as a whole and try to streamline its mission statement so that it is aligned with the organization's mission. A strong knowledge of the company's strategic intent will be crucial for successful integration of HR with the company's strategic planning process. In the Society for Human Resource Management (SHRM) white paper titled *Business/HR Alignment* by David E. Ripley (1996), SPHR, he states:

> Human resource planning is a subset of the business planning process and is designed to work through four key issues:
>
> - The human resource contributions required if the goals and objectives of the business plan are to be achieved.
>
> - The process and activities required to accomplish business plan goals and objectives that must be retained in the organization, and those that could or should be outsourced.
>
> - The extent to which existing HR programs and policies are aligned with goals and objectives of the business plan, are legally required, or are necessary in view of the organization's stated values.
>
> - Realigning existing HR programs and policies with the goals and objectives of the business plan or eliminating them, and implementing any new HR initiatives required to make the necessary HR contribution to the accomplishment of business goals and objectives.

HR contributes to organizational business goals and objectives by (a) projecting future staffing and employee training needs; (b) deciding which functions should continue to be performed within the company or which should be outsourced; (c) examining existing HR programs to ensure that they are still necessary; and (d) continuing to provide a valuable contribution to the organization, as well as implementing new action plans to help the organization better achieve its desired goals.

The involvement of HR in the company's strategic planning process can vary greatly within each organization and also depends on the type of relationship that HR currently has with both management and employees. Although this information is intended to provide a basic understanding of some contributions that HR can make to the strategic planning process, it cannot nearly do justice to the amount of commitment and effort required for a true HR/business partnership to exist. A rapidly changing global economy has resulted in a greater need for value-added HR programs that do not jeopardize individual employees' needs in its pursuit of attaining business goals. Because an organization's most valuable asset is its human capital, it has become increasingly important for most organizations to involve HR in the strategic planning process in order to ensure that action plans meet both organizational and individual employees' needs.

Q 5:   What should we include in our HR mission statement?

A: A mission statement details the purpose and priorities of an organization: that is, what it stands for and where it is headed. Each company is unique; therefore, no two mission statements will be exactly alike. There will be several common elements, however, to the field of HR.

First, HR must be involved in the design and development of programs and services that meet the needs of the company and its employees. For HR to achieve success, potential areas of focus include the following:

- Recruitment
- Selection and placement
- Compensation and benefits
- Employee training and development
- Employee productivity and morale
- Legal compliance
- Retention

Second, HR must support and advise line managers in their efforts to effectively manage their employees and, in turn, achieve business goals. The success of the organization and of HR depends on how well line management carries out its programs, policies, and services.

Third, HR must participate as management's partner in building a successful and competitive organization. HR must understand the company's business, its competitors, and the factors that must be considered in both short-term and long-term planning.

All of these elements should be incorporated into the mission statement. As you develop an HR mission statement, it is important to keep in mind the overall goals of the organization. The HR mission and vision should be tied into that of the company, which will increase the support HR receives from upper management.

Some sample HR mission statements are available on the SHRM web site at <www.shrm.org/whitepapers/mission>.

Q 6: What should we include in an HR audit?

A: HR audits are used to evaluate HR policies and practices. An audit can help to evaluate how effective the programs and services are; how well HR delivers on the programs and services; or where there are opportunities to either enhance, change, or remove programs and processes.

Before conducting an audit, you should determine what aspects of the function need to be evaluated. The overall function can be evaluated, followed by a more in-depth consideration of each of the functional areas, as well as each of the programs and services offered so you make sure the company is in compliance and is meeting customer demands. For example, it may be that a certain benefit program is no longer effective. This ineffectiveness may prompt an audit of that particular benefit program. Individual and company needs dictate whether the audit should be conducted at the departmental or organizational level.

The following questions are for a brief sample audit. This sample audit is not exhaustive, rather it provides examples of the kinds of questions an HR professional should ask. (See Table 1–1).

A sample of a functional audit of performance management is available on the SHRM web site at <www.shrm.org/whitepapers/documents/61123.asp>. A useful publication on this subject is by Business and Legal Reports and is titled *HR Audit: How to Evaluate Your Personnel Policies and Practices"* (Hatsfield, 1990). Another publication is *Employment–Labor Law Audit* (Laurdan Associates, 1999).

Q 7: What are some of the quantitative measurements used for determining HR effectiveness?

A: Despite a common perception of HR as a soft science that is difficult to quantify, numerous calculations are actually available to evaluate the success of the HR Department. Performing bottom-line assessments is critical to becoming the business partner the company needs in the HR role.

These primary general HR measures reflect the employee ratios and costs.

- Ratio of HR employees to staff members
- HR budget in relation to total operational budget
- Revenue per employee in relation to expenditure per employee
- Percentage of employees compared to managers who seek HR's help
- Average turnaround time for a request

TABLE 1–1
SAMPLE AUDIT

Organization and Structure

1. Is there an organizational chart?
2. Does the chart include both employees' names and position titles?
3. Does the chart show reporting relationships?
4. Is the chart updated as changes occur?
5. As the needs of the organization change, does its structure change?

HR Department Organization

1. Is the department sufficiently staffed for the industry and the size of organization?
2. Is the budget in line with other organizations of similar size and industry?
3. Has the company been involved in any employment lawsuits?
4. If there have been suits, what were the outcomes?
5. Is there a job description for each position in the department?
6. To what position does the top HR position report?
7. Does the HR Department have a mission statement?
8. Is the HR mission statement consistent with the vision and mission of the organization?

Functions of the HR Department

1. For what functions is the HR Department responsible?

Payroll	Recruitment	Safety
Benefits	Training	Strategic planning
Salary administration	Labor relations	Others

2. Should the HR Department be responsible for all of the functions listed above?
3. Should the HR Department be responsible for functions that are not listed above?

Tracking these issues may take only a few moments with each encounter and will provide critical data.

Most HR professionals are familiar with the selection statistics that you work with every day. Such measures include the following:

- Time to fill

- Time to start

- Turnover

- Ratio of applicants to offers and of offers to acceptances

- Time for response to applications

- Cost per hire

- Cost of turnover

Each HR Department has different concerns, needs, benefits, and techniques. If there is a function that HR provides, then there is a way to analyze success. For example, for compensation you can analyze complaints by employees, complaints noted in exit interviews, worker's compensation and unemployment claims, benefit costs in relation to total payroll, average "compa-ratio," average increases, ratio of overtime pay to regular pay, and breakdown of exempt and nonexempt ratios.

Training, performance appraisals, succession planning, and legal matters can all be analyzed in a similar fashion. Whatever the issue, its success can generally be measured by examining the percentage of employees (a) who are affected by the issue, (b) who are satisfied with the issue, or (c) who are complaining about the issue (tracked as incidents occur).

Q 8:   What types of questions should be included in an HR customer satisfaction survey?

A: A customer satisfaction survey is useful in determining the adequacy of the products and services provided by the HR Department. To ensure that you obtain different perspectives, your respondent group should include members of the HR staff, line managers, top executives, and employees. Survey questions should address the following topical areas:

- Employee Demographics. At a minimum, ask for the respondents' supervisory status and years of service. Some optional demographic questions such as race, age, and gender may also be included. Assure respondents that they need not indicate their names on the survey nor will any effort be made to identify individual responses.

- Interaction with HR Staff Members. Address issues such as the accessibility of the HR staff, the timeliness of the HR's responses, the location of the HR office, the HR staff's knowledge of HR issues and company policies, and the HR Department's hours of operation.

- Recruitment and Placement. Address examples of services provided in this area such as information about (a) job openings and promotion opportunities, (b) time to fill, (c) qualifications required for specific jobs, (d) career counseling, and (e) other types of employment advice.

- Management-Employee Relations. In this section, address topics such as performance appraisals, disciplinary actions, grievances and appeals, and personal employee counseling.

- Compensation and Benefits. Determine the customers' perceptions of your company's pay and benefits structure, hours of work and overtime practices, employees' awareness of benefits' costs, and overall competitiveness of your compensation and benefits programs.

- Training and Development. Address career development counseling, training opportunities and enrollment information, tuition assistance, career ladders, and any special training programs offered.

- General Administration. Ascertain the timeliness, clarity, and accuracy of such processes as pay adjustments, benefits plan enrollment changes, maintenance of employee records, and in-processing and orientation of new employees.

- Communications. Evaluate the effectiveness, accuracy, and clarity of employee handbooks, newsletters, company goals and mission statement, summary plan descriptions, employee attitude surveys, and bulletin boards.

Although not intended to be an all-inclusive list of areas to cover in an HR customer service survey, the topical areas listed above provide a starting point for developing a survey to meet your company's needs. Sample surveys can be found on the SHRM web site at <www.shrm.org/whitepapers/surveys>.

Q 9:   What issues should be considered in a merger or acquisition?

A: There are many issues to consider when an organization is involved in a merger or acquisition. These issues can include but are not limited to the following:

- Reviewing all employee relations issues
  - HR policies and procedures
  - Employee handbook
  - Employee contracts
  - Organizational charts with key employees' positions
  - Pending employee relations lawsuits
- Gathering information pertaining to all benefits
  - Welfare plans
  - Insured and self-insured plans
  - Pension plans
  - Profit-sharing plans
  - Stocks
  - Form 5500 and other documents pertaining to plans protected under the Employee Employment Retirement Income Security Act (ERISA)
  - Summary Plan Description (SPD)

— Operational questions

— Fringe benefits

— Stock option plans

— Supplemental or excess pension plans

— Benefits regulatory issues (i.e., COBRA and Internal Revenue Service [IRS])

- Gathering information pertaining to compensation

— Executive compensation

— Golden parachutes

— Deferred compensation plans

— Salary administration

— Incentive compensation

— Severance packages

— Payroll issues

- Comparing compliance issues

— Office of Federal Contract Compliance Programs (OFCCP) (affirmative action programs, Executive Order 11246, etc.)

— Equal Employment Opportunity Commission (EEOC) (EE0-1 reports, pending charges, etc.)

— Occupational Safety and Health Act (OSHA) (OSHA-200 logs, reviewing accident rates, etc.)

— Americans with Disabilities Act (ADA), Family and Medical Leave Act (FMLA), Age Discrimination in Employment Act (ADEA) (pending charges, potential charges)

— Wage or hourly charges or audits

Companies should be sure to consult with an attorney who specializes in the complex procedures of mergers or acquisitions. Two SHRM white papers may be helpful in developing a due diligence checklist. Their titles are *Mergers and Acquisitions: HR Transition Model and Issues to Be Considered When Companies Integrate* (Himegarner, 1998) and *Human Resources Acquisition Checklist* (Misor, 1999).

Q 10: How can we create an HR Department organization chart?

A: Organization charts reflect the specialization of positions (horizontal dimension) as well as the authority relationships among positions (vertical dimension).

Organization charts can provide useful information to HR practitioners and organization management. For example, organization charts can help identify how work is coordinated within functional areas of departments and among departments, and how the work is connected with other units or divisions throughout the organization. Charts also provide information about new jobs and position titles, reporting and authority relationships, span of control, and staff duties. Such information is useful for orienting new employees, designing and communicating reorganizations, and so forth.

Charts also have certain disadvantages. They often become quickly outdated and can be misinterpreted. Furthermore, organization charts do not describe the informal aspects of a company or the horizontal linkages of an organization.

The structure of an HR Department is determined by the structure of the parent organization, as well as the HR Department's strategic role within the organization. For the most part, organizational design tends to reflect the functional distinctions (i.e., specializations such as marketing and finance) within the organization. Similarly, the most prevalent HR structure is based on the major HR functions such as benefits, compensation, and so forth. HR's strategic role in such an organization would be that of the specialist, providing state-of-the-art service in each HR function.

Another major organizational design consideration is the size of the organization. Many large companies have multiple geographic locations and diversified lines of business. HR Department structures often depict such a decentralized organization. A centralized HR department could provide overall policy and direction to smaller HR Departments that are located at different geographic sites and that have administrative autonomy. The strategic role of the HR Department would be that of the generalist who provides all aspects of HR administrative support to each location. An autonomous, decentralized HR Department could provide complete HR support to the various business units. The strategic role of the HR Department would then be to match the HR practices with the business requirements of each unit.

SHRM has a few examples of HR Department organization charts. The charts depict the structure of HR Departments in a variety of population sizes and industries. Another source of HR structure charts is The Conference Board, which can be contacted by mail at The Conference Board, Customer Service Department, 845 Third Avenue, New York, NY 10022; or by telephone at (212) 339-0345 and by fax at (212) 980-7014.

Q 11: What is the HR code of ethics?

> **A:** The code of ethics pledges SHRM members to do the following:
>
> - Maintain the highest standard of professional and personal conduct.
>
> - Strive for personal growth in the field of HR management.
>
> - Support SHRM's goals and objectives for developing the HR management profession.
>
> - Encourage their employer to make the fair and equitable treatment of all employees a primary concern.
>
> - Strive to make their employer profitable both in monetary terms and through the support and encouragement of effective employment practices.
>
> - Instill in the employees and the public a sense of confidence about the conduct and intention of the employer.
>
> - Maintain loyalty to the employer and pursue the employer's objectives in ways that are consistent with the public interest.
>
> - Uphold all laws and regulations relating to the employer's activities.
>
> - Refrain from using their official positions, either regular or volunteer, to secure special privilege, gain, or benefit for themselves.
>
> - Maintain the confidentiality of privileged information.
>
> - Improve public understanding of the role of HR management.
>
> For more information on ethics, see *Ethics: A Human Resource Perspective* by Howard M. Pardue (1999), PhD, SPHR. It is available on the SHRM home page at <www.shrm.org/whitepapers/documents/61141.asp>.

Q 12: Once the decision has been made to downsize, what criteria should be used in selecting employees for layoff?

> **A:** In a perfect world, such decisions could be eradicated by ranking all of the jobs within the organization into specific job categories and by eliminating the positions no longer necessary to the continued success of business operations. Unfortunately, this is not a perfect world, and carrying out widespread layoffs can pose greater challenges and risks to employers. Several options are available when planning dreaded, but sometimes necessary, workforce reductions. It should go without saying, however, that you should carefully plan layoff selection before executing an organizational downsizing to ensure that selection criteria do not result in disparate treatment or have an adverse impact on protected groups. In addition, you should research the federal EEOC and the state fair employment

practice laws to minimize inherent risks of potential discriminatory charges.

Although it is virtually impossible for any employer to ever truly obtain risk-free status in implementing workforce reductions, carefully planned and executed downsizing plans used in conjunction with good documentation and layoff policies (which have been reviewed by legal counsel) can be an employer's strongest defense against allegations of discrimination. Employers in unionized environments need to take additional precautions to ensure that an existing collective bargaining agreement is not violated.

Selection for Downsizing

Seniority-Based Selection

With seniority-based selection, the "last hired/first fired" concept is used. Because seniority-based systems reward employees for their tenure, there is a lower risk that older workers will sue employers for age discrimination under the ADEA. However, using seniority does not protect the employer from further risks for potential discrimination against other protected groups.

Employee Status-Based Selection

Employers who have part-time or contingent workers on their payrolls may want to lay off those workers first to ensure greater job security for remaining core workers. Unless an employer's workforce is made up largely of contingent workers, this method alone may not be sufficient to meet downsizing needs, and it may need to be used in conjunction with other selection criteria.

Merit-Based Selection

Although this method of selection is often a preferred choice among many managers because of its added flexibility for weeding out marginal or poorly performing employees, it should be scrutinized carefully. Because merit selection criteria are based either in part or in whole on performance evaluation information (which is not always objective and may contain rater biases), this method has not been proven to provide an accurate qualitative means for ranking the differences among individual employees' performance in selecting employees for layoff.

Skills-Based Selection

With this type of system, it is sometimes possible for employers to retain those workers who have the most sought-after skills. However, be aware that this method may cause a company to retain younger workers with needed and versatile skill sets, and to lay off older workers who may not have the necessary skills. The older workers are protected from discrimination by the Age Discrimination in Employment Act.

Multiple Criteria Ranking

Although all of the above methods can be equally effective when planned carefully, it has been argued that perhaps the most effective method of selection is using a combination of all the criteria previously discussed. Below is a sample of the ranking criteria used by some organizations that have implemented selection policies that are based on multiple criteria such as seniority, skill, and performance considerations.

- Employee's promotability and attitude
- Employee's skills, abilities, knowledge, and versatility
- Employee's education and experience levels
- Employee's quantity and quality of work
- Employee's attendance history
- Employee's tenure within the company

For more information, see the SHRM white papers *Employees in a Downsized Environment* by Marcia Scotty (1999) at <www.shrm.org/whitepapers/documents/61665.asp> and *Tips for Employers Who Want to Avoid Legal Claims for Downsizing* by Sue Erum, Angus Macauley, and Tim Stuckey II (1999) at <www.shrm.org/whitepapers/documents/61112.asp>.

Q 13: What should be considered in making the decision to outsource?

A: Outsourcing can streamline an organization and can allow it to focus attention and resources on its mission; however, outsourcing HR functions can also decrease a company's control over the quality of services its employees receive.

The most common factor to be considered when deciding to outsource HR (or any other function) is cost. However, many other factors that should be considered include the following:

- Will outsourcing help your company to achieve its business goals?

- Is the function or program being considered generally administrative and labor intensive, or is it an integral part of your organization?

- Will outsourcing cause employee relations problems?

- How will outsourcing affect communication with employees?

- Is the technology used by the vendor compatible with your company's?

- Who will manage your company's relationship with the vendor?

- Will the vendor tailor its services to meet your company's needs?

- Will service to your employees improve, decline, or remain the same?

- Is your company's culture compatible with outsourcing?

- Can one vendor provide more than one service?

One advantage of outsourcing is that vendors may assume some of the liability for which the company would normally be responsible. Also, vendors are specialists and are often very experienced in their function. Disadvantages include the possible displacement of current employees and the time-consuming process of initiating a relationship with a vendor. An organization should carefully evaluate its needs, costs, and benefits before deciding to outsource.

There are several articles in *HRMagazine* on this subject: "When Should You Call a Consultant?" by Marilyn Manewitz (1997) and "Outsourced Systems Provide Economy, Improved Service" by Sandra O'Connell (1997).

Q 14: How do we begin a diversity program and make it work?

A: There are many resources available to the HR professional for developing a diversity program. The SHRM Diversity Initiative is a great source for information. See SHRM Online at (www.shrm.org/diversity). Networking with other HR professionals can also provide valuable information in terms of proven methods and potential pitfalls. The white paper titled *Diversity* by William E. Gruer, PhD, SPHR, and Diana M. Osinski (Gruer & Osinski, 1999), SPHR, lists the following recommendations for shaping diversity management and training programs:

- Valuing diversity within the company should begin with the president or CEO, who must and must establish this attitude as a standard for people at all other levels in the organization.

- Evaluate individual workforce demographics to determine the urgency of adopting diversity management policies and programs.

- Evaluate personnel policies, benefits, and employee relations programs to determine how these programs help employees meet their responsibilities to their families, promote the acceptance of diversity, and enhance employee productivity and loyalty.

- Incorporate the subject of managing diversity into supervisory and management training at all levels of the organization. Senior management should hold managers accountable for hiring, developing, and promoting minorities and females. This accountability should be included in managers' incentive pay programs.

- Consider a mentor program, whereby a senior officer is matched with a female or a minority employee to monitor the employee's career progress within the organization.

- Conduct focus group discussions with a sample of employees from each segment of the staff to pinpoint existing differences and to measure the extent to which employees feel that they are valued members of the organization.

- Set specific goals for including minority and female employees in promotion and succession plans.

- Implement formal programs that give employees from every segment of the workforce a nonthreatening medium through which to express their concerns.

- Help employees organize cultural networks. Such networks and groups can arrange multicultural events both within the organization and in the community.

There are several white papers on diversity; they are *Measuring the Success of Diversity Programs* by Gail Majors and Mary Jane Sinclair (1999) at <www.shrm.org/whitepapers/documents/61102.asp> and *Diversity in Business* by Cornelius Grove and Associates (1999) at <www.shrm.org/whitepapers/documents/61103.asp>.

Q 15: What are the benefits of having an HR Call Center? Are there vendors that can assist an organization in setting up an HR Call Center?

A: HR Call Centers are low-cost alternatives for providing information to employees about HR issues. Call Centers offer a large variety of services and may be used as a stand-alone function or to complement other services such as Interactive Voice Response (IVR) systems, employee self-service centers, and intranets. When staffed with an appropriately trained team of HR representatives, a Call Center can offer many benefits to employers and employees alike.

For most HR professionals and line managers, the ability to shift daily responsibilities for administrative functions to a Call Center allows them to focus on more strategic business and HR planning needs. Effective tracking of the types of calls coming into the Call Center equips HR professionals to address many of the issues and concerns raised by employees.

Employees benefit from Call Centers because they can get assistance immediately. Call Centers tend to provide "one-stop shopping" for employees, thereby eliminating potential frustration. Call Centers may also result in increased productivity because employees no longer need to waste company time by calling multiple sources to obtain the answers to their questions.

Listed below are just a few of the many vendors that provide assistance to organizations considering implementation of an HR Call Center:

- Aspect Communications <www.aspect.com>

- Lucent Technologies <www.lucent.com/enterprise/op/docs/oppspa.html>

- Nortel <www.nortel.com>

- Rockwell <www.rockwell.com>

- Siemens <www.siemens.com>

- Vanguard Communications Corporation <www.vanguard.net>

- Associated Call Centers <www.inboundacc.com>

(SHRM does not endorse any of these companies.)

Further information is also available on-line at the ACD Call Center on-line learning center at <www.call-center.net>.

Q 16: What is the typical ratio of HR staff members to employees in an organization?

A: The ratio of HR staff members to the total number of employees that a company maintains depends on the company's structure, actual size, and reliance on in-house staff in relation to the use of outside HR consultants or outsourced functions.

In an annual survey conducted by the Bureau of National Affairs (BNA) and SHRM, employers are reported to have an average of 1 full-time HR professional for every 100 employees in the workforce. Although a recent survey showed that most surveyed employers reported an increase in workforce size, a large percentage of the respondents to the SHRM/BNA survey did not increase their total HR staff to reflect the additional increase in employees within the organization. A complete copy of the

"Human Resources Activities, Budgets, and Staffs Report," which is published annually, is available by contacting BNA at (800) 452-7773 or from the web site at <www.bna.com>.

Q 17: How can we find a Human Resource Information System (HRIS) that is right for our company?

A: Before you even begin looking at the types of HRIS packages available, it is important to go through a careful assessment process to determine your organization's needs. Some questions to ask:

1. What should the system do?

2. If you presently have a system, what works well and what problems exist?

3. What other processes can be automated?

4. Who will have access to the system?

5. What security controls will be needed?

6. Will the system need to be compatible with any other systems (i.e., accounting)?

7. Are there any major organizational changes planned that may affect the choice of system (next 3–5 years)?

8. How long do you expect to use this system?

9. What kind of a budget do you have to work with?

As you answer all of the questions, it is helpful to establish a team to assist with the assessment. Set up a time line for completion of the assessment and prepare an agenda for every meeting. When you are ready to look at vendors, you can draw from a wealth of resources, including directories of HR-related software products, buyer's guides (i.e., Adams, *The HRMagazine HRIS Buyer's Guide*, April issue, annually), and Internet resources linked with SHRM's web page.

Q 18: Where can we get turnover data?

A: BNA produces a quarterly turnover report called the "Quarterly BNA Job Absence and Turnover Report," which can be obtained by contacting BNA directly from its web site at <www.bna.com>, or by calling (800) 452-7773. Highlights of this report appear on the SHRM web site courtesy of BNA.

Q 19: Can we keep our personnel records on the computer or on microfilm instead of on paper?

A: Yes. None of the basic federal employment laws specify in what form you must retain records. Some points are specified by some of the statutes that your company should apply to all of your records.

- Safety. Many of the records are required by law, and all of them are potentially important to your business. Whether you keep your files on paper, computer, or microfilm, make sure they are protected from damage or loss.

- Accessibility. If the Immigration and Naturalization Service (INS), the EEOC, the Department of Labor, or any other government agency conducts an audit, it requires that files be readily accessible and readable. Additionally, those agencies frequently require that certain forms be photocopied, so make sure copying can be easily accomplished.

- Privacy. It is essential, and often mandated, that disclosure of personnel files be made only to those with a "need to know." Therefore, if the files cannot be locked up, passwords or other security tools must be used to protect the privacy of your employees' files. Medical files should still be kept separately from files that are used to make employment-related decisions.

- Special Requirements. Sometimes records must contain information that is not easily scanned or photocopied. In these instances, such as on Form I-9 (which currently requires an original signature), special arrangements may have to be made to ensure compliance. As another example, OSHA specifies that chest x-rays, unlike other x-rays, may not be placed on microfilm.

Record retention is critical in any type of organization. Accurate records frequently reduce potential liabilities. A strong defense in an employment-related lawsuit typically relies on the documentation kept by the managers involved in the situation. All records pertaining to any litigation must be kept for the duration of the litigation. Additionally, most of the federal employment laws do have specific time requirements for how long certain records must be kept (usually ranging from 1 to 4 years). It is crucial that organizations ensure they are complying with these requirements.

After the organization ensures compliance with the record retention time periods of the relevant laws, it is possible to select the type of record-keeping form or method that best suits the organization's needs. Whichever form or method the company selects for the retention of personnel records, the key is to make sure that the records are maintained accurately and efficiently.

Q 20: What is employment practices liability insurance?

A: Employment practices liability insurance (EPLI) is specialized insurance designed to protect against loss incurred in litigating and settling wrongful employment practices liability claims. It is typically structured as gap insurance for the company. It covers such things as discrimination, breach of contract, and wrongful discharge suits, which usually are not covered by general business liability insurance. Directors' and officers' liability insurance just protects the individual and not the company itself. EPLI is most commonly designed to fill this gap in coverage.

EPLI is becoming more common as employment suits become a part of doing business in this litigious age. A poll released by the National Federation of Independent Business found that small employers feel they stand a better than 50–50 chance of being sued in the next 5 years. According to *The EPL Book* by Griffin Communications Inc. (1999), nuisance suits can cost as much as $25,000 or more to resolve. Most employers are not prepared to absorb the risk of loss from such employment practices claims.

When evaluating and selecting insurance policies, companies should review the scope of coverage and adequacy of limits. They should understand who controls the claims handling process—the insured or the insurer. There are currently many variations in coverage and costs as the insurance is still relatively new. EPLI insurance coverage can vary from $250,000 to $25 million. Selection of an appropriate policy for your company's needs can be difficult and should be carefully considered.

EPLI is not meant to replace sound and secure employment practices. In fact, most insurance companies will not insure a company unless it has some basic employment practices in place. Employee handbooks, postincident investigation practices, and arbitration or mediation policies are some of the major items that insurance companies expect an employer to have when applying for an EPLI policy. You should be prepared for the insurance company to scrutinize all of the HR functions. Also, recent employment lawsuits, size of company, geographic location, and type of business or industry all affect the availability and cost of insurance.

References

Chapter 1. Human Resource Management

Adams, J. (Ed.). (Annual April issue). *The HRMagazine HRIS Buyer's Guide.* HRMagazine.

Bureau of National Affairs (BNA). [Quarterly issue]. *Quarterly BNA job absence and turnover report.* Available: BNA, (800) 452-7773 or <www.bna.com>.

Bureau of National Affairs (BNA) & Society for Human Resource Management (Annual). *Human resources activities, budgets, and staffs report.* Available: BNA, (800) 452-7773 or <www.bna.com>.

Erum, S., Macauley, A., & Stuckey, T. II. (1999). *Tips for employers who want to avoid legal claims for downsizing.* (White paper no. 61112). [On-line]. Available: <www.shrm.org/whitepapers/documents/61112.asp>. Accessed 6/99.

Griffin, G. (1999). *The EPL book.* Newport Beach, CA: Griffin Communications Inc.

Grove, C., and Associates. (1999). *Diversity in business.* (White paper no. 61103). [On-line]. Available: <www.shrm.org/whitepapers/documents/61103.asp>. Accessed 6/99.

Gruer, W. E., & Osinski, D. M. (1999). *Diversity.* (White paper no. 61101). Alexandria, VA: Society for Human Resource Management (SHRM). <www.shrm.org/whitepapers/documents/61101.asp>.

Hatsfield, W. (1990). *HR audit: How to evaluate your personnel policies and practices.* Madison, CT: Business and Legal Reports.

Himegarner, A. 1998. *Mergers and acquisitions: HR transition model and issues to be considered when companies integrate.* (White paper no. 61189). Alexandria, VA: Society for Human Resource Management (SHRM). <www.shrm.org/whitepapers/documents/61189.asp>. Accessed 6/99.

Laurdan Associates. 1999. Employment–labor law audit. Potomac, MD: Laurdan Associates.

Majors, G., & Sinclair, M. J. (1999). *Measuring the success of diversity programs.* (White paper no. 61102). [On-line]. Available: <www.shrm.org/whitepapers/documents/61102.asp>. Accessed 5/99.

Manewitz, M. (1997). When should you call a consultant? *HRMagazine, 42*(10), 84–88.

Misor, M. (1999). *Human resources acquisition checklist.* (White paper no. 61108). Alexandria, VA: Society for Human Resource Management (SHRM). <www.shrm.org/whitepapers/ documents/61108.asp>. Accessed 6/99.

O'Connell, S. (1997). Outsourced systems provide economy, improved service. *HRMagazine, 42*(1), 36–41.

Pardue, H. M. (1999). *Ethics: A human resource perspective.* (White paper no. 61141). [On-line]. Available: <www.shrm.org/whitepapers/documents/61141.asp>. Accessed 6/99.

Ripley, D. E. (1996). *Business/HR alignment.* (White paper no. 61127). Alexandria, VA: Society for Human Resource Management (SHRM). <www.shrm.org/whitepapers/documents/61227.asp>. Accessed 6/99.

Scotty, M. (1999). *Employees in a downsized environment.* (White paper no. 61665). [On-line]. Available: <www.shrm.org/whitepapers/documents/61665.asp>. Accessed 6/99.

Society for Human Resource Management (SHRM). (1999). Sample of a functional audit of performance management. (White paper no. 61123). [On-line]. Available: <www.shrm.org/whitepapers/documents/61123.asp>. Accessed 6/99.

CHAPTER 2

GENERAL EMPLOYMENT PRACTICES

Laws

Q 1: **What laws are we required to comply with once we reach the 50-employee threshold?**

> **A:** Once a company reaches the 50-employee threshold, it is responsible for complying with most of the employment regulations. The following breakdown should be helpful:
>
> - Employers with 1 to 14 employees must comply with
>   - Fair Labor Standards Act (FLSA)
>   - Employee Polygraph Protection Act of 1988
>   - Immigration Reform and Control Act (IRCA)
>   - Equal Pay Act (EPA)
>   - Federal Income Tax Withholding
>   - Uniformed Services Employment and Reemployment Rights Act of 1994
>   - Federal Insurance Contribution Act (FICA)
>   - National Labor Relations Act (NLRA)
>   - Consumer Credit Protection Act
>   - Fair Credit Reporting Act
>   - Labor Management Relations Act
>   - Uniform Guidelines for Employment Selection Procedures
>   - Employment Retirement Income Security Act (ERISA)
> - Employers with 11 or more employees must comply with
>   - Occupational Safety and Health Act (OSHA)
> - Employers with 15 or more employees must comply with
>   - Pregnancy Discrimination Act
>   - Civil Rights Act

   — Title I of the Americans with Disabilities Act

- Employers with 20 or more employees must comply with

   — Age Discrimination in Employment Act (ADEA)

   — Consolidated Omnibus Budget Reconciliation Act (COBRA)

- Employers with 50 or more employees must comply with

   — Family and Medical Leave Act (FMLA)

- Finally, employers with 100 or more employees must comply with the Worker Adjustment and Retraining Notification Act (WARN) and must complete and submit the "Employer Information Report" (EEO–1) form to the EEOC. (Executive Order 11246 requires federal contractors with 50 or more employees and $50,000 in government contracts to file the "Equal Employment Opportunity Report" (EEO–1) in September of each year.)

Q 2: What laws does the EEOC enforce and how do these laws apply to a business?

  A: EEOC covers the following:

- Title VII of the Civil Rights Act of 1964 (Title VII). This law prohibits race, color, religion, sex, and national origin discrimination. Title VII applies to employers with 15 or more employees.

- Age Discrimination in Employment Act of 1967 (ADEA). This law prohibits age discrimination against individuals who are 40 years of age or older. The ADEA applies to employers with 20 or more employees.

- Title I of the Americans with Disabilities Act of 1990 (ADA). This law prohibits employment discrimination against qualified individuals with disabilities. The ADA applies to employers with 15 or more employees.

- Equal Pay Act of 1963 (EPA). This law prohibits wage discrimination between men and women in substantially equal jobs within the same establishment. The EPA applies to most employers.

- Civil Rights Act of 1991. This law includes provisions for monetary damages in cases of intentional discrimination and clarifies provisions regarding disparate impact actions.

- Section 501 of the Rehabilitation Act of 1973. This law, as amended, prohibits employment discrimination against federal employees with disabilities.

Q 3: When can we require an employee to take a polygraph test?

A: The Employee Polygraph Protection Act of 1988 prohibits employers from requiring applicants or employees to take a polygraph test. Furthermore, employers cannot discriminate against employees and applicants for refusing to take the test or by using their polygraph test results against them. However, an employer may request a polygraph test if all of the following circumstances exist:

- The test is in conjunction with a current investigation involving economic loss or injury to the employer's business.

- The employee(s) had access to the property that is the subject of the investigation.

- The employer has a reasonable suspicion that the employee(s) was (were) involved in the incident under investigation.

Q 4: What are the requirements for the Fair Credit Reporting Act (FCRA)?

A: Amendments to the FCRA effective September 30, 1997, require employers (a) to disclose to applicants or to employees before they obtain a consumer or an investigative report, (b) to obtain written authorization from the applicant or the employee, and (c) to certify their compliance with the FCRA to the credit-reporting agency.

To obtain a consumer report, the FCRA requires the following:

- On a separate page, make a clear, written disclosure to the applicant or to the employee that a consumer report may be obtained.

- Obtain written authorization from the applicant or the employee.

- Certify to the credit reporting agency that the above steps have been followed and that the information obtained will not be used in violation of any federal or state equal opportunity law.

- Ensure that a copy of the report and a summary of the consumer's rights will be provided to the employee or the applicant if adverse action is taken based on the consumer report.

For you to obtain an investigative consumer report, the FCRA requires the following:

- Obtain written disclosure no later than 3 days after the date on which the report was requested.

- Include a statement informing the employee or the applicant of the rights.

- Include the summary of consumer rights.

One of the federal agencies that enforces the FCRA is the Federal Trade Commission, which has prepared three notices to explain the amended law. To obtain the notices and additional information, contact the Federal Trade Commission, Consumer Response Center-FCRA by telephone at (202) 326-3761 or from the web site at <www.ftc.gov>.

Affirmative Action Plans

Q 5:   Our company has recently obtained a federal government contract. Does this contract mean that we are now required to file an Affirmative Action Plan?

A: Affirmative action is designed to correct the effects of past or present discrimination by taking steps to increase the use of protected groups. An Affirmative Action Plan (AAP) sets objectives for achieving this result. All Affirmative Action Plans must be renewed and updated annually.

Affirmative Action Plans are mandated by law as a condition of doing business with the federal government. Title VII of the Civil Rights Act, the 1973 Rehabilitation Act, the Vietnam Era Veterans Readjustment and Assistance Act, and Executive Order 11246 require that all federal nonconstruction contractors must act affirmatively to hire minorities, women, certain veterans, and persons with disabilities, while larger employers with at least 50 employees and general contracts of $50,000 or more are required to develop and implement written Affirmative Action plans.

Executive Order 11246 requires all federal contractors and subcontractors with 50 or more employees and contracts for $50,000 or more to have a written AAP for women and minorities. This plan should include (a) an EEO policy statement; (b) a statistical analysis of the female and minority workforce, which includes an availability analysis of the labor force and an analysis of areas where the contractor is not using female and minority employees; (c) goals and timetables to correct the underutilization; and (d) a conclusion.

Section 503 of the Rehabilitation Act requires federal contractors and subcontractors with 50 or more employees and with contracts for $50,000 or more to have a written AAP for people who have disabilities. This plan should include (a) an Affirmative Action clause, (b) an invitation to join the plan, (c) a course of action for implementing the plan, (d) a procedure for internal auditing and monitoring, and (e) an analysis of employment practices.

The Vietnam Era Veterans Readjustment and Assistance Act requires federal contractors and subcontractors with 50 or more employees and with contracts for $50,000 or more to have a written AAP for Vietnam-era and other disabled veterans. This plan should include (a) an Affirmative Action policy statement, (b) an invitation to veterans to identify themselves in order to join the plan, (c) a procedure to communicate the policy, (d) an auditing and monitoring process, and (e) a self-analysis.

A court order or an EEO enforcement agency may mandate such Affirmative Action Plans. Employers can also develop and implement voluntary plans under specific guidelines.

In addition to Affirmative Action requirements, several reports are required under Title VII, Executive Order 11246, and the Vietnam Era Veterans Readjustment and Assistance Act. The Equal Employment Opportunity Commission (EEOC) has developed several different reporting forms for meeting the requirements of Titles VII and VI of the 1964 Civil Rights Act. The "Employer Information Report" (EEO–1) is developed jointly by the EEOC and the Office of Federal Contract Compliance Programs (OFCCP) to report workforces by race, ethnicity, and gender. Those employers who are obligated to file an Affirmative Action Plan, as well as all private employers who are not exempt from Title VII requirements and who employ 100 or more employees, are required to file the report annually by September 30.

Federal contractors awarded contracts in excess of $50,000 and employing 50 or more employees are also required to file the report each year under Executive Order 11246. The "State and Local Government Information Report" (EEO–4) must be filed every other odd-numbered year by state and local jurisdictions with 100 or more employees. The Labor Department also requires federal contractors with contracts of $10,000 or more to file a "Form Vets-100" (VETS–100) annually. The form is intended to disclose the number of employees in the contractor's workforce who are Vietnam-era veterans with a 30% or higher disability rating (10% or more if the disability poses a handicap to the employer) as specified by the Vietnam Era Veterans Readjustment and Assistance Act.

The report covers the total number of employees newly hired during the reporting period who are Vietnam-era veterans or special disabled veterans. As with the EEO–1 report, the VETS–100 report must be filed annually by September 30. There are other reporting and recordkeeping requirements set forth by federal and state laws that are not covered above. With this warning in mind, employers should contact local federal and state reporting agencies to obtain further information on what records and reports they may be required to keep and file as either a government contractor or a private employer.

Q 6: As a federal contractor, our organization is required to have an Affirmative Action Plan. Where can we locate resources to assist us with developing such a plan?

A: The development of an Affirmative Action Plan is a complicated process that is critical for federal contractors and others that are required to have a formal plan. The first point of contact should be the OFCCP, the agency responsible for ensuring that federal contractors meet their obligations in doing business with the federal government. The web site can be reached at <www.dol.gov/dol/esa/public/ofcp_org.htm>.

To locate a consultant with expertise in developing a plan, you can access the *Consultants' Database* under the *Consultants' Forum* at the SHRM web site. For a list of software packages with ready-to-modify Affirmative Action Plans, see the Human Resource Information System listings in the HRLinks section of our web site. The SHRMStore ((800) 444-5006) generally has books that will help employers develop a plan available for purchase. Finally, to network with other members who may have expertise in this area, post a query on the HRTalk bulletin board.

Q 7: Are we required to notify the employees if our company is closing?

A: The answer depends on the total number of employees and the number of employees who will be laid off. The federal law for layoffs is WARN (Worker Adjustment and Retraining Notification Act). WARN requires that 60 days notice be given to affected workers and their representatives, to the state dislocated-worker unit, and to the local government.

In situations of plant closings of a single work site, WARN covers employers of 100 or more full-time employees or with 100 or more full-time employees and part-time employees who work at least 4,000 total hours per week. If an employer of this size experiences a layoff or plant closing that affects 50 or more employees by laying them off or terminating them for at least 6 months over a 30-day period, the employer must comply with the requirements of WARN.

In addition, WARN is triggered in situations where mass layoffs include single sites and include 50 or more employees if they represent 33% of the workforce. WARN protections are triggered if the total affected is 500 or more employees, even if the 500 employees do not meet the 33% threshold. State laws with more stringent provisions may also be in place.

For more complete information, see the white papers at our web site under Management Practices, *The WARN Paper* (De la Cruz & Walters, 1999), and *Tips for Employers Who Want to Avoid Legal Claims for Downsizing* (Erum, Macauley, & Stuckey, 1999).

Q 8:   As a government contractor, should we still invite applicants to disclose whether they have a disability for Affirmative Action purposes?

> **A:** Yes, but you should wait until after you have extended an employment offer. Effective August 29, 1996, OFCCP modified its regulations implementing Section 503 of the 1973 Rehabilitation Act to bring the regulations in line with the ADA. Under the revised rule, contractors are required to invite applicants to identify themselves as disabled *after* extending a job offer but *before* starting them in a position. Preoffer invitations to self-identify are permitted only in very limited circumstances, such as when a contractor is actually undertaking Affirmative Action at the preoffer stage.
>
> The invitation to self-identify should state that (a) the information is being requested on a voluntary basis, (b) the information will be kept confidential, (c) refusal to provide the information will not subject the applicant to any adverse treatment, and (d) the information will not be used in a manner inconsistent with the act.
>
> Because OFCCP also made similar changes to the regulations implementing the Vietnam Era Veterans Readjustment and Assistance Act of 1974, you should wait until after extending a job offer to inquire about veteran's status. Contractors must still collect information on each applicant's gender and ethnicity, but you may choose to use one form that allows the applicant to disclose gender, ethnicity, disability, and veteran's status at the postoffer stage.
>
> Both the Rehabilitation Act and the ADA allow you to ask whether an applicant can perform the essential functions of a position either with or without accommodation, but you should wait until after extending a job offer to discuss the details of potential accommodations.

Americans with Disabilities Act

Q 9:   What health problems are considered disabilities under the Americans with Disabilities Act (ADA)?

> **A:** The ADA does not provide a listing of health conditions that constitute disabilities for determination of coverage. Employers should treat any person with an obvious physical or mental impairment or any other person who claims to have an impairment as legally disabled and protected by the ADA. Employers should follow these guidelines: the person (a) has a physical or mental impairment that substantially limits one or more of the major life activities of such individual, (b) has a record of such an impairment, or (c) is being regarded as having such an impairment.

Although the types of physical or mental conditions that are covered under the ADA are too numerous to list, the congressional committee's report on individuals with disabilities states that the above-mentioned definition of a disability includes but is not limited to conditions such as orthopedic problems, hearing and speech impairments, epilepsy, muscular dystrophy, heart disease, cancer, diabetes, mental retardation, cerebral palsy, emotional illnesses, certain learning disabilities, multiple sclerosis, and past alcohol or drug addiction, just to name a few.

Physical or mental characteristics such as hair and eye color, height and weight (with the exception of morbid obesity, defined as 100% or more of normal body weight), and so forth are not considered disabilities under the ADA. In addition, the ADA does not consider impairments that are temporary in nature such as broken bones, pregnancy, influenza, appendicitis, gall bladder attacks, or other types of temporary conditions to be covered under the current regulations.

Conditions such as pyromania, kleptomania, current alcohol or drug abuse, current illegal drug use, homosexuality, bisexuality, transsexualism, transvestism, exhibitionism, voyeurism, pedophilia, and any type of sexual behavior disorders are not given any scope of coverage under ADA guidelines.

Additional information on coverage and accommodations for specific disabilities can be obtained through the Job Accommodation Network at <www.janweb.icdi.wvu.edu>. Information on employment of people with disabilities is available from the President's Committee on the Employment of People with Disabilities whose web site is at <www50.pcepd. gov/pcepd>, or through the white papers section of the SHRM web site at <www.shrm.org>.

Q 10: Can we speak to an employee's doctor to understand more about a condition and the accommodation that may be needed?

A: Various federal and state laws exist that regulate how medical information can be collected, used, and disclosed by employers and health care providers. Failure to abide by those regulations could lead to a lawsuit for invasion of privacy or violation of the law. Examples of such laws include the Rehabilitation Act of 1973, the Vietnam Era Veterans Readjustment and Assistance Act of 1974, the Health Insurance Portability and Accountability Act of 1996 (HIPPA), and the Occupational Safety and Health Act (OSHA). Various states such as Maryland and California have laws governing the collection and dissemination of medical information. Two important laws, the ADA and the Family and Medical Leave Act (FMLA), are discussed below.

- If an employee requests an accommodation under the ADA, the employer must know the nature of the disability so that possible accommodation(s) can be sought. The employee (or candidate) must advise his or her physician to release relevant medical information to the employer. Many employers forward a job description to the physician to obtain a medical opinion regarding the employee's (or candidate's) ability to perform the various duties of the position, as well as ideas on how to accommodate.

- The information that is provided by a physician on the Department of Labor's "Certification of Health Care Provider" form (Form WH–380) is the only information an employer can obtain regarding an employee's medical condition for FMLA purposes. However, a health care provider representing the employer can contact the employee's physician (with the employee's permission) for clarifications and for authentication of the medical certificate.

Q 11: What is the definition of essential functions? How can we determine what they are for a specific job?

A: The essential functions of a job are those functions that are fundamental or a business necessity. Marginal functions are those tasks that can be exchanged or given to another individual if a reasonable accommodation is requested from an individual with a disability.

- The regulations state several reasons why a function would be essential:

- The position exists to perform the function.

- A limited number of other employees are available to perform the function or among whom to distribute the function.

- The function is highly specialized, and the person in the position is hired for having a special expertise or an ability to perform it.

According to the technical assistance manual published by the EEOC, *Technical Assistance on Title I of ADA*, the first consideration an employer should make is whether an employee must perform that function to do the job. The second consideration is whether removing that function fundamentally changes the job.

The EEOC considers the following to be relevant factors in determining whether a function is essential:

- Employer's judgment
- Prepared job descriptions
- Amount of time spent performing the function
- Consequences of not requiring the person to perform the function

- Terms of a collective bargaining agreement

- Work experience of the people performing the function or who have performed similar jobs

- Nature of the work operation

- Employer's organizational structure

Although the ADA does not require employers to conduct a job analysis to identify essential functions, it is probably the most accurate way to determine whether a function is essential for a position. A job analysis should focus on the job purpose and the importance of the functions of the job.

For more information on the ADA and essential functions, try the Job Accommodation Network at (800) ADA-WORK (232-9675) or the web site at <www.janweb.icdi.wvu.edu>.

Q 12: Do we have to accommodate a pregnant employee who cannot do any lifting? What if 90% of the job is loading a truck?

A: Pregnant women who are temporarily unable to do their jobs because of a pregnancy-related condition must be treated the same as nonpregnant employees who suffer a temporary disability. Pregnancy is not covered as a disability under the ADA, because it is a short-term condition and is not an impairment that substantially limits a major life activity.

Any modification of working conditions is because of Title VII or the company's policy on temporary disabilities. If it is your company's policy or past practice to provide a modification of working conditions or to provide unpaid leave for an employee with a temporary disability, the same must be done for a pregnant employee.

Performance Reviews

Q 13: What are some guidelines for managers to follow when writing performance reviews?

A: Managers should try to follow these guidelines:

- Don't focus on one specific incident. Review the entire period that the appraisal covers.

- Don't go solely by memory. Base the review on accurate and factual data.

- Avoid the "halo and horns" effects. Just because the employee performs badly in one area does not make overall performance poor. The same goes for good performance.

- Look carefully at the individual's performance within the job. Length of service or job grade does not necessarily equal better performance.

- Avoid biases about an employee that are based on your personal feelings for the individual.

- Don't rate current performance on past performance. Look at performance for the current period being reviewed.

- Don't overate poor performance and use it as a motivational tool.

- Analyze each employee's performance carefully; establish a performance ranking. Not all individuals are the same.

- Don't rush through the appraisal. Take time to record accurate information that truly reflects the individual's performance.

- Don't be afraid to provide honest information.

Q 14: What are some guidelines we can provide to our managers for conducting performance review meetings?

A: Employee participation and cooperation are essential building blocks to a successful appraisal system. Because the performance appraisal system is usually the main feedback vehicle between employers and employees, careful preparation and skillful handling of the performance review meeting is necessary. The value of an appraisal system can be lost if the results are not communicated clearly and effectively to employees. Results should be communicated in ways meant to encourage employees to take positive actions to improve their overall performance and effectiveness. Listed below are some tips for effectively handling a performance appraisal interview with an employee:

- Choose an appropriate time and place for the review meeting.

- Allow at least one-half hour but no more than one hour for the interview.

- Be sincere and interested in the interview process.

- Put the employee at ease by trying to relieve any tension that may exist.

- Review the positive aspects of the performance appraisal first.

- Approach problems positively and seek solutions.

- Address issues in broad terms first. Next, narrow them down to specifics.

- Avoid lecturing employees.

- Don't focus on past performance issues. Instead, focus on future performance expectations.

- Encourage employees to provide their input.

- Allow the employee to speak without being interrupted.

- Use the individual employee's strengths as a basis for making necessary changes in performance.

- Avoid discussing personal issues or problems with the employee.

- Discuss plans for improvement.

- End the interview on a positive note.

Once all of the issues have been addressed and the employee has had the opportunity to discuss any relevant matters or concerns, summarize the main points of the meeting and develop an action plan for the employee. It is important to remember that performance appraisals are a continuous process and must not be treated as a one-time exercise. It is important to have a scheduled routine follow-up to determine whether the goals discussed during the interview are being attained.

Q 15: When should we use a 360-degree performance appraisal?

A: Multirater, or 360-degree, performance appraisal systems are enjoying popularity among employers with a focus on customer service. They're called 360-degree performance appraisals because a circle of people, which typically includes superiors, co-workers, subordinates, and customers, reviews the employee. The employee also reviews himself or herself.

The use of 360-degree performance appraisals can help employers achieve special outcomes:

- Improved Customer Service. The objective of a multirater performance appraisal system is to obtain a broad-based view not only of the employee's performance but also of the quality of the products and services. The feedback provided by customers who interact with the employee is valuable in providing a more complete picture of the employee's and the company's performance. The feedback may provide clues as to problems that are not limited to that employee or that employee's department.

- Team Initiatives. The use of a multirater performance system supports team initiatives and objectives because the multirater feedback makes employees more accountable for their actions that affect superiors, co-workers, subordinates, and customers.

- Reduced Risk of Discrimination. In a multirater performance appraisal system, employees assume more responsibility, so their ability to shift blame for their actions diminishes. Because a number of individuals are reviewing one employee, the effects of bias and discriminatory views are reduced.

A 360-degree feedback program typically includes between 5 and 10 raters. The group of raters should be large enough to include superiors, co-workers, subordinates, and customers, but not so large that the system becomes unmanageable. The individuals chosen as raters should be those who routinely interact with the employee. The raters should be chosen so they do not favor or disfavor the employee. You should take care to not use the same employees repeatedly as raters because the task of providing frequent feedback could hinder the process.

One of the main concerns of using a multirater feedback system is that the raters fear repercussions from providing candid feedback. For this reason, you may want to consider ensuring the anonymity of each rater. Although anonymity restricts the employee from obtaining follow-up feedback, a fully open program requires a high level of trust and cooperation.

For information on multirater feedback, please see the May 1998 and May 1999 issues of *HRMagazine*. The following books may also be of interest to you:

- *Maximizing the Value of 360-Degree Feedback* by Walter Tornow and Manuel London (1998)

- *The Art and Science of 360-Degree Feedback* by Richard Lepsinger and Antoinette Lucia (1997)

- *360-Degree Feedback: The Powerful New Model for Employee Assessment and Performance* by Mark Edwards (1996)

Q 16: What exactly is Management by Objectives? How is this technique different from standard performance appraisals?

A: Management by Objectives (MBO) is a tool for performance management and strategic planning. The MBO technique requires the supervisor and the employee to develop and agree on realistic, achievable, and measurable objectives and then to determine how those objectives will be met. The supervisor or manager sets the ground rules.

- First, set objectives for the manager's or supervisor's own upcoming project or time period (presumably in consultation with the next highest managerial level). Next, plan the larger objectives that must be imposed on each lower-level employee.

- Second, meet with each employee, outline his or her larger objectives, and guide each person in selecting the smaller objectives that will accomplish the larger objectives. The smaller objectives will be the employee's job or work objectives.

- Third, at the end of the project or the set period of time, meet with the employee and guide him or her in evaluating whether the objectives selected were achieved. A written summary of the joint evaluation, signed by both the supervisor and the employee, with a copy given to each, assures each of them that the other will keep this evaluation in mind in the upcoming rating period.

- Finally, select the next set of objectives. A whole new set of duties may await the employee on the next project, so this evaluation will be strictly confined to closing out the previous project.

The advantage of the MBO process is that it allows employees to actively participate in goal setting. MBO can increase motivation by relating organizational goals to individual goals. Expectations and the evaluative measures are defined in advance. The process concentrates on results achieved rather than on personality traits, so the MBO may offer a relatively high level of objectivity.

The potential drawback of MBO is setting goals in advance that can be difficult to achieve; sometimes goals are set too high or too low. Goals can be affected by external factors beyond the employee's control, such as economic changes, that are difficult to take into account. There could be difficulty in coordinating the individual's goals with the overall goals of the organization and difficulty in making comparisons among different employees, for example, for promoting or setting salary levels.

Q 17: Do we have to test the validity of our performance appraisals? How do we do that?

A: Yes. The EEOC will hold employers' performance appraisals to the same standards as those for determining whether employee selection or testing programs are discriminatory. For a performance appraisal to be considered nondiscriminatory, it must be both reliable and valid.

A performance appraisal is reliable if it provides consistent data regardless of who conducts it.

The courts accept three ways to measure validity: content validity, predictive validity, and construct validity.

- Content validity is determined by looking at the measurable job factors for which the employee is being reviewed. Two examples of measurable job factors would be a typist's speed and error rate. An employer should make sure that the performance appraisal accurately reflects the key behaviors for the jobs being performed. Conducting a job analysis and having job descriptions are two ways to help ensure that the factors being measured are, in fact, job related.

- Predictive validity is determined by showing that there is a statistical correlation between the employee's performance appraisal and the employee's future performance. To indicate predictive validity, you must usually take a large employee sample to show a correlation between past appraisal results and performance on the job.

- Construct validity is determined by demonstrating that the measurable job factors an employer uses are critical to the successful performance of the job. For example, you would not measure an entry-level position on leadership skills; however, you would measure a manager on such skills.

Age Discrimination in Employment Act

Q 18: My organization has 10 employees who are over the age of 50. The company wants to lay them off. Isn't there a law protecting older workers?

A: Employers are prohibited by the Age Discrimination in Employment Act (ADEA) from discriminating against any individual who is 40 years of age or older when they make employment decisions regarding whom to hire, job assignments, employee training, compensation, transfers, promotions, demotions, and layoffs.

In past years, layoffs have been extremely fertile ground for age discrimination claims with some courts ruling that certain types of layoff systems are an unlawful attempt to try to force mandatory retirement, which is prohibited (with limited exceptions) by the ADEA. A layoff plan that is designed for the sole purpose of eliminating older workers from the workplace is a violation of the ADEA.

Employers who display a pattern of laying off older, higher paid employees will leave themselves susceptible to charges of age discrimination under the ADEA. Employees who are 40 or over are protected by the ADEA from adverse actions that are based strictly on age rather than performance. An employer's defense that laying off all employees over the age of 40 is a necessary cost-cutting measure will not, in itself, suffice as a justifiable reason for laying off or demoting only older workers. The safest route to take in designing a layoff plan would be to select employees for layoffs according to a bona fide seniority system, or to select employees on the basis of performance or merit rankings. Conferring with legal counsel before initiating any plan of action that can potentially have an adverse impact on protected groups of employees is highly recommended to ensure compliance with federal and state fair employment practice laws. For additional information on the ADEA, see the SHRM white paper titled *A Brief Overview of the Age Discrimination in Employment Act (ADEA)* (Quirk, 1993) which can be found at <www.shrm.org/whitepapers/documents/61215> or at the EEOC web site at <www.eeoc.gov>.

Q 19: Can we ask employees to sign releases that are offered in conjunction with early retirement benefits?

A: Early retirement incentives are allowed under the ADEA, provided that the early retirement is voluntary. Because the vast majority of employees who would accept an early retirement package are close to retirement age, the organization may want to protect itself against age discrimination lawsuits under the ADEA. In addition, in 1990 Congress amended the ADEA with the Older Workers' Benefit Protection Act (OWBPA), which changed the rules for age discrimination releases by setting stricter criteria for releases of both protected rights and disputed claims. For an age release to be considered as knowing and voluntary under the federal law, the OWBPA has set forth specific requirements that must be met so the release may be considered binding.

With a release of ADEA rights, an employee gives up all potential age bias claims in return for the early retirement benefit. For these releases to be valid and enforceable under both the ADEA and the OWBPA, they must meet the following criteria:

- They must be in writing.
- They must use plain and understandable terminology.
- They must refer to rights or claims protected under the ADEA.
- They must address the rights or claims that arose on or before the date each release was executed.
- They must be in exchange for a benefit to which the employee would not otherwise have been entitled.
- They must give the employee 21 days to review and consider (45 days if in conjunction with an incentive for voluntary termination or group workforce reduction).
- They must give the employee 7 days to revoke after signing.
- They must advise that the employee consult and discuss the waiver with a lawyer before signing.

As with any agreement, employers are strongly encouraged to have an early retirement incentive plan and to have the accompanying release of ADEA rights reviewed by legal counsel. For a sample ADEA waiver and release to help you draft your plan, call the SHRM Information Center at

(800) 283-7476, option 5. For additional information on releases, see the March–April 1999 SHRM Legal Report titled *The Older Workers' Benefit Protection Act: Are Waivers Worth the Paper They're Written On?* (Pierson & Fulkerson,1999) under the white papers heading of the SHRM web site at <www.shrm.org/whitepapers/documents/61629>.

Employee Terminations

Q 20: Are there any best practices related to terminating employees?

A: Before an organization decides to terminate an employee for performance reasons, there are several issues to consider:

- Thoroughly investigate and review the facts. If action is required after a major incident, walk away from the situation for a brief period to cool down before making any important decisions. If suspension of the employee is necessary to allow time for the investigation, then consider that alternative.

- Allow time for all parties to review the details of the situation.

- Find and obtain statements from witnesses, if applicable.

- Talk with the employee to get his or her perspective.

- Obtain and review all related current and prior documentation.

- Outline the facts of the most recent situation.

- Examine the employee's previous discipline history.

- Examine records of employees with similar infractions, and compare the disciplinary actions imposed on them with the disciplinary action considered now.

- Determine whether the employee is in a protected class. If so, determine whether there has been disparate treatment (intentional) or treatment that has resulted in disparate impact (not intentional, but nevertheless discriminatory) for this employee.

- Review the facts of the investigation with an objective third person.

- Pinpoint the basis for the possible discharge.

- Determine if the discharge violates any federal or state laws.

- Discuss your decision with an HR professional, employment attorney, corporate council, or final decision maker.

- Determine the best time and place to carry out the discharge calmly, in a direct but compassionate manner. Consider including a witness in the meeting, if appropriate.

- Document what was said and what was done at the termination meeting.

Q 21: What is employment-at-will, and what does it mean to our company?

A: When an employee is hired for an indefinite period of time without a written contract or a collective bargaining agreement, that employment is an at-will situation in which either party is free to terminate the employment relationship at any time for any reason. Employment-at-will laws vary according to state provisions and case law. Employment-at-will is often subject to exceptions that include the following:

- Terminations resulting in discrimination against any protected class

- Terminations for reasons that violate public policy such as refusing to break a law, performing a public duty such as jury duty, exercising a right such as filing a discrimination claim, whistle blowing, or participating as a witness in a federal investigation

- Terminations that breach an implied contract or covenant

Employers' rights to terminate employees-at-will have diminished in recent years, and it is never advisable to rely solely on the at-will doctrine when terminating an employee.

To protect your company from claims related to discrimination based on protected status or public policy violations, keep detailed documentation to verify that an employee was not terminated for any of the reasons listed above. You should link severance agreements to written agreements releasing the employer from potential claims and should use the advice of counsel in drafting such agreements.

To protect your company from breach of implied contract or covenant claims, include an at-will employment statement on your application, in your employee handbook, and in each offer letter. You should have your attorney review your handbook to avoid any language that might imply a contract. Train supervisors and managers to avoid implying a promise of continued employment to employees, either orally or in writing.

Q 22: An employee just provided us with a 2-week notice of resignation. Can we decline the notice and inform the employee that today will be the last day of employment?

A: Although there is no requirement to accept a 2-week notice, providing that there is no existing employment contract between the parties to honor such a notice of a resignation, there are several reasons employers should not respond to a 2-week notice by terminating the employee.

If an employer declines to accept a 2-week notice, the employer is, in effect, terminating the employee. Therefore, the former employee has the right to claim unemployment insurance if his or her future employment plans should, for some reason, be eliminated. Also, such a termination may provide former employees with a possible wrongful termination claim if they leave under adverse circumstances. Consult an attorney for more information on wrongful termination.

Employers generally expect professionalism from their employees, including the expectation that departing employees will provide a 2-week notice before leaving their position. In fact, some employee handbooks specifically state that employers expect such a notice. If employers terminate employees on receiving a notice of resignation, future departing employees may be reluctant to provide such a notice for fear that they will be terminated immediately and they will not receive compensation for their last 2 weeks of employment.

If you feel strongly that a resigning employee should leave immediately for any reason, we suggest that you tactfully inform the employee that he or she will be compensated for the following 2 weeks and that it is not necessary to remain on the premises after the close of business that day.

Q 23: If an employee admits that he or she has been drinking while working, can we terminate that person?

A: The ADA states an employer may require that employees shall not be under the influence of alcohol and shall not be engaged in the illegal use of drugs at the workplace. However, this is a sensitive issue where the answer will depend on the specifics of the situation. The ADA does not restrict the ability of employers to discharge employees who report to work under the influence of alcohol (or illegal drugs). Employment actions should be based on work performance and disciplinary- and attendance-related issues and should focus on the problematic behavior rather than a suspected cause.

Employees who have alcohol or drug abuse conditions but who are not active drug or alcohol users should be given the same consideration as those who suffer other disabilities. To avoid a charge of discrimination, an employer should make every effort to accommodate an employee's disability. An employer can gain protection from a simple agreement (legal counsel is suggested) that states the terms required for the employee to avoid discharge and should include mandatory attendance at a rehabilitation program and acknowledgment that any further violation will result in immediate termination.

Q 24: We know that someone who applied for a job with us has a very serious charge against him or her and may end up being convicted of a crime. How do we proceed through the application process without discriminating?

A: You may not base a hiring decision on the fact that an applicant has a pending charge. Remember that people are "innocent until proven guilty." You may, however, ascertain the applicant's ability to attend work during the hours required for the position.

Q 25: We have an employee who is just not working out? Can we terminate this employee?

A: Yes and no. Employment-at-will states allow employers and employees to end the employment relationship at any time, for any reason, and at the will of either party. However, employees could potentially bring suit for wrongful discharge if they are terminated without cause. If your disciplinary policy requires corrective action procedures or progressive discipline procedures, it is best to follow that policy. If employees are normally taken through the progressive discipline steps (verbal, written, etc.), this employee should be treated the same way. Documentation of progressive discipline could be your best defense in a suit of wrongful discharge. Thus you will be able to show that the termination was for just cause. A good resource on this subject is an article that was printed in the May 1999 edition of *HRMagazine* titled "A Legal Dichotomy? Employment-at-Will Doesn't Mean You Should Ignore Progressive Discipline" by Paul Falcone (1999).

Q 26: Can we require an employee to sign a noncompete agreement?

A: A noncompete agreement is a contract that prohibits an employee from working in a related business for a certain length of time after the employee leaves the company. It is intended to protect a company's business in terms of confidential information or client base. Because such agreements restrict an individual's choice of employment, they are subject to legal review in many states. A few states have banned noncompete agreements entirely.

Even in states that do not regulate noncompete agreements, the courts will closely scrutinize those agreements to make sure that they are necessary to protect the company's interests. A company must be able to show that it has a protectable interest and that the restrictions placed on the departing employee, either in length of time or geography, are reasonable. The courts will also look at other factors such as whether similarly situated employees were required to sign such agreements and if consideration was given (i.e., the employee was given something) in exchange for signing the agreement. When an employee is required to sign a noncompete agreement at the time of hire, it can be argued that giving the employee a job is sufficient consideration. The same cannot be argued when requiring an employee to sign a noncompete agreement upon termination. Even if the employee signs the agreement, some courts may rule that it is not binding because no consideration was given.

It is advisable to consult with an attorney and with state and local regulations before developing and implementing noncompete agreements. See the SHRM Legal Report on this subject, *Noncompete Agreements: Considering the Ties That Bind* (Sandler, 1998) at <www.shrm.org/whitepapers/documents/61219.asp>.

Q 27: We have been informed that one of our employees has been arrested for criminal activity outside the workplace. Can we terminate this employee?

A: Many employers find themselves in a position where they need to determine the current employment status of an employee who has been arrested or incarcerated. Depending on the employer's current policy or past practices, several options are available for handling such situations as they arise. An employer's policy may simply call for treating such situations as unexcused absences and, therefore, for applying any disciplinary action that is in accordance with the current policy for unexcused absences. Another approach may be to consider handling such situations under any current company-approved unpaid policy relating to personal leave of absence.

For employers who tend to experience a higher prevalence of arrested or incarcerated workers, and depending on the nature of your business, you may find it necessary to draft a more detailed policy that specifically addresses what action the company will take when an employee is arrested or incarcerated and is going to be unavailable for work for a specified number of days (e.g., a suspension or a termination).

When you draft policies regarding arrested or incarcerated workers, it is imperative that you keep in mind that an important distinction must be made between an employee who has been arrested for a crime versus an employee who has been convicted of a crime. With this distinction in mind, you may find it more suitable to place an arrested employee on a suspended status and to terminate him or her only when the nature of the offense has a direct relationship with the employee's job function and when the offense results in an actual conviction.

When you are faced with making decisions regarding the employment status of an employee who has been arrested or incarcerated, it is advisable that you first consult with legal counsel to ensure that the policy does not violate any federal EEO or state fair employment practice laws. You should further discuss any potential liability that may exist for negligent hiring or retention claims if you choose not to take any disciplinary action.

Regardless of what approach you as an employer decide to take in handling the issue of arrested or incarcerated employees, policies and practices should be applied and enforced fairly and consistently for all employees throughout the organization.

Q 28: Assuming there are valid grounds for termination, can an employer offer an employee the opportunity to resign instead of being fired for poor performance?

A: Yes, and if you give employees this choice, it may lessen hard feelings and the likelihood of a lawsuit. If the employee accepts your offer, obtain the resignation in writing. It is also a good idea to explain what information you will provide to prospective employers and the unemployment compensation board about the separation. Although your records can characterize it as a resignation, it will typically be considered a constructive discharge or involuntary termination for unemployment compensation purposes.

Q 29: We have an outstanding employee who is always 15 minutes late. What can we do to make this employee come to work on time?

A: Attendance and tardiness are components of an employee's overall performance. Such problems should be addressed as you would any other performance issues. Communicate to the employee what is expected, and explain the impact that habitual tardiness has in terms of both individual performance and team effort. Provide the employee with a defined period of time in which to improve, and be prepared to follow your disciplinary policy if the problem continues. Ensure that the same standards are applied equitably and fairly to all employees.

Q 30: How many incidents should we allow before termination for excessive absenteeism?

A: It has been reported that absenteeism costs employers billions of dollars nationally per year in lost productivity. In addition, absenteeism can be extremely disruptive to the organization, creating a drain on productivity and efficiency. Employees who are at work must often bear the responsibilities of those who are absent. Further, absenteeism is consistently ranked as one of management's most common disciplinary problems. In lieu of those issues, it has become increasingly important for employers to define what constitutes excessive absenteeism or tardiness and to establish written policies. A good attendance policy will draw a definition between scheduled and unscheduled absences and will address how each will be treated. It will also define how many absences or tardinesses in any given period of time will be considered acceptable or unacceptable.

The number of absences considered to be excessive and disruptive to the operation of a business will vary considerably among different organizations. Although some employers set policy standards of 10 to 12 absences per year as being excessive, others may allow employees 1 to 3 absences per month before initiating disciplinary action to improve employee attendance. Patterns of repeat attendance issues such as consistently being absent from work on a Monday or a Friday or on days either preceding or following a holiday may need to be addressed. In addition, specific limits on tardiness should be established by either using a point system based on the types of absences taken, or by implementing a policy that limits tardiness to 5 to 10 incidents per year before initiating disciplinary action.

Employers must take the Family and Medical Leave Act and the Americans with Disabilities Act into consideration when developing an attendance policy. Absences that are covered by these laws cannot be counted against employees for disciplinary purposes. Employers should keep this set of laws in mind when designing their attendance policies.

Regardless of which standards an organization ultimately decides to set forth in its attendance policy, the policy needs to be implemented carefully and should be communicated to all employees, as well as to managers and supervisors. Managers and supervisors must be able to understand their roles in the entire process so they can make decisions regarding whether an employee is in violation of the policy and whether the appropriate disciplinary action must be taken.

Employee Survey

Q 31: Morale seems sort of low, and turnover seems sort of high. We want to use an attitude survey to check things out. Should we use one? If so, what should we keep in mind?

> **A:** Attitude surveys are a good idea only if the leadership of the company is open to feedback and is prepared to take action that is based on the survey's results. If company leadership does not welcome feedback from company employees, a survey may serve to be divisive. If the leaders of the company do not respond to the surveys by making changes based on such survey results, employees will resent having their feedback ignored.
>
> A company can purchase surveys off the shelf, hire a consultant to design a survey, or design its survey in house. From the outset, the company leaders need to define carefully what insight they hope to gain from the survey.

This plan will serve as a guide for selecting a survey or formulating questions. It is a good idea to announce that a survey will be conducted a week or more before it is administered so you can give employees time to put some thought into their answers. To get a good response from employees, you should make the survey short enough that it doesn't burden employees to fill it out.

Experts advise that survey results be collected and analyzed by an outside entity to ensure confidentiality and to avoid any appearance of bias. Once the data are processed, the outside source should report to the company's top leaders first. Some companies then inform management before sharing the results with the staff members at large. Other companies provide management and staff members with the survey results at the same time.

Last, and perhaps most important, leadership should begin the process of planning a course of action to remedy any issues that are discovered. A follow-through on such issues should include participation from employees at all levels.

Employee Handbook Versus Policy Manual

Q 32: What is the difference between an employee handbook and a policy manual?

A: A policy manual is the formal, full set of policies that your company has in effect for the workforce. It is usually written for the company management team to use to make decisions relating to workplace issues.

An employee handbook is written for employees in a style and format that is easy to use. It may reference the policy manual, but the handbook is not written in such a formal way. For example, the policy manual may have a section on vacation, including (a) exactly how vacation time is accrued, (b) when and how vacation time can be requested, (c) if earned vacation is paid upon termination, and so forth. The employee handbook would be a more informal listing of how many days of vacation time are available each year and, perhaps, would provide a form for requesting vacation time.

Although a policy manual could be several hundred pages long, depending on many factors, the employee handbook is usually a booklet. Employees can speak with their managers if they have questions that the handbook does not address, and the manager will look in the policy manual to find the answers.

Q 33: We need to revise our employee handbook. Are there any resources that will help make this process faster?

A: The following resources are available through SHRM to help in preparing or revising an organization's employee handbook:

- SHRM has a white paper, *Preparation of the Employee Handbook* (Scharinger, 1996).

- SHRM Policies Databank is a database of sample policies collected from members and is located at <www.shrm.org/whitepapers/policies>.

- A list of "Policy Manual/Employee Handbook Creation" software exists from the *Personnel Software Census* by Advanced Personnel Systems (1999). This list is not directly available from SHRM, but the vendor may be contacted at (916) 781-2900 or on the web site at <www.hrcensus.com>.

- SHRM's *Consultants' Database* and *Buyer's Guide* can both be accessed through SHRM's web page. The *Consultants' Database* and *Buyer's Guide* both provide consulting resources on a variety of HR-related topics, including employee handbooks and policy manuals.

- You can link to a number of HR-related web pages through SHRM's web page by selecting HRLinks. Once in HRLinks, under the Legal Issues and Resources category, you will find links to handbooks and policies resources.

Q 34: What should we include in our employee handbook?

A: As you determine what issues to address in your company's handbook, you should consider several factors, including legalities and company culture. Certainly, there are legal issues that should be covered in an employee handbook. For example, employment at-will and sexual harassment policies are usually addressed in handbooks for employees. Also, a company's culture will affect which topics are chosen for inclusion in a handbook. For example, some companies intentionally avoid creating an environment with a lot of rules and regulations and, therefore, will include only the most basic information in their handbooks. Other companies try to proactively address issues and, therefore, address a great many potential problems in the handbook. The employee handbook can be a useful tool for telling new employees about the company's history, culture, and mission.

Items that are often included in handbooks include the following:

- Miscellaneous
  - Welcome
  - Company history
  - Mission statement

- — Equal Employment Opportunity (EEO) statement
- — Union-free statement
- — Employment at-will statement
- — Current handbook supersedes all prior editions

- Policies and Procedures
  - — Probationary period
  - — Hours of work
  - — Breaks and mealtime
  - — Overtime
  - — Attendance
  - — Clocking in and out
  - — Performance appraisals
  - — Dress code
  - — Use of company property
  - — Business conduct
  - — Confidentiality
  - — Conflict of interest
  - — Discipline
  - — Electronic communications
  - — Gifts and gratuities
  - — Grievance procedures
  - — Harassment
  - — Safety and security

- Benefits
  - — Insurance
  - — Leave
  - — Tuition assistance
  - — Holidays
  - — Bonuses
  - — Consolidated Omnibus Budget Reconciliation Act (COBRA)
  - — Employee assistance programs
  - — Relocation

— Retirement

— Disability

— Worker's compensation

Sexual Harassment

Q 35: With all the discussion on sexual harassment, what do we have to do to help safeguard our company?

A: An organization should take several steps to minimize the risk of liability in cases of sexual harassment:

Issue a written policy against sexual harassment. Clearly define and provide examples of both *quid pro quo* (this for that) and hostile environment harassment, including same-sex harassment. Outline complaint procedures for employees, and explain disciplinary actions that will be taken against proven harassers. Guarantee that no retaliatory action will be taken against employees who file sexual harassment complaints. Require that all supervisory personnel report suspected sexual harassment immediately.

Establish complaint procedures. Specify the person to whom employees can report a complaint, as well as what they can expect regarding the ensuing investigation. Clearly provide employees an alternative in the event the immediate supervisor is the alleged harasser.

Communicate the policy and train the employees. Educate employees and managers about what type of conduct constitutes sexual harassment. Make all employees aware of the company's policy and their obligations, including how to report or file a complaint. Emphasize that employees can come forward with complaints without fear of retaliation or reprisal. Tailor training for managers and supervisors to include identifying sexual harassment before it is reported and handling complaints.

Promptly investigate every complaint. Conduct a prompt investigation involving only those employees who are instrumental in resolving the complaint. Document the investigation. Ensure confidentiality to the extent possible. Inform the complainant of the results of the investigation. If the investigation reveals that harassment did occur, take immediate and appropriate corrective action.

Additional information can be found in the SHRM Legal Report titled *Sexual Harassment: Prevention and Avoiding Liability* by Gilbert F. Casellas and Irene L. Hill (1998) at <www.shrm.org/whitepapers/ documents/61636.asp>.

Q 36: What guidelines should an employer follow when investigating allegations of sexual harassment?

A: When an employee complains of sexual harassment, the employer must take the complaint seriously. Employers have an obligation to investigate promptly and to take appropriate action to minimize legal liability, not to mention restoring the trust and morale of their employees. The individual conducting the investigation must be knowledgeable about the organization and its employees and must be able to gather all the facts in an objective and professional manner. Listed below are steps to follow when conducting an investigation:

- First, interview the employee claiming sexual harassment. Assure the employee that no retaliatory actions will be taken and that he or she should report any incident of retaliation. Listen carefully and write down all the facts such as dates, times, witnesses, and so forth. Use open-ended questions such as what, when, where, and how. Let the employee tell the story without interruption.

- Second, interview any potential witnesses.

- Third, interview the accused (use the same guidelines as for the first item). Inform the accused that retaliation is strictly prohibited.

- Fourth, attempt to reconcile conflicting statements.

- Fifth, make a final decision. If sexual harassment has occurred, apply the appropriate discipline and document it.

- Sixth, follow up periodically with the employee who claimed sexual harassment to ensure that no further incidents or retaliation has occurred.

- Seventh, document such follow-up visits.

- Eighth, keep all investigative documentation separate from personnel files.

- Finally, consider reiterating the sexual harassment policy to all the employees.

Employee Conduct

Q 37: What can an employer do when a supervisor and an employee are dating?

A: Some employers have implemented a dating policy in an attempt to manage this situation and its potential ramifications. Problems can include charges of sexual harassment and favoritism and the possibility of unprofessional behavior in the workplace. All of the factors that should be considered in formulating a policy are beyond the scope of this page, but employers need to be aware of the challenges they may encounter. For example, a policy that requires the resignation, transfer, or termination of the subordinate employee when two employees are dating may be found to be discriminatory if a disproportionate number of women are adversely affected.

Disparate impact can occur if the workforce is predominately male and if men hold the majority of senior or supervisory positions. A better alternative is to allow employees to make the decision about who is going to make a change. An employer's enforcement of a dating policy may also be subject to claims of invasion of privacy, especially if it is perceived that the employer is attempting to regulate an employee's behavior and actions outside the office.

In lieu of a dating policy, employers should increase awareness of their sexual harassment policy and complaint procedures. For your supervisors and employees, conduct regular training sessions about sexual harassment, and include as a part of the curriculum a discussion on the problems that can surround office romances, especially those between a supervisor and a subordinate.

Address all job performance problems as they arise. Even though you cannot prevent an office romance, you can still manage an employee's behavior.

Before choosing a course of action, an employer should consult with an attorney to assess the impact a decision will have on the organization.

Q 38: Can we require that employees speak only English in the workplace?

A: Although an employer can generally have an English language requirement as part of the job, he or she should be careful about imposing English-only rules on employees. The EEOC views English-only rules as a burdensome condition of employment and will closely scrutinize them.

Limiting employees' ability to speak their language of origin at all times can create an atmosphere of inferiority, isolation, and intimidation that is based on national origin. Rules such as those restricting language could discriminate against employees because of their national origin and, therefore, could violate Title VII.

It is perfectly legitimate to require employees to speak English during certain periods of time as long as the employer can justify it by business necessity. Some examples of business necessity would concern maintaining safety, speaking English to English-speaking customers and co-workers, and achieving productivity. When courts review English-only rules, they tend to give employers quite a bit of latitude if language rules are reasonable and can be connected to the duties of the position.

For more information, see the spring 1995 SHRM Legal Report titled *Beware the Native Tongue: National Original and English-Only Rules* (Carey & Seegull, 1995), located on the SHRM web site at <www.shrm.org/whitepapers/documents/engonly.asp>. EEOC's *National Origin Discrimination Guidelines* can be found on the EEOC web page at <www.eeoc.gov>.

Q 39: Is it a good idea to have a policy regarding employee use of the Internet?

A: Yes. Having an Internet policy is a sensible measure for any employer that allows employees access to the Internet. By having a policy in place and effectively communicating it to employees, an employer can avoid incidents that may create embarrassment and potential legal problems for both the employer and the employees.

Internet use policies can be beneficial in (a) setting limits for the personal use of Internet resources and e-mail; (b) reducing the employer's claims to invasion of privacy by explaining that employees should not expect Internet communications to remain private and confidential; and (c) forbidding the receipt or transmission of obscene, illegal, discriminatory, or other information that may result in harassment or defamation.

Although no policy can eliminate employee misconduct completely, having an Internet use policy and guidelines that are clearly communicated to employees will certainly help employers in disciplining employees for improper use of such resources. Further information and a sample policy are available through the white papers section of the SHRM web site.

Q 40: Can employers monitor employee e-mail?

A: In this era of developing technology, many companies are faced with a dilemma of whether to monitor employees' e-mail. Employees may perceive monitoring as an invasion of privacy. Employers perceive e-mail monitoring as a method of ensuring security, controlling network communication costs, and monitoring job performance. Employers have been apprehensive about monitoring e-mail because they are sensitive to employees' privacy expectations. Many courts have found that monitoring e-mail in the regular course of business is not an invasion of privacy. Establishing a policy is the best way to balance the employee's right to privacy and the employer's need to know. An e-mail policy should address the following issues:

- Business Use. The policy should state that e-mail is strictly for business use.

- Security. Security-sensitive information should not be allowed to be communicated through e-mail.

- Personal Messages. E-mail should not be used for personal business. No solicitations should be conducted through e-mail.

- Offensive Messages. Offensive and harassing communication should be unacceptable and prohibited. References should be made to the company's harassment policy.

- Privacy. Employees should be made aware that all communications over the e-mail are not private. They are open to scrutiny by company personnel. The policy should lessen the expectation of individual privacy.

- Right to Monitor. The employer should reserve the right to monitor e-mail at any time.

- Disciplinary Procedures. Guidelines for violation of company policy should be communicated.

The two documents listed below are available on the SHRM web site at <www.SHRM.org>.

- *Sample E-Mail Policy* (SHRM, 1999) at <www.SHRM.org/whitepapers/documents/emailsamp.asp>

- *E-Mail in the Workplace: How Much Is Private?* (Underhill & Lintharst, 1996)

Q 41: What should and should not be included in the employee's personnel file?

A: The following should be included in a basic personnel file:

- Employment application and résumé
- College transcripts
- Job descriptions
- Records relating to hiring, promotion, demotion, transfer, layoff, rates of pay and other forms of compensation, and education and training records
- Records relating to other employment practices
- Letters of recognition
- Disciplinary notices or documents
- Performance evaluations
- Test documents used by an employer to make an employment decision

- Exit interviews
- Termination records

The following should not be included in a basic personnel file:

- Medical or insurance records
- EEO or invitation to self-identify disability or veteran's status records
- Immigration (I–9) forms
- Child support or garnishments
- Litigation documents
- Worker's compensation claims
- Requests for employment or payroll verification
- Reference checks

Q 42: Is our company (private) obligated to allow current employees to review their personnel files? What about former employees? Is the employer obligated to make copies of employee personnel files as well?

A: There is no federal law that requires private employers to provide employees access to their personnel files. Requirements to access personnel files are guided by state law. Seventeen states have some provisions governing an employee's right to access his or her personnel file: Alaska, California, Connecticut, Delaware, Illinois, Iowa, Maine, Massachusetts, Michigan, Minnesota, Nevada, New Hampshire, Oregon, Pennsylvania, Rhode Island, Washington, and Wisconsin. The provisions and wording vary widely from state to state.

The provisions often address issues such as (a) who has access (current and former employees), (b) how much frequency of access, (c) how to obtain copies, (d) what are exceptions to the information accessible by employees, (e) what are prohibitions on the kinds of records to be kept, (f) how can record corrections be made, (g) what legal remedies are available, and (h) what can be disclosed to third parties. Please keep these items in mind when developing a company personnel file access policy.

Although you may not be required by state law to allow access, it is simply good practice to allow your employees an opportunity to review their personnel files. Honesty and openness create a positive environment where employees are aware of documentation about their employment. Thus they won't feel that their employer is trying to hide something. Certainly, nothing should go into the file without the employee's awareness and usually not without his or her signature. A copy of the information should be provided to the employee as well. Your employee handbook should provide clear guidelines about how to handle access, frequency, reproduction of information, and disagreements with the information. Be sure to check your specific state provisions when making such policy decisions.

Q 43: Is it a good practice for the supervisor to maintain a file separate from the one in the HR Department?

A: Many supervisors keep a working file on employees. While the file is not wrong in and of itself, the supervisor should not hide documentation that has been used to make an employment decision. Any backup documentation for disciplinary or promotion purposes should be kept in the HR file. Maintaining double files as a means of evading disclosure of the information should be discouraged. For example, attempts to keep one clean and safe version of the file in the HR Department and another with discriminatory comments in the supervisor's possession can be dangerous because of the possibility of discovery and required disclosure. Educating supervisors about potential problems associated with keeping such files is a good way to prevent potential problems.

Q 44: What concerns should we have when planning a company-sponsored event?

A: Many organizations enjoy sponsoring events such as sports teams, holiday parties, and other fun activities. Such events are considered to be great morale builders, but employers may be concerned that mishaps or injuries will occur and that problems may result.

Injured employees are entitled to worker's compensation. The employee is likely to be covered by worker's compensation if the event is held on company property during work hours. However, if an employee was attending a function or another fun activity without the company officially sponsoring the event, the employee may not be covered by worker's compensation. Listed below are some issues to consider while planning a company social event or other sponsored activities:

- Who plans the activity?
- Who financially supports the activity?
- When will the activity take place?
- Will the activity be held during work hours?
- Where will the activity take place?
- Who benefits from the activity?
- Will attendance at the activity be voluntary or involuntary?
- Will employees be penalized for not attending the activity?

- Will alcohol be served at the activity?

To alleviate their concerns, employers may want to consult with legal counsel. Some companies develop a form that states that the employee is voluntarily participating in the activity. Establishing a well-thought-out plan and providing clear communication for company-sponsored events will always be helpful.

Q 45: It has always been our company's practice to celebrate the holiday season with an office party. This year we would like to explore other options for our employees. Are there any creative alternatives for year-end holiday activities?

A: There are many alternatives to traditional office parties when employers are planning year-end holiday activities. Because of the diverse nature of today's workforce, employers are choosing to help employees celebrate the holiday season with a wider variety of special year-end activities.

Some less traditional activities include things such as food or gourmet baskets, gift certificates, year-end bonuses or gifts, contests and raffles for prizes, holiday dinners, additional paid holidays, community projects to help assist the underprivileged, gift matching to employees' local charitable organizations, coupons for theater or musical events, or the traditional formal holiday parties.

For some employers, budgetary constraints may not allow much room for things such as parties, gifts, or bonuses for employees. However, those employers can still convey their greetings and express their appreciation by sending workers holiday cards or special letters of thanks signed by supervisors or members of upper management, or by devoting the final issue of the company newsletter to workers' religious and holiday observances. Another option for employers is to consider teaming up with other employers in their area to share any combined costs of offering a formal holiday party outside the workplace.

Because such a variety of options is available to fit a variety of different budgets, employers should make every effort to provide employees with some type of year-end activity or special holiday acknowledgment. Doing so can be a great way to increase productivity and boost employee morale.

Q 46: Our company has decided to have a holiday party, which will include serving alcohol. What are some potential liabilities, and what can we do to minimize the company's risks?

A: At any type of company-sponsored party, an employer may be held liable for employees' actions during the party, as well as for any injuries incurred. Additionally, employees who are injured at company-sponsored holiday parties may be eligible to receive worker's compensation benefits.

Employers can incorporate the following suggestions into their holiday party plans so they can minimize liability when alcohol is a factor:

- Before the party, be sure to communicate to employees that excessive drinking will not be tolerated. Also state that intoxication and inappropriate behavior at the party will be grounds for disciplinary action.

- Convey to employees that the holiday party is purely a social event and that attendance is voluntary.

- Involve employee participation in holiday party planning.

- Hold the party at an off-site location, and use professional bartenders to serve and monitor alcohol consumption.

- Do not provide open bars. Instead provide cash bars and implement a drink limit per individual (i.e., a ticket system).

- Do not permit managers or supervisors to buy alcoholic beverages for employees.

- Stop serving alcohol early, well before the party's scheduled ending time.

- Offer a wide variety of nonalcoholic beverages, and serve protein-rich foods to slow digestion and alcohol absorption.

- Provide a variety of entertainment (i.e., dancing, games) so that drinking is not the focus of the party.

- Hold the party at a location that is easily accessible by public transportation.

- Collect employees' car keys when they arrive at the party.

- Arrange for volunteer spotters and volunteer-designated drivers to monitor the party, to determine if individuals are intoxicated, and to drive them home.

- Arrange for alternative transportation (i.e., taxis) for intoxicated individuals.

- If held at a hotel, arrange for a block of rooms that employees can reserve at a discount.

Although these suggestions won't eliminate liability, they will minimize employer risk and will promote a holiday season of happiness and safety.

Q 47: One of our employees recently came in to work with her tongue pierced. Can we discipline her for violating our dress code?

A: Maybe. Because personal appearance is a matter of personal taste, company dress codes can be difficult to develop and even harder to enforce. However, even in our litigious society, companies do retain some rights. One of them is the right to expect that employees will be dressed, will be groomed, and will behave in a manner appropriate for their positions, their workplace, and the community in which they work. Nonetheless, even the most specific and carefully crafted dress code may need to be modified to address the newest vogue—body piercing. The days when only women wore earrings are gone. Now, depending on where your company is located, you may encounter multiple earrings; earrings on men; and pierced noses, lips, eyebrows, and tongues. Although body piercing is not widespread in business environments across most of the United States as of this writing, there are certainly communities and workplaces where it is considered socially acceptable.

If an employee's personal appearance or hygiene is such that it causes offense to co-workers or customers, it is appropriate for a company to address the problem. If additional earrings present a problem, it may be possible to ask the employee to remove them while at work or when dealing directly with customers, rather than resorting to more drastic forms of discipline. A company without a written dress policy will have difficulty defending its position.

In developing a policy, or dealing with a potential violation of policy, be sure to focus on the business reasons for the standards you have. Make those reasons consistent with the company's image. It is generally considered more reasonable to require strict adherence to a dress policy in situations where employees have regular customer contact or where safety or hygiene is of particular importance. Be sure to eliminate the potential for discrimination by considering racial, ethnic, religious, and other stereotypical assumptions that may arise from specific provisions of your policy. Finally, be certain to consistently enforce dress codes to prevent employees from feeling singled out.

Standards for acceptable business dress are undergoing constant metamorphosis. What may be inappropriate today may be fine tomorrow. Develop a strong, clear policy and modify it as necessary according to changing circumstances. Include provisions in your policy that allow for variations based on type of position and amount of customer contact, if appropriate. Deal with problems and complaints quickly and respectfully. Focus on the business or job reasons for corrective action.

Q 48: Can we prevent employees who smoke from taking breaks during the day?

A: There are several issues here. The primary one is that of discrimination. About half of the states currently have smokers' rights laws in effect; these laws protect smokers from discrimination that is based on the fact that they are smokers. Even in the states that do not have current laws in effect, preventing the smokers from taking breaks solely because they are smokers is not a wise practice. There could even be adverse effect if the majority of smokers in your workplace are in a protected class. Therefore, the company must first make sure this employment decision is not one that is punitive or discriminatory in nature.

If the company wants to prevent smoking breaks because of productivity concerns, those concerns are a safe place to start. The next concern is fairness. Policies cannot be implemented to affect some of the employees and not to affect others (especially when the rights of the former group are protected as stated above). Therefore, if the company wants to crack down on the number of breaks taken, it must do so for all of the employees. Other employees may be taking breaks as frequently as the smokers are; however, their breaks may not be as visible to others. To be fair, you must address these other breaks as well.

The next step is to write and implement a clear policy and to determine at what point the breaks will become cause for disciplinary action. How many breaks will the company allow? How long will they be? What will the consequences be when there is abuse of the allowances? You need to carefully write the policy and to carry out the penalties consistently in all instances. Once you put the policy in writing and begin to apply it, your company must apply it in all cases, not just for the smokers. Otherwise, legal problems, as well as morale problems, will probably arise.

Q 49: We are considering rehiring a former employee. What are the issues in doing so?

A: Although former employees may represent a source of well-qualified applicants, there are several issues to consider before instituting a practice or policy of rehiring:

- Why did the individual leave in the first place? Naturally, if the individual was terminated for cause, companies are not interested in inviting him or her to return to work. If, however, the individual left in good standing and if, in retrospect, the organization favorably remembers the person's contributions, then re-employment may be highly desirable.

- Will the organization give preference to rehires or merely include them in the pool of other applicants for an open position? A couple of risks to preferential treatment are that (a) employees have little incentive to stay with an organization in the first place when they know they can leave and easily return, and (b) organizations struggling to improve the diversity of their workforce as a result of required or voluntary Affirmative Action efforts may find preferential treatment works against them if they rehire members of the majority group over the groups they are working to increase.

- Is the individual fully qualified for the position for which he or she is applying? What experience has the person gained since leaving your company? Is the individual's education and experience comparable to that of others who have applied for the position? There may, in some cases, be a tendency to rush to rehire popular employees who performed well in one position because you assume they will perform equally well in another. Using objective selection criteria for these individuals will help to eliminate such favorable (or unfavorable) biases.

- Will employee benefits be reinstated at the same level as when the employee departed? With the exception of ERISA (in general, ERISA requires prior periods of service to be counted following a break in service for vesting purposes), the decision to reinstate benefits is left to the company and is based on policy and plan requirements. Some considerations are (a) the amount of time elapsed between the dates of resignation and rehire, (b) the number of years of service before resignation, (c) the plan's requirements (such as waiting periods), and (d) the prior receipt of benefits (such as severance pay). Will the individual be eligible for such benefits again at the same level?

- Does the organization have a seniority policy in place? If so, are rehired individuals reinstated to their prior level of seniority for purposes of promotions, recognition programs, and so forth?

Finally, there may be legal or policy requirements to re-employ workers who are on extended periods away, such as military leave, or who are guaranteed re-employment as a result of an employment agreement, union contract, or layoff policy.

It is sometimes said that you can't go back, an expression that may best describe the subjective issue behind this question. Although there will always be circumstances when an organization is delighted to re-employ a star employee, or where a tight labor market or specialized job makes it a necessity, all too often former employees are compared against their replacements and may not, in retrospect, be missed as much as expected. Guarantees or preferential treatment for rehires may then be a disadvantage. A better solution may be a policy (a) that discusses what will happen IF a person applies for rehire, (b) that does not promise such preferential treatment, and (c) that includes a conservative policy for reinstating benefits.

Q 50: An employee has requested to use an empty conference room during lunch to hold a prayer group. Should we allow this usage?

A: Generally, yes. Employers have an obligation under Title VII to reasonably accommodate the religious practices and beliefs of employees and applicants, unless the employer can demonstrate that accommodation would result in undue hardship on the conduct of business. Undue hardship exists if a proposed accommodation would require (a) a variance from a bona fide seniority system (e.g., when to do so would deny another employee his or her job or shift preference as guaranteed by the system), (b) violation of collective bargaining agreements, (c) more than a *de minimus* cost, or (d) discrimination against those employees who do not share the beliefs of the employee seeking accommodation.

Your employee should be allowed to engage in religious exercise and religious expression with fellow employees to the same extent that you as an employer allow employees to engage in comparable nonreligious exercise or expression. For example, if you permit employees to meet during lunch for Weight Watchers meetings or book clubs in the workplace, you must allow this employee to hold a prayer group under similar conditions. If the employees sponsoring those meetings are permitted to invite their coworkers to the meetings at work, for example, on a bulletin board or by e-mail, your employee must also be allowed to invite attendees to the prayer group under similar conditions. It is important to note that the law protects employees against religious demands by their employers and against unwelcome religious intrusions by both employers and co-workers. It is also advisable to consult state and local laws to determine what additional requirements exist concerning religious discrimination.

References

Chapter 2. General Employment Practices

Advanced Personnel Systems. (1999). Policy manual/employee handbook creation. [List of software]. In *Personnel Software Census*. Advanced Personnel Systems, (916) 781-2900 or <www.hrcensus.com>.

Carey, J. H., & Seegull, L. (1995). *Beware the native tongue: National original and English-only rules*. (White paper). [On-line]. Available: <www.shrm.org/whitepapers/documents/ engonly.asp>. Accessed 5/99.

Casellas, G. F., & Hill, I. L. (1998). *Sexual harassment: Prevention and avoiding liability*. (White paper no. 61636). [On-line]. Available: <www.shrm.org/whitepapers/documents/ 61636.asp>. Accessed 5/99.

De la Cruz, J., & Walters, R. (1999). *The WARN paper*. (White paper warn.asp). [On-line]. Available: <www.shrm.org/whitepapers/documents/warn.asp>. Accessed 6/99.

Edwards, M. (1996). *360-degree feedback*: *The powerful new model for employee assessment and performance.* New York: American Management Association.

Equal Employment Opportunity Commission (EEOC). *Technical assistance on Title I of ADA.* Washington, DC: EEOC.

Erum, S., Macauley, A., & Stuckey, T. II. (1999). *Tips for employers who want to avoid legal claims for downsizing.* (White paper no. 61112). [On-line]. Available: <www. shrm.org/whitepapers/documents/61112.asp>. Accessed 6/99.

Falcone, P. (1999). A legal dichotomy? Employment-at-will doesn't mean you should ignore progressive discipline. *HRMagazine,* 44, 5: 110–120.

Lepsinger, R., & Lucing A. (1997). *The art and science of 360-degree feedback.* San Francisco: Jossey-Bass.

Pierson, G., & Fulkerson, S. (1999). *The Older Workers' Benefit Protection Act: Are waivers worth the paper they're written on?* (White paper no. 61629). [On-line]. Available: <www.shrm.org/whitepapers/documents/61629.asp>. Accessed 5/99.

Quirk, J. (1993). *A brief overview of the Age Discrimination in Employment Act (ADEA).* (White paper no. 61215). [On-line]. Available: <www.shrm.org/whitepapers/ documents/61215.asp> or <www.eeoc.gov>. Accessed 5/99.

Sandler, D. R. (1998). *Noncompete agreements: Considering the ties that bind.* (White paper no. 61219). [On-line]. Available: <www.shrm.org/whitepapers/documents/61219. asp>. Accessed 6/99.

Scharinger, D. (1996). *Preparation of the employee handbook.* (White paper no. 61171). [On-line]. Available: SHRM, (800) 283-7476) or <www.shrm.org/whitepapers/ documents/ 61171.asp>. Accessed 5/99.

Society for Human Resource Management (SHRM). (ongoing database) *Buyer's guide.* [On-line]. Available: <www.shrm.org>.

Society for Human Resource Management (SHRM). (ongoing database) *Consultants' database.* [On-line]. Available: <www.shrm.org>.

Society for Human Resource Management (SHRM). (1999). *Sample e-mail policy.* (White paper). [On-line]. Available: SHRM, (800) 283-7476 or <www.shrm.org/ whitepapers/ documents/emailsamp.asp>. Accessed 5/99.

Tornow, W., & London, M. (1998). *Maximizing the value of 360-degree feedback.* San Francisco: Jossey-Bass.

Underhill, M., & Lintharst, T. (1996). *E-mail in the workplace: How much is private?* (White paper no. 61662). [On-line]. Available: SHRM, (800) 283-7476 or <www.shrm. org/documents/61662.asp>. Accessed 6/99.

CHAPTER 3

STAFFING

Pre-employment

Q 1:   How do we develop a staffing plan?

> **A:** Staff planning is a systematic process to ensure that an organization has the right number of people with the right skills to fulfill business needs. You must take into account internal and external changes and must integrate HR planning with the company's business plan. The following list describes the various steps needed to develop a staff-planning program:
>
> 1. **Job description**. Develop a job description with input from the manager.
>
> 2. **Job requirements**. Develop a detailed and useful set of job requirements with the manager. This information can help you determine whether qualified candidates already exist or whether they can be developed within the company before recruiting externally. Some of the questions to ask are (a) what skills, knowledge, and abilities are required for the job; (b) what are some of the characteristics of the people who succeed or fail in the job; (c) what qualifications are needed for the job; and (d) how does the job relate to others.
>
> 3. **Fair employment considerations**. To avoid illegal screening of applicants with disabilities, list job duties describing only what the necessary tasks are, not how the tasks are normally performed.
>
> 4. **Assessment of current employees' skills**. Gather skills information from your employees to help you find qualified internal candidates before recruiting from outside.
>
> 5. **Turnover trends**. Document turnover trends to help you predict how many people will leave an organization. This information will prepare you for peak recruitment times.
>
> 6. **Business trends**. Consider two issues when analyzing business trends: the internal changes and the external factors. Internal adjustments such

as changes in work shifts, workforce demographics, and downsizing, as well as external factors such as a merger or acquisition, legislation, and so forth will affect staff planning.

Once all relevant information has been collected, the HR Department can forecast its staffing and recruitment needs.

Q 2:   What is situational interviewing?

A: The situational interview is a method of conducting a structured interview. Structured interviews are the result of HR professionals seeking fairer, more reliable, and more valid selection methods. The situational interview (Taylor & O'Driscoll, 1995) addresses three main issues: "... the ability to consistently identify people who can do the job; the ability to make selection decisions which are capable of withstanding legal scrutiny; practicality in implementation."

In a situational interview, applicants are asked a series of questions regarding how they would respond in hypothetical job situations. The theory is that the applicant's response to the hypothetical situation is a predictor of how the applicant will respond in an actual incident. Hence, a critical factor in using situational interviews is ensuring that the situations presented are representative of important job duties and of incidents that actually occur in the position.

The elements of situational interview questions are a brief synopsis of the situation and then a question similar to "What would you do?" An example of a situational question for interviewing an applicant for an HR Director position is "You are approached by an employee who tells you that she has AIDS and will need time off for the required treatment and its effects. How would you handle this situation?"

One of the primary advantages of situational interviewing is the minimization of the effects of some interviewers' inability to obtain and to interpret meaningful information about applicants. The structured nature of the situational interview puts the interviewers—and more important, the job candidates—on the same playing field.

For more information on situational interviewing, the following resources may be of interest to you:

- *Structured Employment Interviewing* by Paul Taylor and Michael O'Driscoll (1995)

- *Topgrading* by Bradford Smart (1999)

- *Extraviewing: Innovative Ways to Hire the Best* by Arthur Bell (1992)

Q 3:   What compliance issues are involved in creating a pre-employment test?

A: Pre-employment testing is a selection tool that can provide valuable information to aid the selection process. Pre-employment tests can add objectivity to the selection process if applicants for the same position take the same test under the same conditions and if the test accurately measures skills essential to job performance. Pre-employment tests should be validated (content validity, construct validity, criterion-related validity) to ensure that they measure the knowledge or skills that an applicant would need to perform the job.

Many compliance issues should be considered when implementing a pre-employment testing program. The Uniform Guidelines on Employee Selection Procedures of 1978 is one tool that can help with compliance issues. The Guidelines set forth a single set of employment standards on all employers covered under Title VII or Executive Order 11246, and they aid in determining whether an employer policy or practice causes a "disproportionate adverse impact" on the employment opportunities of any race, sex, or ethnic group. To determine whether a selection procedure causes an adverse impact, you should apply the "4/5ths rule" or 80% rule. The 80% rule involves comparing the hiring rates for different groups. If the selection rate for a protected group (defined by race, ethnic origin, sex, etc.) is less than 4/5ths (or 80%) of that for the group with the highest selection rate, the procedure is considered discriminatory.

Pre-employment testing must adhere to the employment provisions of the Americans with Disabilities Act (ADA). If a test screens out or tends to screen out a person with a disability, the test must be job related and must be consistent with business necessity. Even if a test is job related and justified by business necessity, an employer has an obligation to provide a specific reasonable accommodation, if necessary. The reasonable accommodation obligation applies to testing by protecting persons with disabilities from being excluded from jobs that they actually can do, because a disability either prevents them from taking a test or negatively influences a test result. However, an employer does not have to provide an alternative test format for a person with an impaired skill if the purpose of the test is to measure that skill.

Employers are encouraged to check their state laws before implementing a pre-employment testing program. If a testing program involves medical examinations, AIDS testing, or genetic testing, other rules and regulations govern those types of tests.

Q 4:   What do we need to do to implement a pre-employment drug screen?

A: The design and implementation of a pre-employment drug screening program should involve the input and cooperation of HR, legal counsel, and security. Make sure that the policy for testing complies with the drug testing laws in your state.

The requirements of relevant laws should be incorporated into the program. Local and state laws, in addition to federal laws, may need to be reviewed. Federal laws that may be applicable include the following:

- The Omnibus Transportation Employee Testing Act of 1991. This law mandates pre-employment testing. Employers in the transportation industry should review this legislation for procedural requirements.

- The U.S. Department of Defense (DOD). This federal agency specifies drug-free workplace requirements for its contractors.

- Executive Order No. 12564. This order establishes drug testing policies and procedures for federal employees.

- The ADA. This law allows pre-offer tests for illegal substances; however, only post-offer tests for blood alcohol level are permitted. In addition, the ADA protects applicants who have successfully completed a drug rehabilitation program. Therefore, an employer should establish a timeframe within which an applicant who previously tested positive can reapply.

- The Rehabilitation Act. This law applies to the federal government, government contractors, and those receiving financial assistance from the federal government. The Act protects those in drug rehabilitation programs or those who have successfully completed such programs.

The types of substances to screen for and the acceptable level of use should be identified. Legal requirements pertaining to the screening of the substances should also be identified.

Determine whether urine or blood sampling will be used. Urine sampling requires the establishment of procedures to prevent substitution or debasing of the sample by the addition of foreign materials.

The privacy of samples should be maintained by establishing a sample identification method that does not include the applicant's name. In addition, a sound chain-of-custody procedure must be used.

When selecting a lab to conduct the testing, choose one that meets your organization's testing needs. In addition,

- The lab should have a history of highly reliable results and a methodology to confirm initial positive results. Gas chromatography or mass spectrometry are reliable methods for verification. Also, the lab should be enrolled in a minimum of one independently administered program to monitor its success rate.

- Check whether the lab is licensed and accredited per applicable local, state, and federal laws.

- Determine the complete services provided and the associated fees so that testing costs can be determined.

- Set up a procedure to frequently check the quality of service provided by the lab.

Notice of the substance-screening policy should be placed on employment applications. Notify the applicant of the testing procedure and test the applicant only after he or she has been notified of the test and procedures and has given his or her consent. Test all applicants for all jobs.

Employees should be given an opportunity to retest, as well as a means to challenge results. The consequences of a positive test result should be made clear to the applicant.

Sources:

- Bureau of National Affairs (BNA)

- *Minding Your Business* by M. J. Lotito and L. C. Outwater (1997)

Q 5:   How do we track our applicants for our Affirmative Action Plan (AAP)? What is the definition of an applicant?

A: The definition of an applicant depends on the company's hiring practices. A company is free to define what it considers an applicant as long as its practice is consistent. For example, an applicant can be anyone who has expressed interest in the job and who is qualified for the position. In its recruitment policy, the company should communicate whom it considers an applicant. Some of the questions a company should consider when defining an applicant are these: Will walk-ins or unsolicited resumes be accepted? Does an individual have to apply for a specific job?

Once an applicant is defined, an employer with an AAP needs to maintain an applicant flow log. Although employers without AAPs are not required to maintain an applicant flow log, the EEOC advises employers to have one to support their selection practices.

To track the personal information of the applicants, companies should ask applicants to complete a *tear sheet*. A tear sheet is a voluntary form that is completed by the applicant and that tracks information such as name, address, referral source, sex, race, position applied for, veteran's status, handicap status, and employment type (i.e., full-time, part-time, etc.). According to the Office of Federal Contract Compliance Programs (OFCCP), an applicant log must provide at least data for sex, race, veteran's status, or handicapped status, if applicable.

Tables 3–1 and 3–2 are examples of applicant flow data charts that could be used for tracking the required data.

Some additional data that a company may want to track would cover apparent age (without asking the employee his or her age), the reason the job was turned down, where and when the job opening was advertised, and how many responses were received.

For more information on AAPs and applicant flow logs, see the following books that are available from the SHRMStore:

- *Forms Used in Human Resources* by SHRM (1997)

- *How to Write an Affirmative Action Plan* by S. Bruce (1994)

Or visit the OFCCP web site at <www.dol.gov/dol/esa/public/ofcp_org. htm>.

Q 6: What are the compliance issues involved in conducting pre-employment criminal background checks?

A: Employers who use police records to screen applicants must take care not to tread on risky legal ground. The first thing to consider is that an arrest is not the same as a conviction. Basing an employment decision solely on an applicant's arrest record can be discriminatory, because it has been shown that certain protected classes tend to have a higher arrest rate. To help minimize potential discrimination charges, an employer should limit record checks to convictions rather than arrests. If an applicant's background check does show a record of a conviction, then the employer should consider whether business necessity warrants rejecting the applicant on the basis of that conviction. The EEOC's guidelines for weighing the business necessity standard state that an employer should consider the following when basing employment decisions on conviction records:

- The nature and severity of the offense(s)

- The amount of time that has lapsed since the conviction or sentencing

- The relevancy of the conviction to the job for which the applicant is applying (job relatedness)

State laws vary regarding an employer's using criminal records or inquiring about them. Some states require employers to conduct criminal record

TABLE 3–1
APPLICANT FLOW LOG: NUMBER OF HIRES

Job Group/Title	EEO-Category	White		Black		Hispanic		American Indian		Asian	
		Male	Female	Male	Female	Male	Female	Male	Female	Male	Female

TABLE 3–2
APPLICANT FLOW LOG: RECORD OF HIRES

Date Hired	Name	White		Black		Hispanic		American Indian		Asian		Veteran		Disability		Position	Starting Salary
		Male	Female	Male	Female	Male	Female	Male	Female	Male	Female	Yes	No	Yes	No		

checks before hiring for certain types of positions such as prison staff, security personnel, public school personnel, and so forth. Other states grant a greater amount of protection to applicants regarding criminal record disclosures. Although protections vary from state to state, generallyspeaking, prospective employees are not normally required to disclose any information concerning arrests or criminal charges that did not result in an actual conviction, nor are they required to disclose information regarding convictions that have been pardoned or protected by the courts in some other way. Last but not least, some states require employers who use criminal records to advise applicants that criminal records will be used and to obtain written authorization for release of such records.

Criminal record inquiries can be a valuable tool when used properly and within the guidelines of federal and state laws to ensure that an employer will not be charged with negligent hiring or retention claims. To ensure compliance with both federal and state laws, an employer must carefully consider employment decisions that will be based on past criminal history.

Q 7: What are the compliance issues involved in conducting pre-employment physical examinations?

A: The law that most affects an employer's ability to require pre-employment physical examinations is the ADA. Essentially, an employer may require a physical examination only after a contingent offer of employment has been made. No physical examination can be required before an offer is made. Physical examinations can be required only if the following exist:

- All other candidates in the job category are also required to have a physical examination.

- The candidate's medical history is treated confidentially and is kept separate from other employment-related records.

- The results of the examination are not used to discriminate against persons covered by the ADA.

A physical exam should assess whether the person is currently able to perform the duties of a job with or without accommodation. To make this assessment, the medical practitioner who conducts the examination must have a clear understanding of the job. The medical practitioner assumes no responsibility for the ultimate hiring decision. Also, it is wise to have only job-related physical attributes or conditions examined.

Contingent offers of employment may be withdrawn based on the results of a physical examination if the reason for withdrawing the offer is job related, is consistent with business necessity, or is imperative to avoid a direct threat to health or safety. Contingent offers may also be withdrawn (a) if there is no reasonable accommodation that the employer could make to allow the person to perform the job, or (b) if providing the needed accommodation would cause undue hardship. Offers of employment cannot be legally withdrawn because of speculation about a person's future attendance or use of benefits.

Q 8: Can we ask if an applicant has a disability?

A: The ADA prohibits employers from asking this question or any question whose intent is to find out about possible disabilities. If the applicant has an obvious disability or voluntarily discloses the disability, an employer can ask if reasonable accommodation is needed. If the answer is yes, the employer can ask what type of accommodation is needed. If the answer is no, the employer is prohibited from asking any further questions about accommodation but may ask the applicant to describe or demonstrate performance. Interviewing candidates with known disabilities should be no different from interviewing candidates without disabilities. You should always focus on the functions of the job, not the disabilities.

Q 9: What accommodations should we make for applicants with disabilities?

A: The ADA requires employers to provide reasonable accommodations to employees or job applicants who are qualified individuals with disabilities, unless doing so would cause undue hardship. An accommodation is any change in the work environment or the way things are usually done that will enable an individual with a disability to enjoy equal employment opportunities. Accommodations are also required during the job application process, if needed.

An employer is obligated to provide accommodations for known disabilities. Generally, it is the responsibility of the individual with the disability to inform the employer of the need for accommodation. This need can be stated in "plain English," and the individual is not required to mention the ADA, to fill out forms, or to use the term "reasonable accommodation." The employer must inform employees and applicants of its obligation under the ADA to provide reasonable accommodations. Notices should be posted in conspicuous places where employees and applicants can see them. Notices can be included in job applications, in job vacancy notices, or in internal postings or can be communicated orally.

The Equal Employment Opportunity Commission (EEOC, 1999) has issued specific guidelines on reasonable accommodation and job applicants. When the applicant has not asked for an accommodation, the employer

... may tell applicants what the hiring process involves (e.g., an interview, timed written test, or job demonstration), and may ask applicants whether they will need a reasonable accommodation for this process.

During the hiring process and before a conditional offer is made, an employer generally may not ask an applicant whether [he or she] needs a reasonable accommodation for the job, except when the employer knows that an applicant has a disability—either because it is obvious or the applicant has voluntarily disclosed the information—and could reasonably believe that the applicant will need a reasonable accommodation to perform specific job functions. If the applicant replies that [he or she] needs a reasonable accommodation, the employer may inquire as to what type.

After a conditional offer of employment is extended, an employer may inquire whether applicants will need reasonable accommodation related to anything connected with the job (i.e., job performance or access to benefits/privileges of the job) as long as all entering employees in the same job category are asked this question. Alternatively, an employer may ask a specific if [he or she] needs a reasonable accommodation if the employer knows that this applicant has a disability—either because it is obvious or the applicant has voluntarily disclosed the information—and could reasonably believe that the applicant will need a reasonable accommodation. If the applicant replies that [he or she] needs a reasonable accommodation, the employer may inquire as to what type.

The EEOC guidelines clearly state that individuals with disabilities who meet initial requirements to be considered for a job should not be excluded from the application process because the employer speculates (a speculation based on the request for reasonable accommodation to complete the application process) that the individual will be unable to perform the job. The need for reasonable accommodation for the application process should be evaluated separate from any accommodations needed to perform the job.

Q 10: If we lay off employees, do we have to rehire them?

A: No, unless the employer has promised or has a policy to rehire laid-off employees when work is available. Unionized employers must follow their collective bargaining agreement on recall status. Failure to comply with the terms of the union contract could lead to an arbitration decision overturning the employer's action. Everyone involved in communicating the layoff must avoid making promises, verbally or in writing, that could create a legally binding obligation.

Staffing Changes

Q 11: What are some guidelines for sound termination procedures?

A: A sound termination policy begins with the training and the accountability of supervisors in performance management issues. Supervisors are responsible for communicating company policy and disciplinary procedures for violating company policy, conducting regular performance reviews, and counseling employees who underperform. In addition, managers should be thoroughly trained in what the acceptable grounds or procedures are for terminating an employee.

Each termination should be carried out in accordance with your company's termination policy. A sound termination policy is made up of the following components:

- The manager should obtain approval from HR or senior management before terminating an employee. This practice will help to ensure that rash actions are not taken and that there are legitimate reasons for the termination. Though supervisors should seek approval for terminations, they should be empowered to immediately suspend employees in cases of gross misconduct.

- The manager should provide supporting documentation for the termination, such as performance reviews, disciplinary actions, and notes from meetings held with the employee.

- The HR Department and senior management should investigate the grounds for the termination. If the grounds are legitimate and the documentation is in order, then the termination should be carried out.

- The employee should be given the opportunity to review and to respond to the reasons for the termination. Including grievance procedures in the termination policy will give the employee an opportunity to express complaints that otherwise might be expressed to a lawyer or a judge.

- The employer should ensure that all alternatives to termination have been explored, particularly with long-term employees. For example, is transferring or demoting the employee an option?

Q 12: What is constructive discharge?

A: Constructive discharge refers to the resignation of an employee because the employer deliberately made the work environment so intolerable that the employee could not function effectively and, thus, resigned as the only recourse. Such a situation is viewed as a type of discriminatory discharge and often comes up in cases involving union activity, sexual harassment, age discrimination, and disability accommodation.

It is often difficult to prove constructive discharge. Some courts require that the complainant prove that the employer intended for a resignation to occur. Other courts require only a demonstration that any reasonable person would have felt compelled to leave under the same circumstances. The complainant may be required to prove that he or she took other, less drastic steps to resolve the problem before resigning. For example, a complainant may be required to show that the sexual harassment he or she experienced on the job produced a work environment so intolerable that any reasonable person would have felt compelled to resign, and that the employer either intended resignation to occur or was aware of the sexual harassment and neglected to take appropriate action.

The cost to an employer can be high if the employee is successful in proving the case. Costs can include back pay, damages, and attorneys' fees. Reinstatement may also be a requirement. If the complainant shows that the employer's motive was discriminatory or otherwise illegal, the supervisor and the employer can be liable for both punitive and the actual damages under certain state laws.

It is important for an employer to realize (a) that certain states have laws that govern constructive discharge claims and (b) that the requirements for substantiating a claim differ among the courts. Company policies should include a request for employees to provide resignation letters and to participate in exit interviews as a way to ensure that an employee is terminating voluntarily rather than through constructive discharge.

Adverse Staffing Practices

Q 13: Do you have a sample employment requisition? What should be included on an employment requisition?

A: An employment requisition form is an internal form that can be used for requesting staff members or making changes to current staffing. The form can be a check-and-balance system to ensure that managers, HR, and

Human Resource Management
75

finance are all aware of staffing requests and budgetary requirements. (See Table 3–3.)

TABLE 3–3
SAMPLE EMPLOYMENT REQUISITION

Supervisor name: _____   Supervisor title: _____
Date of request: _____   Date needed: _____
Department: _____   Location: _____
Job title: _____   Salary grade: _____
Proposed corporate title: _____   Salary range: _____
Exempt: _____   Regular full-time: _____
Nonexempt: _____   Regular part-time: _____ hrs/wk
Supervisor: _____   Temporary full-time: _____
Nonsupervisor: _____   Temporary part-time: _____ hrs/wk
                                                                  (Estimated term date): _____

Addition is within budget: _____
Addition is approved as over budget: _____
Replacement: _____ If replacement, who is vacating position and why? _____
_____

Job description? _____ Yes (please attach) _____ No
If no, give a complete description of the work to be performed: _____
_____

Special qualifications and experience required: _____
_____

Originated by: _____   Date: _____
Approved by: _____   Date: _____
Received in HR by: _____   Date: _____

Q 14: What are disparate impact and disparate treatment?

A: Disparate impact occurs when an employer's practice (such as using employment selection criteria) has a disproportionate adverse impact on the employment opportunities of a group of individuals because of their sex, race, color, religion, or ethnicity. One way to determine if disparate impact is present is by using the 4/5ths rule.

The 4/5ths rule is used to determine disparate impact by looking at the selection rate of a minority group and by comparing it to the selection rate of the majority group. If the minority selection rate is less than 4/5ths, or 80%, of the majority group, the practice could be discriminatory. The most notable case regarding disparate impact was *Griggs v. Duke Power Co.* (1971), a case in which requiring a high school diploma and passing a standardized test were shown to have a negative effect on African-American applicants when compared to white applicants. If employers are able to show that the employment practice in question is a business necessity and is job related, the courts may uphold the practice.

Disparate treatment is intentional treatment that results in discrimination against a protected group on the basis of sex, race, color, religion, or ethnicity. In cases of disparate treatment, employees or applicants must show that intentional discriminatory practices took place. In response, an employer must show a legitimate reason for the practice.

Q 15: Who is required to file Form Vets–100 (VETS–100) form? Where do we obtain a copy?

A: All nonexempt recipients of federal contracts or subcontracts are required to complete the VETS–100 form for furnishing supplies and services or using real or personal property in the amount of $10,000 or more. Services include, but are not limited to, utilities, construction, transportation, research, insurance, and fund depository—irrespective of whether the government is the purchaser or the seller.

There are three options for filing VETS–100 data: (a) by electronic means on a 3 1/2 in. high-density diskette in an *ASCII comma delimited* text file, (b) by providing the current year's hard copy of the VETS–100 form, and (c) in the near future by using the Internet web site at <www.nvti. cudenver.edu/vets.vet100.asp>.

For questions about any of these filing formats, call the VETS–100 help desk at (703) 461-2460 or send e-mail to <VETS100@dyniet.com>.

Equal Employment Opportunity

Q 16: What are the Equal Employment Opportunity (EEO) recordkeeping and reporting requirements?

A: Title VII of the 1994 Civil Rights Act requires that all private and public employers with 100 or more employees file an annual "Equal Employment Opportunity Report" (EEO–1) on or before September 30. The report requires that employers provide a statistical breakdown of their workforce by gender and race. The EEOC currently has no requirements that specific records be maintained other than a copy of the most recent EEO–1 report. However, the EEOC recommends that any records that are maintained and that were used to classify an employee's racial or ethnic identity be kept separate from other employment records that are available to individuals responsible for making personnel decisions.

Labor organizations with 100 or more members at any time during a 12-month period are required to file a "Local Union Equal Employment Opportunity Report" (EEO–3) with the EEOC by December 31 in even-numbered years. EEO–3 requires local unions to provide a statistical breakdown of their membership, applications for membership, referrals, and applications for referrals by gender and race. Records necessary to complete the EEO–3 report must be kept for 1 year from the date the report is due. Membership applications and referral applications must be kept for 6 months from the date they were made.

Political jurisdictions with 100 or more employees are required to file a "State and Local Government Information Report" (EEO–4) by September 30 in odd-numbered years. The EEO–4 report requires a statistical breakdown of the workforce by gender, race, and salary. Political subdivisions with 15 or more employees are required to keep for 3 years all records and statistics used to complete EEO–4.

Public elementary and secondary school systems or districts and separately administered schools must file an "Elementary-Secondary Staff Information Report" (EEO–5) by November 30 of even-numbered years if they employ 100 or more employees or if they employ 15 or more employees and the EEOC has requested a report to be filed. This report consists of two parts—one part is for the school district as a whole; the other part is for each school within the district and provides a statistical breakdown of all full-time and part-time staff members by assignment classification, gender, and race. Records used for completing the EEO–5 report must be maintained for 3 years.

Institutes of higher education with 15 or more employees are required to file an "Integrated Post-secondary Education Data Systems Report" (IPEDS–S), which replaces the former "Form EEO–6" (EEO–6), by November 30 in odd-numbered years. IPEDS–S requires that all institutions provide a statistical breakdown of their workforce by length of contract, salary classifications, primary occupational activity, tenure, and rank by gender and race. All records used for completion of IPEDS–S must be kept for 3 years.

In addition to the above reporting requirements, government contractors and subcontractors that have 50 or more employees and $50,000 or more in government contracts or that are receiving federal funding in any amount are required to file an EEO–1 report annually by March 31. The report needs to be filed with the contracting agency within 30 days after an award of a contract or subcontract, unless a report was submitted within the previous 12-month period before the award date.

The above information summarizes the reporting and recordkeeping requirements imposed by federal EEOC laws. Employers who are required to complete any of those reports should contact the EEOC at <www. eeoc.gov> or call (202) 663-4264 to obtain copies of report forms and instructions, as well as the recordkeeping requirements for each report to be filed.

Q 17: What are the steps in an EEO compliance investigation?

A: The Equal Employment Opportunity Commission enforces Title VII of the Civil Rights Act of 1964, the Age Discrimination in Employment Act, the Americans with Disabilities Act, and the Equal Pay Act. Acts of discrimination that are prohibited under those laws are related to hire, placement, promotion, discipline, wages, layoffs, termination, benefits, and terms and conditions of employment.

Complaints related to EEO compliance should be filed with the local agency that enforces state and local antidiscrimination laws or, in jurisdictions that do not have such laws, with the U.S. EEOC.

- Step One. The EEO compliance investigation process begins with an "intake interview" with the complainant. An Equal Opportunity Specialist (EOS) conducts the interview. When the complainant has provided enough information to show that he or she is entitled to file a charge, the EOS assists the person with formally filing the charge, which includes a written statement made under oath. After the charge has been filed, the complainant receives further counseling and is given a copy of the "Information Sheet for Charging Parties and Complaints." The EEOC then notifies the employer within 10 days of the charge and, depending on the circumstance, may supply the respondent with a copy of the charge.

- After the charge is filed, the EEOC has three approaches to processing investigations: (a) *rapid processing* is reserved for time-sensitive cases such as those involving expiration limitations for claims under the ADEA, (b) *extended processing* is used for cases that will require ongoing legal aid and considerable EEOC resources, and (c) *systemic cases* involve pursuing discrimination that may affect a broad class of complainants who may be employed by different employers in the same type of business.

- Step Two. An EEOC investigation must establish whether there is reasonable cause to believe that the allegations in the claim are true. As part of the investigation, the EEOC may, in writing, request information from the employer, including a request for documents to be mailed to the EEOC office or a request for an on-site investigation. Interviewing witnesses is usually an important step in the investigation process. In some circumstances, EEOC investigators carry out on-site investigations that may include visiting facilities, inspecting records, copying evidence, and interviewing witnesses. Either employers can submit to on-site visits voluntarily, or the EEOC can use its subpoena power to force submission.

- Step Three. After the EEOC investigation, the investigator may feel that a fact-finding conference would be useful. This type of meeting helps to define the issues, establish undisputed facts, and decide whether a settlement is possible.

- Step Four. The final step is the predetermination interview with the party against whom the EEOC feels it will rule. The EEOC investigator reviews the information with the party and ensures that all relevant information has been considered. If the interview is with the employer, the investigator also discusses the possibility of settlement. If the interview is with the charging party, the EEOC investigator discusses the party's right to file a private suit.

If a settlement is not reached between the two parties, the EEOC issues a determination letter indicating whether there is reasonable cause to believe that the allegations contained in the charge are true. For ADA and Title VII charges, this occurrence is called a *reasonable cause determination*, and the determination letter is usually sent within 120 days. Decisions for ADEA and EPA cases are sent by what is known as a *letter of violation*.

If reasonable cause is found, the EEOC is obligated to attempt to conciliate the charge through voluntary settlement. If attempts of conciliation are not successful, either the EEOC or the charging party has the right to file in court. If no reasonable cause is found, the EEOC is no longer involved, but the charging party still has the right to file in court.

Q 18: What is a bona fide occupational qualification (BFOQ)?

A: *Bona fide occupational qualification* is a legal term to describe discriminatory job requirements that are permissible exceptions under Title VII for employers when the discriminatory requirements are reasonably necessary for the normal operation of each employer's business. Under BFOQ, an employer is permitted to disqualify an employee or applicant only on the basis of religion, gender, and national origin. Race and color are excluded. For example, a Catholic school may disqualify a non-Catholic applicant from a teaching position because the Catholic religion is the educational mission of the employer.

Recruitment

Q 19: How can we measure the success of our company's recruiting efforts?

A: A variety of methods can help you evaluate your company's recruitment level of success. Perhaps the most important thing you can do is to ask, at every opportunity, where applicants learn of job openings. Simply tracking the key issues can provide critical money-saving information that will tell you how to proceed in the future.

Keep records of where you advertise, what the ad cost, how many applications are received, how many people are hired as a result of the ad, and how long the hiring process takes to fill the position. Next, calculate your average cost for one hire. This type of information will indicate your most cost-effective source versus your quickest source versus your most productive source. Newspaper ads may yield the greatest number of responses, but a career fair may get the highest ratio of hires to applicants. By using this information, you can target the best strategy.

Other factors that are important in evaluating your recruiting success are turnover rate, longevity once hired, number of hires per year, time to fill broken down by salary, and average starting salaries compared to those of your competitors.

See the SHRM white papers on benchmarking, turnover, retention, and recruitment strategies for further information.

Q 20: We are implementing an internal job-posting system. What should we consider?

A: Internal announcements are an effective and efficient recruiting tool. Announcements may be made by using job-posting boards, newsletters, e-mails, voice mails, flyers, or other means. Your corporate culture will determine which methods are most suitable for your organization.

The elements of an internal job posting are (a) position title, (b) level or grade, (c) standard work hours, (d) reporting structure, (e) qualifications, and (f) instructions and deadline for applying for the position.

You may consider implementing eligibility rules for employees to apply for a vacancy. Some common eligibility rules are related to minimum service in current position, performance review scores, supervisory approval, and disciplinary actions. You may also consider limiting the number of positions an employee can apply for at any given time. This limitation helps to ensure that employees are applying only for the positions in which they are seriously interested.

Your job-posting policy should be clear and consistent as to what types of positions will not be posted internally and what the relationship is between the internal posting and the external recruiting. Let employees know at what point the external recruiting process will begin. Recruiting may be deferred so that internal applicants have a greater opportunity, or external recruiting may be conducted at the same time. You may decide the external recruiting issue with each position, but be clear about what the process will be when you post each position.

As with any company policy, one of the keys to the success of your job-posting system is your company's commitment and consistency in administering the policy. When employees see that the program is fairly and consistently administered, they will be more apt to participate in and accept the outcomes of your job-posting system.

Q 21: Our company wants to institute a nepotism policy. What are some of the issues?

A: Nepotism policies address allowing family members or friends of current employees to work in the organization. Perceptions of nepotism can depend on a firm's limited resources, its recruiting sources, and its size. Nepotism can expand on the labor pool from which employers draw applicants. It can be an efficient way of identifying readily available, qualified talent. Allowing family members to work at the company can help foster a family-oriented environment, thus boosting morale.

However, nepotism policies can create many problems. A big challenge is the perception of favoritism. Co-workers resent the "privileged" status or special treatment they think the relative receives. The relative who is receiving the perceived "special treatment" has the problem of not knowing if he or she was hired or promoted because of performance or because of a blood or a marital relationship. There is also hiring pressure on the HR Department and HR managers. For example, senior managers may request you hire their children for summer jobs or internships. This can give the relative an unfair employment advantage over nonrelated applicants. Discipline problems can be a challenge if two relatives are in a supervisor-subordinate role. Another problem that could cause an intimidating situation would be if the first-line manager has to discipline his or her boss's relative.

A further area of concern would be family members who bring personal disagreements into the workplace. Such disputes can be disruptive to operations and to the morale of nonrelated employees. Scheduling and leave issues can become a problem if two relatives or a married couple wishes to take time off together, or if one partner needs to be absent to care for the ill spouse. Confidentiality issues become a concern if one relative has access to information that can directly benefit another relative elsewhere in the company.

Federal and state laws should be checked before implementing nepotism or antinepotism policies. Discrimination based on marital status, race, and gender can be upheld if nepotism policies cause a disparate impact on protected groups. Employers should consult with their legal counsel about the legality of their nepotism policies.

Q 22: What should we consider when selecting an external recruiter?

A: In general, when selecting an external recruiter, you should do the following:

- Thoroughly analyze what your recruitment needs are.

- Review various sources (yellow pages, Internet, other employers) for external recruiters and ascertain each recruiter's reputation, reliability, and experience.

- Develop a good relationship with the recruiter by (a) visiting the recruiter's work site to view the operations, (b) inviting the recruiter to visit your work site, and (c) trying to do as much work as possible with one recruiter. Such a relationship tends to give the recruiter an incentive to provide good referrals. It also allows the recruiter to become familiar with the needs of your organization.

- Obtain these assurances from the recruiter:

  — The employer will not be misrepresented in any dealings, and the confidentiality of the employer will be maintained.

  — The recruiter will keep the employer updated on all progress.

  — The references and qualifications of each referral will be thoroughly checked, and each candidate will be interviewed.

- Execute a written contract with the recruiter, and include statements pertaining to the following:

  — How the recruiter complies with relevant federal and state employment and labor laws

  — What method the recruiter uses to obtain a qualified referral

  — How the recruiter's fee is determined

  — Whether the recruiter will refund any fees charged to the employer if a referral does not stay longer than some preset period (e.g., 90 days)

— Whether the agreement between the recruiter and the employer is exclusive or nonexclusive (i.e., the recruiter receives a fee from the employer only if a referral is hired by the employer)

It is important to note that when an employer uses an external recruiter (e.g., an employment agency) to recruit job candidates, both the employer and the recruiter can be held liable for any violations of the ADA. The Immigration Reform and Control Act (IRCA) requires that the job eligibility of all persons hired as the result of recruitment or referral for a fee must be verified under IRCA rules. If the employer performs the verification, then the employer must forward a copy of the completed "Form I–9" to the recruiter or referrer.

Q 23: What are the direct and indirect costs associated with cost per hire?

A: Each company's direct and indirect costs associated with cost per hire may differ depending on the company's industry and staffing needs. In addition, depending on the job market and the economy, the cost per hire will fluctuate from year to year.

The direct costs include these:

- Advertising fees (internal and external)
- Employment agency fees
- Employee referral or signing bonuses
- Relocation costs
- Overhead costs for HR staff (travel, supplies, salaries and benefits, etc.)
- Background check costs
- Pre-employment test costs (medical and nonmedical)
- Telephone calls
- Training costs

The indirect costs include these:

- Turnover costs
- Effect on production
- Effect on employee morale
- Increase in employee relations issues
- Disruption of the business

Q 24: What is succession planning?

A: Succession planning is the formal process of business planning that is used to identify candidates for future key managerial or leadership positions within an organization before there is an actual need. The objective of succession planning is to include all positions within an organization that are critical to the organization's future success, which may include managerial positions or positions that are not of a supervisory or managerial nature. A well-thought-out succession plan can be a company's best resource for developing and retraining people because it can assist in pinpointing skill or experience deficiencies within the organization. It is worth mentioning that succession planning is not a technique used solely to plan individual career advancement, nor is it meant to reward individual performance.

Traditional succession plans normally require the Chief Executive Officer (CEO) and other top executives to identify their own future replacements. For a succession plan to be effective and to achieve its desired goals, it should incorporate certain key elements into its design such as CEO and top management support, integration with the strategic business plan, identification of critical positions to be included, and time lines for succession—both for organizational needs and for identification of individual readiness.

Succession planning is not to be considered a luxury, because the consequences of not being prepared to replace key personnel can have a detrimental impact on the organization's success and productivity. Organizations that prepare in advance for changes will remain more competitive and will be better equipped to meet future challenges as they arise.

Additional information on succession planning is available through the SHRM white paper titled *Succession Planning: Lessons from Kermit the Frog* by Tim Orellano (Orellara & Miller, 1999), SPHR, and Janice A. Miller, SPHR, (1999) at <www.shrm.org/whitepapers/documents/61203.asp>.

Q 25: What are the factors for determining if someone is an employee or an independent contractor?

A: Employers that misclassify workers as independent contractors instead of employees are subject to tax, interest, and penalties enforced by the Internal Revenue Service (IRS). Also at issue are a worker's rights to benefits, overtime, minimum wage, and protection under employment laws such as antidiscrimination laws. Therefore, it is important that employers accurately classify their workers. The most important issue in determining the status of a worker is control.

Under common law, courts have used the economic reality test to determine which workers are employees. The following factors are considered:

- The amount the worker has invested in the equipment used

- The potential for profit and loss on the part of the worker

- The degree to which the employer exercises control over the work

- The extent to which the service performed is integral to business

- The permanency of the business relationship

The IRS considers three categories of evidence in assessing the control a company exercises over a worker:

- Behavior control

- Financial control

- Nature of the relationship

The IRS considers 20 factors in determining employee versus independent contractor:

- Employer and not worker has risk of profit and loss.

- A continuing relationship exists.

- Worker is required to comply with instruction.

- Employer has required training.

- Services are required to be rendered personally.

- Services provided are integral to the business.

- Employer has control over hiring and supervising assistants.

- Employer has control over the hours of work.

- Employer requires full-time work.

- Employer requires work be done on its premises.

- Employer controls the sequence in which the services are provided.

- Employer requires progress reports.

- Worker is paid by the hour, week, or month.

- Employer furnishes tools or materials.

- Employer pays business or travel expenses.

- Worker has an investment in facilities.

- Work is done for more than one firm.

- Worker makes services available to the public.

- Employer has the right to discharge the worker.

- Worker has the right to terminate the relationship.

Q 26: What are some of the concerns in a joint employment relationship?

A: A joint employment relationship exists when two or more companies share control over the same employee or group of employees. This arrangement is most often seen in the use of staffing agencies such as temporary help and employee leasing. The staffing agencies pay the employee, withhold taxes, have the right to hire or to fire, and so forth, while the client supervises the employee, directs day-to-day work, and determines the length of the assignment.

A joint employment relationship can create legal liability in several areas. These areas of liability can include the following:

- Title VII

- Age Discrimination in Employment Act (ADEA)

- Americans with Disabilities Act (ADA)

- Equal Pay Act (EPA)

- Family and Medical Leave Act (FMLA)

- Fair Labor Standards Act (FLSA)

- Worker's Compensation

- Labor Relations

- Occupational Safety and Health Act (OSHA)

- Unemployment Insurance

- Consolidated Omnibus Budget Reconciliation Act (COBRA)

- Employee Retirement Income Security Act (ERISA)

- Worker Adjustment and Retraining Notification Act (WARN)

Different federal laws and, in some cases, individual states will apply varying tests and standards to determine the existence of a joint employment relationship and the accompanying legal responsibility. A central factor in such tests is the amount of control each party has over the individual employee.

Q 27: What information should be included on an application? What should be omitted?

A: Although it is not illegal to ask some questions, their inclusion may be ill-advised. The information the questions elicit can later be used to support discrimination charges so it is not advisable to use those questions. The cardinal rule for employment applications is to request information that is job related and that you can use to make an employment decision. Do not ask about anything else.

Most applications are divided into five general sections: (a) biographical or personal, (b) education, (c) work experience, (d) references, and (e) a disclaimer. Below is a section-by-section review of the most commonly found errors. Although this review is not comprehensive, it should provide some guidance on how to create or revise your application.

Questions for Employment Applications

Biographical or Personal

Age. Questions about age can lead to discrimination complaints under the ADEA (which applies to people age 40 and over).

Don't Ask: How old are you? Are you age 70 or older? What is your date of birth?

Do Ask: If you are under 18, will you be able to furnish a work permit after employment?

Medical or disability. Questions in this category can lead to potential discrimination complaints under the ADA.

Don't Ask: Do you have any health-related problems or disabilities that may limit your ability to perform this job?

Do Ask: Are you able to perform the essential functions of the job listed on the attached job description?

Don't Ask: How many days were you absent from work last year?

Do Ask: Our company offers a maximum of 10 sick days per year. Will you be able to comply with this requirement?

Don't Ask: Have you ever filed a worker's compensation claim?

Do Ask: You may ask this question only postoffer and only after you become aware of the need for access to second-injury funds.

Relatives. Antinepotism policies could violate some state statutes prohibiting discrimination on the basis of marital status. It might be advisable to limit such policy to the supervisory relationship during employment. There is also a potential adverse impact on women and minorities, so check your state laws before including this question.

Don't Ask: Do you have any relatives who work for this company?

Do Ask: If employed in the position for which you have applied, would you be in a supervisory relationship to any relative or member of your household? Yes or no?

National origin or race. The IRCA and Title VII prohibit discrimination based on national origin and race.

Don't Ask: The application should not have questions requesting EEO or affirmative action information.

Do Ask: This request should be made on a tear-off section or on a separate form and should allude to the fact that providing such information is voluntary and will not be considered in the employment decision.

Don't Ask: Please provide a recent photograph.

Do Ask: Avoid this request completely. Personal appearance is not normally job related.

Don't Ask: Are you a U.S. citizen? If not, do you have a current work permit? (Unless U.S. citizenship is required for this position.)

Do Ask: Are you legally eligible to work in the United States? (Verification will be required upon hire.)

Don't Ask: What language do you most commonly speak at work and speak at home?

Do Ask: The job requires fluent speaking and writing in English (asked only if fluency is, in fact, a bona fide requirement for this position). Can you meet this requirement?

Convictions. Requesting arrest records has been shown to have a potentially adverse impact on some minority groups.

Don't Ask: Do not include any questions about "any arrests or convictions."

Do Ask: Have you ever been convicted of a crime, other than a traffic violation? (Conviction will not be an absolute bar to employment.)

Religion. Title VII prohibits discrimination on the basis of religion.

Don't Ask: Please list any clubs, fraternal or sororal groups, and charities to which you belong.

Do Ask: List memberships in any professional organizations that you feel would enhance your application, excluding any organizations whose name would indicate the race, religion, creed, color, national origin, or ancestry of its members.

Sex. Title VII prohibits discrimination on the basis of sex. The Pregnancy Discrimination Act is part of Title VII.

Don't Ask: Are you pregnant? Avoid this subject completely.

Don't Ask: Do you have any children?

Do Ask: This job requires overnight travel. Would you be able to meet this requirement?

Or Ask: Will you be able to work overtime when needed? Yes or no?

Education and Schools Attended

Dates of school attendance. This information could reveal the applicant's age and, thus, create the potential for age discrimination under ADEA.

Don't Ask: What are the dates of school attendance?

Do Ask: How many years of schooling have you attended?

Work Experience

Military service. Questions about military service are acceptable, but questions about discharge may be discriminatory, because some ethnic groups have received a higher proportion of general and dishonorable discharges. Also, questions about reserve or guard status should be avoided, because they may violate a veteran's re-employment and leave laws.

Personal and Professional References

This section usually requests a list of references, either personal or professional. Professional references have more relevance to the job qualifications than personal references and would be less likely to elicit extemporaneous information. Ask the applicant to sign an authorization giving permission to verify credentials and to check references.

Disclaimer Statements

Disclaimers and notices should be as direct and as explicit as possible. Make sure that you are consistent with your policies and practices. The disclaimer statement should address items such as drug testing, employment-at-will, or other conditions of employment. The entire application form should be reviewed by legal counsel.

Q 28: Did immigration legislation during the late 1990s change the documents we can accept for completing a new employee's I–9 form?

A: Yes, the Illegal Immigration Reform and Immigrant Responsibility Act of 1996 (IIRIRA) reduced the number of documents an employer can accept as proof of eligibility to work in the United States. After September 30, 1997, employers could no longer accept certificates of naturalization, certificates of citizenship, foreign passports, or birth certificates.

As provided on the reverse side of the I–9 form, documents acceptable for verifying both identity and employment eligibility (List A) will be limited to (a) a U.S. passport, (b) an alien registration card, and (c) other documents designated by the Attorney General. There have been no changes to the documents establishing identity only (List B). Those that establish employment eligibility only (List C) will be limited to (a) a U.S. social security card and (b) other documents as determined by the Attorney General.

If employers make a technical or procedural mistake in meeting IIRIRA's verification requirements, they will not be penalized as long as the error was made in good faith. Once the Immigration and Naturalization Service (INS) has pointed out the failure, the employer will have 10 days to correct it. This grace period has been applicable only to good faith efforts occurring on or after September 30, 1996, and is not available to employers engaging in a pattern or practice of paperwork violations.

Note that as of March 20, 1996, "Alien Registration Cards" (INS Form I–151) (which are also known as green cards) issued before 1979 were no longer valid as proof of eligibility to work. To obtain a replacement "Alien Registration Receipt Card" (INS Form I–551), holders of Form I–151 must apply in person at a local INS office.

Employers should continue to verify employees' identity and eligibility to work within 3 business days after they are hired. Until INS issues a new I–9 form reflecting the changes described above, you may want to contact your local office if you have questions about which documents are acceptable.

Q 29: Can we keep employees' I–9 forms in their regular personnel files?

A: It's better to keep them in a separate file for both legal and practical reasons. Although employers must be able to provide INS inspectors with completed I–9 forms for review, they should not allow INS agents to view employees' full personnel files, because doing so would violate privacy laws. Also, because I–9 forms often include information about an employee's national origin, it makes sense to separate them from the regular personnel files, just as you maintain EEO or Affirmative Action forms separately.

Q 30: Can we develop an employment test to help screen applicants?

A: Yes, but you should consider a few things before investing in the testing process. Employment tests have been a frequent target of lawsuits. To avoid extensive time, energy, and the cost of a legal defense, you would be wise to research the federal and state laws and regulations regarding employment testing before instituting a testing process.

The 1978 law titled Uniform Guidelines on Employment Selection Procedures (UGESP) makes it clear that any selection processes that adversely affect employment opportunities for any protected group should be validated. Generally, adverse impact can be determined by using the 4/5ths rule, which measures the selection rate of any race, sex, or ethnic group that is less than 4/5ths, or 80%, of the rate for the group with the highest selection rate.

If adverse impact has been established, the employer should consider test validation for job requirements and performance. Under UGESP, validation can be achieved through three methods; they are content validity, criterion validity, and construct validity.

- Content validity establishes that the content of the test is representative of the content of the job itself.

- Criterion validity establishes a statistical relationship between the scores on a test or procedure and the levels or measures of job performance.

- Construct validity identifies a trait (e.g., leadership) that would be important to successful performance in the job for which the candidates are to be evaluated. The test must, indeed, show that it does measure that trait.

In addition to conducting a validation study, the employer should consider hiring methods, other than testing, that would achieve the company's legitimate business purpose with less adverse impact.

There are still a number of details that an employer should consider before instituting an employment test. Spending the time to do a little research in this area can make the difference between your test design withstanding a court challenge and achieving its intended purpose, and its causing a costly legal defense and screening out good candidates. Consult with your employment attorney or a testing professional for help in this area.

Q 31: How do we calculate turnover costs?

A: Quantifying the costs of turnover can be very difficult. Some expenses are more obvious than others. For example, direct costs, such as the cost of advertising for a replacement, are easily measured. However, it is not always easy to assign a dollar figure to indirect costs such as productivity loss and employee morale issues.

According to AlignMark Corporation (formerly the RIA Group), turnover costs can be divided into four categories: separation, replacement, training, and productivity. Separation costs include unemployment compensation, costs of COBRA benefits continuation, and the cost of conducting exit interviews. Replacement costs include advertising, pre-employment testing, and time and materials for new-hire orientation. Training costs include the time and effort from trainers, supervisors, and co-workers. Productivity costs are often hard to quantify but include issues such as morale problems, decreased production, increased error rates, and the effects on the company's reputation.

Q 32: What direct and indirect costs should be included in a cost-per-hire calculation?

A: When calculating cost per hire, you can use direct and indirect costs to measure recruitment effectiveness. Direct costs include, but are not limited to, advertising, employment agency fees, job fairs, employee referrals, credit and reference checks, examination and testing during the selection process, bonuses, relocation, HR overhead, college recruitment, Internet, training, and communication.

Indirect costs can include, but are also not limited to, decreased productivity, turnover, morale impacts, safety (if a higher number of accidents result from the vacancy), disruption of regular business functions, overtime (to compensate for the vacancy), and new hires to maintain production.

Cost-per-hire benchmarking information is available through the Employment Management Association at <www.ema@shrm.org>.

Q 33: How do we calculate monthly turnover rates for our company?

A: Monitoring turnover is an important HR function. Companies like to monitor the movement of employees out of the organization so they can look for and minimize causes of turnover. Controlling turnover is one of the many quantitative ways the HR Department can affect the bottom line.

The formula for calculating turnover on a monthly basis is to take the number of separations during a month and divide it by the average number of employees on the payroll. Multiply the result by 100, and the resulting figure is the monthly turnover rate.

$$\text{Monthly Turnover Rate} = \frac{\text{Number of separations during 1 month}}{\text{Average number of employees on payroll during the month}} \times 100$$

The number of separations during the month should include both voluntary and involuntary terminations. Do not include employees who are laid off.

When employers want to calculate the annual turnover rate, they should add each of the monthly rates together (i.e., January + February + March + April + ... + Dec = annual turnover rate).

After calculating the turnover rate for your organization, you may want to compare it to others in the same industry or to companies of the same size. Some resources you may want to look at include the BNA report titled "Job Absence and Turnover Report," which is published quarterly, as well as the BLS publication titled *Employee Turnover and Job Openings Survey*. Contact BNA at (202) 452-4323 or on the web at <www.shrm.org/bna>. Contact BLS at (202) 606-7828 or on the web at <www.bls.gov>.

Q 34: Where can we find information on recruiting sources such as executive recruiters, permanent placement agencies, advertising agencies, nonprofit organizations, and governmental agencies?

A: With the increased use of on-line technology worldwide, the Internet is an invaluable source for recruiting databases and other recruiting sources. Start with the HRLinks section of our web site for a list of other sites we have identified as being particularly valuable to HR practitioners. But don't hesitate to conduct your own search using Yahoo, Infoseek, or other Internet search tools. Be as specific as you can to narrow the number of hits you will get, and try your search a couple of different ways to be sure you're getting all the possible options.

Executive recruiters can be searched on the Internet at such web sites as "Recruiters On-line Network" at <www.recruitersonline.com> or the "Association of Executive Search Consultants" at <www.aesc.org>. Temporary and permanent placement agencies are another traditional source of candidates. Both the Internet and your local *Yellow Pages Directory* can provide you with listings of such firms.

Larger employers may find the services of a recruitment advertising agency particularly helpful for identifying sources and placing ads in publications across the country and all over the world. One good source for learning about available services is the SHRM Annual Conference and Exposition. Each year, hundreds of companies with HR products and services gather in one place to display information and to be available to discuss your needs. Last year between 20 and 30 such firms were represented.

Professional associations such as SHRM frequently offer some type of job search assistance to their members, and most have a publication that their members receive. Most local libraries carry the *Encyclopedia of Associations* in their reference section. This resource is particularly helpful for identifying individuals in specialized occupations.

Finally, many governmental agencies, both federal and local, help individuals from disadvantaged populations find employment. Look through the blue pages of your local telephone book for resources.

Q 35: What questions should we avoid asking during an interview?

A: Interviews continue to be the selection method of choice for most employers because those meetings allow for an in-depth questioning of a candidate and offer an assessment of a candidate's chances for success within the organization. Interviewers need to exercise a measure of caution in preparing interview questions. Interviewers should avoid asking the candidate discriminatory questions, just as they would with employment applications. Under Title VII of the Civil Rights Act, employers may not consider any information about an applicant's race, religion, creed, sex, national origin, or ancestry in making any type of employment decision. Other laws also prohibit asking applicants questions regarding their age, disability, military history, union membership, or sexual orientation.

To conduct an effective and legal interview, questions such as those listed below should be avoided.

- How old are you? What is your date of birth?

- Have you ever been arrested? Have you ever been convicted of a felony or misdemeanor?

- Have you ever been declared bankrupt? Have you ever filed for bankruptcy?

- Do you have any children? Are you planning to have any children?

- Do you have any diseases? Do you have any physical or mental impairments?

The questions listed above are only a small sampling of what an interviewer should not ask an applicant. Many good books on interviewing procedures and techniques are available through the SHRMStore, as well as at local libraries and bookstores. A SHRM white paper, *Basic Interviewing* (1999), includes appropriate and inappropriate questions; it is found at <www.shrm.org/whitepapers/documents/61202.asp>.

Q 36: Our company is interested in conducting pre-employment testing as part of our selection process. What issues should we be concerned with?

A: It is common for employers to ask applicants to undergo testing procedures as part of the selection process. Although state laws and case law interpretations vary depending on the type of testing being used and its place in the selection process, here are a few general issues to consider before you implement testing:

- **Pre-employment, job, or skill-based testing**

  — Be certain that the tests are job related and are an accurate predictor of performance in the job (tests should be validated to support this prediction).

  — Administer the same tests under the same conditions to all applicants for the same position.

  — Accommodate people with disabilities by modifying the test or testing conditions or by eliminating the testing requirement.

  — Do not rely solely on tests for making decisions about candidates; use tests as one component of your overall selection procedure.

- **Drug tests**

  — Check state and federal laws (especially federal contractors and employers governed by the regulations of the Department of Transportation or other federal agencies) before using drug tests as part of your selection process.

  — Obtain an applicant's consent before testing.

— Although stand-alone drug tests may be administered before an offer, employers who conduct medical examinations after the offer typically combine the two to save money and time. Medical examinations may not be required before an offer of employment is extended.

— Maintain confidentiality and establish procedures for confirmation tests, if they are not already specifically regulated for your industry.

For more information, check these web sites: (a) the Institute for a Drug-Free Workplace at <www.drugfreeworkplace.org> provides some information, and (b) the Substance Abuse Program Administrators Association has an interesting site at <www.sapaa.com>.

Q 37: What are the legal issues related to reference checking?

A: Conducting background checks is an important part of the selection process in today's hiring game. Negligent hiring has become a common legal claim against employers who have made hiring decisions without diligently making an effort to check references. It is particularly important to conduct a reference check on individuals who are dealing with the public or who are in positions of trust, such as jobs that involve entering customers' homes or working with children.

For an overview of reference-checking guidelines, see the white paper called *Reference Checking* (1999) in the SHRM white papers section on the home page at <www.shrm.org/whitepapers/documents/61201.asp>. One of the most important parts of reference checking is to obtain a release from the applicant that allows the prospective employer to check references. This release is especially important when a credit check will be performed. The Fair Credit Reporting Act (FCRA) imposes specific notification guidelines on employers, depending on the kind of credit report done. For more detailed information on the FCRA, see the white papers on the SHRM home page. The SHRM Information Center can provide you with a list of firms that conduct background investigations, as well as sample forms for authorizations.

Q 38: Can we use credit reports as part of our selection process?

A: Yes. However, unless the position requires either handling money or having authority over spending large amounts of money, the applicant's financial condition is not likely to be relevant to the position. Using a credit report can be viewed as a discriminatory basis for making hiring decisions.

The FCRA, which regulates consumer reporting agencies and entities, including employers, makes it legal to procure a consumer report for employment purposes only if the consumer has been notified in a clear and conspicuous written disclosure before the consumer report request, and only provided that the consumer has given written authorization for the report's procurement by the employer. The FCRA also stipulates that information from the consumer report will not be used in violation of either federal or state employment opportunity laws or regulations, and that the consumer is provided not only with a copy of the consumer report, but also with a copy of the consumers' rights under federal law.

Basing employment decisions solely on a consumer credit report may have an adverse impact on one particular group (such as minorities or women). Employers should be prepared to prove that business necessity and job relevancy are factors when basing employment decisions on the results of credit reports. More in-depth information on the use of consumer credit reports and the FCRA, along with sample disclosure letters, can be obtained from the white papers on the SHRM home page.

Q 39: What are some innovative ways to retain high-tech employees?

A: Companies retain good employees by becoming "employers of choice." How can your company be an employer of choice? Employees respond well to working environments that meet their needs whether high tech or not. Assuming that the wages are agreeable (these days that means you are paying at market rate or probably above if high tech), employees need to feel like (a) they make a difference, (b) they have meaningful work, and (c) they have a work and life balance. Employers should set up good communication channels with employees so that employees feel that their views are important to the company and they are being heard. Consider work and life balance options such as flex time, compressed work weeks, or dependent care programs, and make those options a part of your culture so employees can have other priorities in their lives besides work. Hire the right people for the right jobs, and then allow them to do their work free from micromanagement and with the authority to make good decisions. Top off your approach with an innovative benefit plan. Some ideas from the SHRM High-Tech Bulletin Board:

- Generous tuition assistance

- Paid sabbaticals

- Signing bonuses

- Retention bonuses

- Generous vacation time

- Stock options

- On-site fitness facilities

- Concierge services (manicures, dry cleaning pick up and delivery, mobile car detailers, shoe shines, massages)

- Free snacks, drinks, fruit

For more ideas, see the white paper *Retention Tactics That Work* by Catherine Fyock (1999) on the SHRM web site at <www.shrm.org/ whitepapers/documents/61667.asp>.

References

Chapter 3. Staffing

Bell, A. (1992). *Extraviewing: Innovative ways to hire the best.* (Homewood, IL: Business One).

Bruce, S. (1994). *How to write an affirmative action plan.* Madison, CT: Business and Legal Reports. Available: SHRMStore, (800) 444-5506.

Bureau of Labor Statistics (BLS). (current edition) *Employee turnover and job openings survey.* Washington, DC: BLS. Available: BLS, (202) 606-7828 or <www.bls.gov>. Accessed 6/99.

Bureau of National Affairs (BNA). (current edition) *Job absence and turnover report.* [Quarterly report]. Available: BNA, (202) 452-4323 or <www.shrm.org/bna>.

Equal Employment Opportunity Commission (EEOC). (1999). *Guidance on reasonable accommodation under ADA.* Washington, DC: EEOC.

Fyock C. (1999). *Retention tactics that work.* (White paper no. 61667). [On-line]. Available: <www.shrm.org/whitepapers/documents/61667.asp>. Accessed 6/99.

Griggs v. Duke Power Co., 401 U.S. 424 (1971).

Lotito, M. J., & Outwater, L. C. (1997). *Minding your business.* Alexandria, VA: Society for Human Resource Management (SHRM).

Orellano, T., & Miller, J. A. (1999). *Succession planning: Lessons from Kermit the Frog.* (White paper no. 61203). [On-line]. Available: <www.shrm.org/whitepapers/documents/61203.asp>. Accessed 5/99.

Smart, B. (1999). *Topgrading.* Paramus, NJ: Prentice Hall.

Society for Human Resource Management (SHRM). (1999). *Basic interviewing.* (White paper no. 61202). [On-line]. Available: <www.shrm.org/whitepapers/documents/61202.asp>. Accessed 6/99.

Society for Human Resource Management (SHRM). (1997). *Forms used in human resources.* [On-line]. Available 7/00.

Society for Human Resource Management (SHRM). (1999). *Reference checking*. (White paper no. 61201). [On-line]. Available: <www.shrm.org/whitepapers/documents/61201.asp>. Accessed 6/99.

Taylor, P., & O'Driscoll, M. (1995). *Structured employment interviewing*. Brookfield, VT: Gower.

.

CHAPTER 4

HUMAN RESOURCE DEVELOPMENT

Q 1: Where can we find a seminar on sexual harassment, Affirmative Action, or employment law?

> **A:** Sexual harassment, Affirmative Action, and employment law seminars are provided by many organizations throughout the country. Here is a list of resources that will assist you in finding the appropriate seminar on different subject matters:
>
> - <www.astd.org/virtual_community/seminar_agent/>
> -
> - <www.tasl.com/tasl/home.html>
> -
> -
> - <www.amanet.org/seminars/>
> - <www.neli.org/programs.asp>

Q 2: What is meant by the term *learning organization*?

> **A:** A *learning organization* is defined by Michael Marquardt (1996) as an organization that is continually changing and adapting to better collect, manage, and use knowledge for corporate success.
>
> A learning organization has 12 characteristics:
>
> - Learning is accomplished by the organizational system as a whole.
> - Members recognize the importance of organizational learning.
> - Learning is a continuous process that runs parallel to work.
> - There is a focus on creativity.
> - Systems thinking is practiced.
> - People have access to information that is important to the company's success.
> - The company rewards individual and group learning.

- Workers network inside and outside the organization.

- Change is embraced, and failures are viewed as opportunities to learn.

- Quality and continuous improvement drive the company.

- There are well-developed core competencies.

- The organization adapts and changes as the environment changes.

Peter Senge's (1990) book *The Fifth Discipline* identifies six key skills or disciplines that maximize organizational learning:

- Systems thinking—a conceptual framework that makes patterns clearer and helps one see how to change them

- Mental models—our deeply ingrained assumptions that influence how we understand the world and how we take action

- Personal mastery—the high level of proficiency in a subject or skill area

- Team learning—aligning and developing the capacity of a team to create the results its members desire

- Shared vision—a shared vision of the future that fosters genuine commitment

- Dialogue—a high level of listening and communication among people

Q 3:   How should a company go about selecting a trainer?

A: The implementation of a new organizational training program will most likely result in the need to make decisions regarding selection of an appropriate facilitator. When selecting a trainer, an organization should first assess whether it is best to hire an external expert in that particular field, or if it will be more appropriate to turn current on-staff trainers into subject-matter experts. In making such decisions, an organization should carefully analyze (a) which skills will need to be taught, (b) what the managers' or supervisors' assumptions are about how people learn, and (c) what role the trainer is expected to perform. For tasks that are highly complicated or involve extensive on-the-job knowledge, it certainly may be more appropriate to turn an existing employee into a trainer. However, just because a worker may be an expert who performs a certain task well, it does not necessarily mean that he or she will also perform well or adequately as a trainer.

Another determinant that must be considered is the role that the trainer is expected to fill. If the role of the trainer is simply to step into a classroom and present lectures or demonstrations, it may be enough to select a trainer who has subject-matter expertise along with good presentation skills. If the trainer is expected to play a larger role in the training program, such as identifying performance problems and implementing and evaluating training solutions, additional skills may be required.

Tables 4–1 to 4–5 contain selection criteria to be used as a guideline for choosing training staff members on the basis of training program objectives.

TABLE 4–1
WHEN SELECTING TRAINERS FOR THE ROLE OF ANALYZER

Evidence of Experience in	Evidence of Knowledge in
Work observation	Principles and theories of behavioral science
Occupational analysis	Motivational theories
Interviewing	Learning theories
Negotiation with supervisors and managers	Job design
Presentation of written and oral information	

TABLE 4–2
WHEN SELECTING TRAINERS FOR THE ROLE OF DESIGNER

Evidence of Experience in	Evidence of Knowledge in
Design of training programs	Performance-enhancing methods
Selection of alternatives to expensive classroom training	Classroom training
Development of clear performance objectives	The elements of clear performance objectives

TABLE 4–3
WHEN SELECTING TRAINERS FOR THE ROLE OF DEVELOPER

Evidence of Experience in	Evidence of Knowledge in
Developing lesson plans	Media selection
Developing training schedules	Principles involved in developing written instructional material
Developing training aids	Adult learning theories
Developing other instructional materials	
Writing training instructions, workbooks, and job aids	
Planning training events	
Using various training media	

TABLE 4–4
WHEN SELECTING TRAINERS FOR THE ROLE OF DELIVERER

Evidence of Experience in	Evidence of Knowledge in
Speaking in groups	Training objectives
Managing classroom process	Individual and group behavior
Dealing with conflict	Specific methods of public speaking
Giving performance feedback	Use of humor
Using various training media	

TABLE 4–5
WHEN SELECTING TRAINERS FOR THE ROLE OF EVALUATOR

Evidence of Experience in	Evidence of Knowledge in
Observation and measurement of performance	Work-measurement techniques
Presentation of evaluation results in either written or oral form	Statistical-measurement analysis
Application of statistical techniques to data	Collection of data
Comparison of performance to standards	

Q 4:   What should be included in a Request for Proposal (RFP) for a trainer?

A: Here are some elements to consider:

- Specify what type of training you are seeking. If necessary, specify the delivery method that you prefer (facilitation, seminar, multimedia presentation, etc.).

- Identify your company.

- Describe what the company hopes to achieve from the training.

- Define what a successful proposal must include.

- Note any conditions that apply (e.g., extra fees).

- Indicate when the proposal must be submitted.

- List the person to contact for submission and for questions.

- Attach a sheet that spells out additional proposal requirements such as these:
  — Submission deadline
  — Statement of purpose or objectives
  — Support for the proposed development or delivery methods
  — Description of development or delivery methodology
  — Requirement for a project timetable
  — Budget and explanation of expected expenses
  — Credentials and references

Q 5:   How does a company conduct a training-needs analysis?

A: Before you begin a training program, it is important to know what training the organization needs. A training-needs analysis is an important step in determining what areas need to be addressed and in identifying the employees who need training.

A needs analysis involves collecting information to determine if a training need exists and, if so, what kind of training is required to meet this need. The analysis also should address why the need exists. If the problem identified is not attributable to worker performance, training may not be the best solution. For instance, a company might discover that its employees have received appropriate training to perform their jobs but are not motivated to do so. In this situation, it would be more appropriate for the company to reconsider its system of compensation and awards.

There are many different methods for conducting the needs analysis. Among the available assessment methods are the following:

- **HR records**. HR records can include accident and safety reports; attendance records; grievance filings; exit interviews; performance evaluations; and other company records such as production, sales, and cost records.

- **Individual interviews**. People to consider interviewing for information on training needs include Affirmative Action officers, employment recruiters, managers, and top executives.

- **Focus groups**. Unlike individual interviews, using focus groups involves simultaneously questioning a number of individuals about training needs.

- **Observations**. Sources for observation include on-the-job performance, simulations of work settings, or written work samples.

- **Surveys or questionnaires**. Surveys or questionnaires generally use a standardized format and can be administered by mail, phone, or hand.

- **Samples for use**. Sampling is similar to surveying and focuses on a smaller, selected group.

- **Group tests**. Tests can identify areas that need to be addressed, as well as employees who need training.

Each organization selects the most appropriate method, taking into account such factors as organization size, technology, organizational structure, training staff, facilities, and budget.

Q 6:   What should be included in a training budget?

A: A training budget should have the following items:

- Trainer salaries—salaries paid to internal training staff members

- Seminar and conferences—cost for outside vendors

- Hardware—costs for audiovisual and video equipment, computers, copies, and so forth

- Off-the-shelf materials—costs for prepackaged materials in any format (such as books or manuals)

- Custom material—costs for material tailored to meet the designated training program

- Facilities and overhead—costs for classroom building, and like items

- Outside services—costs for outside consultants

In many organizations, training costs are charged back to the departments that use the training. In those cases, each department has a training budget that should be rolled up and reconciled with the training department's budget in order to control the entire training cost of the organization.

Q 7: What should be included on a training evaluation form?

A: Perhaps the most important part of a training program is evaluating the results.

Other than the initial data on the dates, title, instructor, and the participants' occupations, we should get several pieces of critical information from a training evaluation. The following questions should be asked:

- What was your overall view of the usefulness of this course for someone in your job?

- What were the objectives of the program, and were they met?

- Do you feel enough time was spent on each topic?

- Was your trainer prepared for the course?

- Has taking this course changed your awareness of any topic?

- Has taking this course changed your behavior or your job performance?

- Do parts of your job prohibit you from using the skills learned in the seminar?

- What topics would you have liked further information about?

The questions can be open ended or linked to a numeric scale (e.g., a 1–5 scale where 1 is the lowest and 5 is the highest). For either way, you want answers in at least three broad areas: What was the effectiveness of the course? What was the effectiveness of the trainer? What could be done differently?

Q 8: How should our company set up a mentoring program?

A: The coordinator should consider the following in setting up a mentoring program:

- **Winning support for the program.** The key to the success of any new program is to win the employees' support. Early in the process, the program coordinator should do the following:

  — Explain the rationale, goals, and details of the program to the whole organization.

— Emphasize the benefits of the program, both for the participants and for the company as a whole.

— Solicit the employees' input about the process, and ask them about any problems they may foresee.

— Decide early in the communication plan what the rewards will be for those who serve as mentors.

- **Identifying potential jobs to be enhanced**. Some jobs in your organization may not lend themselves well to being enhanced by a mentoring program. The first thing the coordinator should do is identify those positions that can be enhanced. Some examples of potential candidates for enhancement are positions that (a) involve customer service, (b) involve a large financial responsibility or investment, (c) require staff continuity, and (d) have a person who is close to leaving the position.

- **Selecting the mentors**. Your selection strategy should be based on your desired outcome of the program. If the goal is primarily job training, mentors should be selected from the same division and specialty as the trainee. If the goal is more related to communicating corporate culture, an individual with a broad knowledge of the company should be selected.

- **Training the mentors**. The mentor should be well versed on what the trainee's job entails. This analysis should be conducted by the mentor with the trainee and should describe the day-to-day responsibilities of the trainee's position. The mentor and the trainee should together build a learning plan and develop a time line for accomplishing the various components of the lesson plan.

- **Guiding the trainees**. The program's goals should be clearly communicated to the trainee in the form of written and verbal explanations, including program timetables. It should be clear to the trainee that promotion is not an automatic result of participation. The trainee should have a good understanding of what he or she needs to know about the position.

- **Program evaluation**. Ongoing assessment should be built into the program. Some methods of evaluation include interviewing participants at specified intervals, soliciting input for change and improvements, using formal evaluation tools, and having participants discuss problems and concerns with a neutral third party.

Additional resources on this topic include these:

- *Mentoring* by David B. Hutchins, (1999) SPHR. The SHRM white paper is available at <www.shrm.org/whitepapers/documents/61303. asp> under the Information Center and Library.

- *Managers as Mentors* by Chip R. Bell (1996). It is available in the SHRMStore by calling (800) 444-5006 or at <www.shrm.org/shrmstore>.

- *Beyond the Myths and Magic of Mentoring: How to Facilitate an Effective Mentoring Program* by Margo Murray and Marna Owen (1991). The book is available at <www.amazon.com> and other bookstores.

- *The Mentoring Program Coordinator's Guide*. This handbook is for leaders who want to develop or improve mentoring programs. It includes detailed information on how to design, manage, and evaluate a program.

- *Planning, Implementing, and Evaluating a Successful Mentoring Program: A Checklist of Critical Tasks* by Linda Phillips-Jones (1998). This 14-page booklet is for planners and coordinators of formal mentoring and is a planning and accountability tool that contains 65 steps to complete throughout a mentoring program. It is available from The Mentoring Group/CCC; 13560 Mesa Drive, Grass Valley, CA 95949. You can telephone (530) 268-1146, fax (530) 268-3636, or visit the web site at <www.mentoringgroup.com>.

- The American Society for Training and Development has other mentoring resources and can be contacted by telephone at (703) 683-8123 or on its web site at <www.astd.org>.

Q 9:   What is cross training or job rotation?

A: Programs for cross training prepare employees to perform jobs other than the ones they were hired to do. Such programs can help to increase employee morale and can allow a company to have greater flexibility. Companies are finding other ways to make work more meaningful or satisfying to employees. Employees who participate in cross-training programs feel that they play a greater part in the company's success.

Most companies have cross-training programs for three reasons: (a) jobs for certain employees have become obsolete, (b) technological advances demand that employees learn new skills to do their current jobs, and (c) the organization has created new jobs for which the employees need to be trained.

Job rotation is a type of job enhancement that involves stretching an employee's skills, knowledge, and abilities to include other work assignments. Job rotation gives employees a greater sense of expertise in different tasks, as opposed to being an expert at one job. Job rotation also relieves the problem of covering for absent employees in a department.

Cross training and job rotation are two steps that can be taken to increase employee satisfaction along with the more common measures of pay, security, or supervisory techniques.

Q 10: How do we set up an internship program?

A: In general, an internship program should be designed to provide a meaningful job experience for the intern, as well as satisfying the employer's work requirements. Internships administered through a college or university program should be undertaken only if the employer's needs are consistent with the school's program. The school should be contacted for program details. Companies or departments within organizations can also design and administer internship programs.

You will need to decide on various factors. You must determine the duration of the internship (e.g., summer, semester, year) and the number of hours per week the intern will work. In addition, you must determine if the internship will be paid (e.g., competitive salary, minimum wage, stipend) or if the intern will earn college credits. You must also determine the nature of the work (i.e., will the intern work on specific projects, or perform the regular duties of a position).

A successful internship program will require these steps of the employer:

- Develop a job description that details the minimum grade point average, experience, and education level requirements.

- Screen the internship candidates to be certain that each candidate's objectives and expectations match those of the employer.

- Determine the wage and benefit level or credits the intern will receive. Before hiring the intern, the employer must consider certain factors with respect to the Fair Labor Standards Act (FLSA). For example, if the employer benefits from the internship in the form of productive work or if the intern is performing the work of a typical employee, the intern could be considered an employee and be eligible for minimum wage and possible overtime protection. In contrast, if the internship is part of an education program designed and administered by a college or university where the student is receiving academic credit, the FLSA will not apply.

- Determine if a formal internship agreement or, perhaps, release forms are appropriate. Also, determine if the employer's various insurance plans cover an internship program (e.g., worker's compensation, liability).

- Review antidiscrimination provisions (Title IX of the 1972 Education Amendments, Title III of the ADEA, Title VI of the 1964 Civil Rights

Act, Section 504 of the Rehabilitation Act) that apply to student interns from colleges that receive federal funding.

- Provide adequate supervision to support the intern in meeting his or her objectives. In addition, staff members with whom the intern will interact should be prepared to help ensure that the intern's experience is positive.

- Complete regular reports on the intern's progress toward accomplishing his or her objectives.

At the conclusion of the program, the interns should provide the employer with an evaluation of their experience, including suggestions for improvement.

Q 11: What is distance learning?

A: Distance learning can involve satellite communications, computer learning, correspondence, and video and audio technologies. These delivery technologies often involve either self-study or a combination of self-study with onsite lectures and discussion. Distance learning comes in various high-tech and low-tech packages.

Distance learning means that the learner is able to study and learn in a location other than the usual location of the trainer. Distance learning frees both learners and trainers from the constraints of the traditional fixed timetable and increases the availability of the learning opportunity. It allows learners to choose their learning environment, to work their own pace, and to use the material as a refresher. Distance learning needs to be strategically planned and implemented within the organization.

Other issues also need to be considered with distance learning:

- Level of learner support
- Provision for people with special needs
- Administrative control, including statistical information
- Politics and perceived threats
- Conflicts of interests and priorities between different functions
- Issues that deal with the learning environment (e.g., desks, chairs, and lighting)

For more information on distance learning programs, try (a) *Peterson's Guide to Distance Learning Programs, 2000*, 4th ed. (1999) at <www.petersons.com>; (b) the American Society for Training and Development's web site at <www.astd.org>, or call (703) 683-8100; or (c) the United States Distance Learning Association at <www.usdla.org>, or call (800) 275-5162.

Q 12: What should be included in a program to train new supervisors?

A: When a company hires a new supervisor or promotes a current employee into a supervisory position, it is important that the employee be trained properly to ensure success in the new role. A newly promoted supervisor may require assistance in making the transition from an employee to a supervisor, and a newly hired, experienced supervisor may need to be trained in the company's policies and practices. Providing training and assistance to ease this transition period can certainly be beneficial to both the supervisor and the organization, because the benefits of having well-trained supervisors can far exceed the amount of time, money, and effort spent on training them.

The content of a training program for supervisors may vary greatly among different organizations. Generally speaking, managerial competencies can be divided into two categories: knowledge and skills.

The knowledge category may include the following training subjects:

- Management theories and practices

- Business procedures

- Business regulations

- Total quality management

- Change management

- Wage and salary administration

- Strategic planning

- Succession planning

- Performance evaluations

- Equal employment opportunity

- Union contracts and labor relations

- Business ethics and proper conduct

The skills category may include the following training subjects:

- Motivation

- Leadership and influence

- Conflict management

- Coaching and counseling

- Work scheduling and planning

- Time management

- Problem-solving skills

- Negotiation skills

- Decision making

- Team-building skills

- Organizational communication

- Organization and delegation of work

The content and duration of supervisory training programs can vary significantly and should be based on the needs of the organization and on the individual participant's career experience and progress. Supervisory development and training programs are designed to provide exposure to both management and functional responsibilities. Therefore, individual training modules and programs should be customized to develop managers' and supervisors' own special abilities, as well as to delineate the skills and abilities that will be necessary to move along a defined career path from one management position to another within the organization.

Q 13: What should be included in an orientation program?

A: Orientation programs differ from one company to another. What works in one company's culture might not fit in another company's culture. Therefore, the person designing an orientation program in a company should carefully select the topics to cover for orientation. Topics that are often covered in orientation programs include the following:

- Company history, mission statement, and structure

- Employee handbook

- Benefits

- Tour of the company

The supervisor is usually responsible for covering the following:

- Responsibilities and standards

- Tour of the work site

- How the job fits into the company

Q 14: What is an *assessment center*? Where can we find one?

A: An *assessment center* is a process that is often used to evaluate management-level candidates and a process in which candidates are asked to participate in a series of situations that resemble what the employee might be called on to do in the real world. Those exercises should be a simulation that is based on the specific task of the position to be filled. During this process, the candidates are observed on their ability to make decisions, set priorities, and handle conflict, as well as communication skills. Assessment centers provide an effective alternative to the selection process because they can include panel interviews, mock staff meetings, and other work-related exercises involving several employees. Assessment centers enhance the ability to recognize and select the most suitable candidate for the organization. It is important to point out that an assessment center is not a place but, rather, a process that can be established as part of your selection process.

Q 15: What is an on-the-job training program?

A: On-the-job training (OJT) programs tend to be flexible, very relevant to the individual's job, and relatively inexpensive to implement. Trainers must be ever vigilant to use the flexibility to their advantage rather than to allow the program to degrade into a haphazard, ongoing project that is really never completed.

OJT can take several forms. Training can take the form of coaching, which is intensive learning through demonstration. Coaching is usually done in individual sessions where the supervisor will observe, demonstrate, and give feedback to newer employees. Mentoring is another technique used to allow a more seasoned employee to guide a new employee through the global technical and interpersonal skills necessary for long-term success in a role.

Rotation and cross training allow employees to pick up new skills that enable the employees to fill roles wherever there is the greatest need. Cross training is most beneficial where a business goes through frequent fluctuations in product demand. Vestibule training is a technique that is as close to OJT as possible. Employees are trained off-line in an environment that is either a replica of the work environment or the actual work environment when it is not in full operation.

Because adults learn best when they are active participants, the OJT technique is an ideal choice for mature learners. The keys to success are presentation, demonstration, and practice. The most critical elements of OJT are follow-up by the trainer and tracking progress toward an ultimate measurable goal. As with any training program, the starting point is to develop clearly stated objectives. Making sure that a systematic plan is being executed is critical to the success of the program.

Q 16: How do we conduct a cost-benefit analysis to determine return on investment for training programs?

A: One of the most important aspects of training from an organizational standpoint is the ability to determine the costs and benefits that are involved with a training program. Because it should be considered an investment in the organization's HR, training is expected to have (a) a return that can be measured by productivity and (b) efficiency that is substantial enough to justify the costs associated with the program. It should also produce a visible benefit to the organization. Training directors and managers can select from a number of different methods to determine a training function's return on investment (ROI). The steps of one calculation method are shown below.

Training Program Cost-Benefit Analysis

Basic Calculation

1. **Calculate training return**. The training evaluation should have produced some payoff measures such as the increased sales, the value of higher productivity, the costs savings of less equipment damage, and so on.

2. **Figure training investment**. This figure reflects the total costs of conducting training. Add together the following expenses:

   - Program expenses include expenses for trainees' and trainers' travel, lodging, and food, as well as for trainers' salaries and facility rental.

   - Materials and equipment expenses include costs for materials, supplies, and equipment operations.

   To figure total training investment, you must deduct from the total expenses any of these offsetting factors:

   - Program revenues include paybacks from training that might come from the trainees' accumulation of frequent flyer coupons, or from the resale or rental of training materials.

   - Equipment revenues include resale, rental, or reuse of training equipment for other purposes. Such revenues can offset the cost of purchasing the devices.

3. **Figure training return**. Subtract the training investment from the training return to learn the net (after expenses) training return.

4. **Learn return on investment**. Calculate ROI by dividing the net training return by the training investment. This final calculation should yield a figure greater than 1. If not, the company has actually lost money by training its employees.

Averaging Costs over Time

The previous example used simple calculations for the purposes of illustration. In real life, however, figuring the ROI for a training program involves more complex calculations. The initial investment should be divided over the program's life cycle, because the more years a program operates, the more value the company gets for its initial investment. Consider the number of employees who will undergo training during the program's life cycle and the average tenure of those trained employees. Then include those factors, along with the average annual increase in productivity, sales, and so on, when calculating the program's payoff.

The following examples show how to use these additional factors in evaluating a training investment.

Averaging Costs over the Program's Life Cycle

An organization has decided to purchase equipment to produce in-house training videos but is debating what type of equipment to buy. Camera A has a purchase price of $10,000, a $2,000 savings over the higher-priced Camera B. But after getting information on repair and maintenance, the cost breakdown over the equipment's life cycle of 15 years proves Camera B to be the better investment, as shown in Table 4–6.

TABLE 4–6
COST BREAKDOWN

	Camera A	Camera B
Initial investment	$10,000	$12,000
Maintenance	300	240
Operating costs (annual)	240	180
Repair costs (annual)	200	100
Total annual costs	$ 740	$ 520
Costs in year 1 (annual)	10,740	12,520
Costs from years 2 to 15	10,360	7,070
Total life cycle costs	$21,100	$19,590

Determining the Payback Period

The payback period is the number of years it takes for a company to recover its initial investment. Programs with the lowest payback period are the most economical. Using the payback method to estimate the value of training is simple to calculate and easy to explain. Although this calculation provides a good rough indicator of the risk involved in making a training investment, it does not take into account factors such as the time value of money and the effect of cash flows beyond the payback period.

The above calculation model was provided courtesy of AlignMark Corporation (formerly the RIA Group). Additional information can also be obtained from AlignMark Corporation at <www.alignmark.com> or from the American Society for Training and Development at <www.astd.org>.

Q 17: What resources can the Information Center suggest we use to develop training programs?

A: The best collection of training-related resources is just a click away. The list found in the HRLinks section of the SHRM web page includes a variety of sources that will provide the resources you need to learn more about training. Of note is the American Society for Training and Development (ASTD) Info-line series. For a small fee per item, ASTD will provide information sheets on various training-related topics. The SHRMStore also contains several training-related books. Call (800) 283-SHRM (7476), extension 3315, to order a catalog or to visit our on-line store. Finally, SHRM members can request information on specific training-related topics by contacting the Information Center by e-mail or by telephone at (800) 283-SHRM, option 5.

References

Chapter 4. Human Resource Development

Bell, C. R. (1996). *Managers as mentors*. San Francisco: Berrett-Koehler Publishers. Available: SHRMStore, (800) 444-5006 or <www.shrm.org/shrmstore>.

Hutchins, D. B. (1999). *Mentoring*. (White paper no. 61303). [On-line]. Available: <www.shrm.org/whitepapers/documents/61303.asp>. Accessed 6/99.

Marquardt, M. (1996). *Building the learning organization: A systems approach to quantum improvement and global success*. New York: McGraw-Hill.

The Mentoring Group. (n.d.). *The mentoring program coordinator's guide*. Available: The Mentoring Group/CCC, 13560 Mesa Drive, Grass Valley, CA 95949; (530) 268-1146; fax (530) 268-3636; or <www.mentoringgroup.com>.

The Mentoring Group. (n.d.). "Planning, implementing, & evaluating a successful mentoring program: A checklist of critical tasks." [Booklet]. Available: The Mentoring Group/CCC; 13560 Mesa Drive; Grass Valley, CA 95949; (530) 268-1146; fax (530) 268-3636; or <www.mentoringgroup.com>. Accessed 6/99.

Murray, M., & Owen, M. (1991). *Beyond the myths and magic of mentoring: How to facilitate an effective mentoring program.* San Francisco: Jossey-Bass. Available: <www.amazon.com>.

Senge, P. (1990). *The fifth discipline.* New York: Doubleday.

Peterson's. (1999). *Peterson's guide to distance learning programs.* 4th ed. [On-line]. Princeton, NJ: Peterson's. Available: <www.petersons.com>.

CHAPTER 5

COMPENSATION

General

Q 1: **What is meant by the term *comparable worth*? How is it different from *equal pay*?**

> **A:** *Comparable worth* is the concept of equal pay for similar or comparable work. Using this theory, individuals—most often women— seek increased compensation on the basis that the work is just as valuable to society or as difficult as other jobs that pay more. When we apply comparable worth doctrine, we compare jobs in different locations that have been typically occupied by one sex. Comparable worth is the idea that because women have typically held a position, such as nursing, the job pays less—not because the market, through supply and demand, creates a lower wage for the job.
>
> *Equal pay* is often an issue of pay between genders. Women historically have been and continue to be paid less than men, even when working in the same job. The Equal Pay Act is an amendment to the Fair Labor Standards Act that prohibits employers from discriminating between men and women by paying one gender more than the other "for equal work on jobs the performance of which requires equal skill, effort, and responsibility, and which are performed under similar working conditions." This definition does not mean that the jobs must be identical but that they should be substantially equal according to the four criteria mentioned above. When we consider differences in pay under the Equal Pay Act, the jobs in question must also be at the same physical establishment to incur a violation. Seniority systems, merit systems, and incentive plans can cause differences in pay if an employer can show that one of those systems is in place and administered fairly.

Q 2:   Where can we get sample job descriptions?

> **A:** There are many different sources for obtaining sample job descriptions. When trying to decide what source to access, first decide how many descriptions you plan to write. If you are writing or revising all

or most of your company's current job descriptions (and yours is a rather large company), we would suggest one of three methods:

- One method is to hire a consultant to write them for you. This method can be very costly but is worth the investment if your company has limited human resources to invest in the project. To find a listing of potential consultants, access the SHRM member *Consultants' Database* from SHRM's home page.

- A second method is to purchase one of the many job description software packages on the market. Most tend to be very simple to use and can provide boilerplate language for many job descriptions that can be modified to fit your company's needs.

- The third method is to purchase books of sample job descriptions from among the many on the market. Watson Wyatt, Business and Legal Reports, and the American Management Association are all publishers of job description books.

If your project is on a smaller scale, other options may be more appropriate. The SHRM Information Center can provide up to three job descriptions when members call and make a request. SHRM also has a job description databank accessible through its home page at <www.shrm.org/whitepapers/descriptions>. The Internet has sites where job descriptions can be downloaded for a fee. One of them, "Job Descriptions Now," is linked to the SHRM home page. To obtain the occasional hard-to-find description, you should contact fellow SHRM members who might have a similar job. If a particular company or industry is similar to yours, use the member directory on the SHRM home page to see if any SHRM members are listed with whom you can network. Or post your question on HRTalk to see if anyone responds with a good sample.

Q 3: We are revising our performance appraisal process. What resources are available?

A: The Information Center can provide general information on the performance appraisal process, as well as lists of books and articles available for rental and reprints (a small charge exists for these services). Because of the number of requests we receive for sample forms, the Information Center asks members to submit copies of their performance appraisal forms every few years for possible inclusion in our book of sample forms. The 1996 edition is available through the SHRMStore and contains 30 sample forms used by members, reviewed by the Information Center staff, and sorted into categories (i.e., 360-degree, peer, team, etc.). It is item number 61-12, *Performance Appraisal Forms: A Collection of Samples*, and costs $25 for members. In the near future, many sample appraisal forms will appear on the SHRM web site. Additionally, a number of general HR-related web sites are listed in the HRLinks section of our home page and other resources, such as consultants and networking opportunities.

Q 4:   Where can we find salary data for a wide range of employee job titles?

A: One of the most frequently asked questions at the SHRM Information Center is where to find salary survey data. The Information Center has salary data only for HR professionals. The William M. Mercer consulting firm prepares the *HR Management Compensation Survey* in cooperation with SHRM annually. One suggestion we always have for those seeking data is to contact any professional associations that your employees belong to in order to see if they conduct a salary survey. The Special Libraries Association, for example, conducts salary surveys for the library profession.

Where else should you look for salary data? Large consulting firms conduct salary surveys on just about every occupation. If you look at the SHRM *Consultants' Forum Directory* on the SHRM Internet page, you can search the directory to find compensation consultants in many states. (See <www.shrm.org>, and select the Consultants' Forum section of our home page.)

In addition, many other sources that provide salary data are linked to the SHRM Internet page. Visit our page at <www.shrm.org>. Select HRLinks from the list of choices on the left side of the page. Then at HRLinks, see the section on compensation. One of the subsections is about salary surveys. In March 1999, SHRM had 24 links to sites with salary data, and the HRLinks are constantly being updated. Some of the items that those linked sites have to offer are below:

- "Abbott, Langer & Associates" allows you to determine current pay rates for many jobs and industries.

- Both *DataMasters* and *Money* magazines have U.S. cost-of-living comparisons. If you enter the places you want to compare, the difference in cost of living will be computed for you.

- The "JobSmart" link provides salary data in scores of occupations.

- The "Recruitment Extra" and also "Wage" web sites list salaries for hundreds of jobs.

- A significant find in the HRLinks section is the "Employment Cost Trends" link to the Department of Labor's Bureau of Labor Statistics. Click on "National Compensation Survey" for specific city data; much of the information looks brand new.

The advent of salary data on the Internet provides the largest free source of this kind of information that we have ever seen. A note of caution: Be aware of the sources of this data. If you have questions about how it is computed or where it comes from, contact the source (most provide e-mail addresses on the page). Although SHRM makes every effort to link our members to reliable sources, every site on the Internet is not as authoritative as the next one. Use such information with care. You may want to compare several sources to see how closely they match before you use their data.

Q 5: How do we conduct a salary survey?

A: If an organization has staff members with enough statistical expertise to conduct a salary survey and to make determinations on matters such as the proper size of the sample to be surveyed, the next step is to decide whom to survey and what types of questions to ask. Generally speaking, in making the decision as to whom to survey, an organization should, whenever possible, survey companies that are either people competitors or product or service competitors.

Product and service competitors can be described as those who compete for the same product or service. They can be located close to your geographic region or facility, or they can be spread throughout the country. People competitors are best described as companies with which your organization competes for people and are most likely located within the same geographical region. Identifying product or service competitors is normally pretty easy; however, it is not always as easy to identify people competitors.

It may be helpful to use exit interview information or new hire information to note where new hires have worked in the past and where terminating employees are going to work. This information should give employers a fair idea of who their people competitors are in the market. It is important to note that once you decide what companies to survey, you assure these organizations that the information they give you will be kept confidential and that you will provide them with a copy of the survey results.

In addition to your deciding which companies to survey, it is equally important to decide what jobs you want to obtain wage and salary data about. When selecting benchmark jobs, employers should try to survey (a) job families as opposed to single jobs, (b) jobs that other companies are likely to have, (c) highly populated jobs, and (d) jobs that are experiencing high turnover or that are difficult to recruit for. Once your organization has made its final decisions regarding which companies to survey and which jobs to use as benchmarks, the next step is to determine the type of information that will be needed.

The obvious answer to this question is to ask what you really need to know. You may want to ask about the organization's size, union presence, pay program procedures, total compensation packages, or benefit programs. To ensure that you will receive data that will be useful to you, you should ask questions specific to the benchmark jobs, such as the number of people in the company being surveyed, the average monthly salary of individuals in those jobs, the salary of the highest paid employees in those jobs, the salary of the lowest paid employees in those jobs, and the maximum and minimum salary limits for those jobs.

The time frame for obtaining survey results is usually underestimated. Although it is typical for individuals who are not accustomed to conducting salary surveys to estimate that a survey can be designed and conducted in a matter of weeks, most surveys can take from 10 to 12 weeks to design and implement (for a short survey) and as long as 6 months (for a larger survey). We also recommend that you involve the management team in the initial processing of the survey. It is important for managers and executives to participate in the design, content, and selection of the companies you are going to invite to participate in the survey.

The above information briefly summarizes some of the components that go into conducting a salary survey. Completed salary-survey questionnaires need to be verified and analyzed carefully when they are returned, and individuals with expertise in the compensation area will be required to properly conduct and interpret survey results that are to be used for internal salary planning and administration purposes. Organizations that do not have internal staff members with the appropriate expertise to tackle such a project are probably better off bringing in a consultant who specializes in salary surveys to provide assistance with processing the survey questionnaires and the results.

Employers should be careful when conducting salary surveys themselves. Some employers have been found to violate anti-trust laws when conducting their own surveys. It is best to let a third party conduct the salary survey for your company. If hiring an outside firm is not possible, then look at surveys conducted by various companies and not just within the same industry. Make sure that the surveys are conducted blindly so that the individual companies cannot be identified in the results. The more it appears that you are surveying your direct local competitors, the more it appears that you may be violating anti-trust laws. Having legal counsel evaluate your process could prevent problems in the long run.

Q 6: What is a *competency* and where can we find general information or sample models for developing competencies?

> **A:** A *competency* is defined as a set of related knowledge, abilities, and skills that directly affect a major part of an individual's job. Competencies usually correlate with performance on the job and are used to measure against well-accepted industry standards. Competencies can also be used to improve individual employee training and development programs, as well as to develop variable pay systems such as skill-based or competency-based pay plans. Regardless of the reasons to develop competencies or to use competency models, an employer should first make a careful assessment to identify individual competencies that are weaker than desired. This assessment should be accomplished by using a means that is valid, reliable, and relatively simple to administer.
>
> Three different methods are currently being used to assess competencies: (a) 360-degree feedback tools that provide feedback from peers, management, customers, and so forth; (b) assessment centers or labs that typically involve the use of role playing, and (c) interactive multimedia systems where an individual is given the opportunity to view a series of videotapes and respond appropriately to various situations.
>
> Because competency models have increased in popularity, many books and articles have been written on the subject. The SHRM Foundation has recently sponsored and published two publications that can prove to be very valuable resources for understanding and developing competency models. The study *HR Competencies for the Year 2000: Take the Wake Up Call* (Schoonover, 1998) and *HR Competencies for the Year 2000: A Professional's Toolkit for Performance Development* (Schoonover, 1998) are available from the SHRMStore at <www.shrm.org/shrmstore> or by calling (800) 444-5006.

Q 7: What is the difference between a *job evaluation* and a *job analysis*?

> **A:** A *job evaluation* is a systematic way to determine the value of a job in a company. It is usually used to determine a position's relative worth within an organization and to help provide detailed information so employers can establish an equitable pay practice program. A *job analysis* is a process that helps the company determine what the functions of a position are. A job analysis is a tool used mainly to assist a company to set its equitable pay program.
>
> The first two steps used to evaluate a position's relative worth within an organization are (a) performing a job analysis (a discussion on job analysis follows) and (b) writing a job description. Completing those two steps will help the company create a hierarchy of jobs.

The two main approaches in conducting a job evaluation are *job content* and *market-based* evaluations.

A *job content evaluation* focuses on internal equity and the job's worth to the organization. Job content evaluations are broken into two categories: nonquantitative and quantitative.

- A nonquantitative evaluation of job content compares the jobs within an organization to one another by using a ranking or classification system. The most common nonquantitative evaluation systems are the ranking, slotting, and classification systems.

- A quantitative job content evaluation uses a statistical approach to determine the relative worth of a position. In a quantitative system, the job functions are broken into compensable factors. Those compensable factors are then assigned a numerical value. The most common quantitative evaluation systems are the point factor, the comparison factor, and the scored questionnaire.

A *market-based evaluation* measures a position's value within a specific industry or market. Gathering market data from published salary surveys usually completes this type of an evaluation. Smaller companies or those that are competing for a limited talent pool usually complete market-based evaluations. In addition, this type of evaluation system usually does not take into consideration the internal value of the position or function.

A job analysis is usually the first step in building a pay program. The information gathered from a job analysis is used to complete job descriptions that, in turn, are used to help measure the comparative worth of a position.

Information for a job analysis is gathered by using a combination of the following: observation, employee interviews, and questionnaires.

- **Observation.** This method is very popular in a production environment. Direct observation is very time consuming. Observing employees could make them feel as if they are being watched and could affect their productivity. Observation could also provide incomplete data because the entire function may not be observed.

- **Interviews.** The success of interviewing will depend on the skill of the interviewer. The main challenge of interviewing is making the employee feel valued. The interview method is extremely useful for positions that are at the management level or that are technical. By interviewing employees in these types of positions, you will be able to determine how much decision making or judgment will be required. This method is probably the most costly but the most accurate way to determine a position's compensable factors.

- **Questionnaires**. This method is more commonly known as Position Analysis Questionnaires (PAQs) and is the most efficient because it allows measurement of several jobs at one time. However, because it depends on the incumbents' understanding of the position and their writing and verbal skills, this method does limit confidence in the results. PAQs can be formatted as open-ended or highly structured questionnaires. Open-ended questionnaires require incumbents to provide a written response, whereas the highly structured PAQ allows the jobholder to select the answer that best describes the duties and responsibilities at hand.

By using a combination of job analysis techniques, an employer obtains the information necessary to (a) determine the expectations of the employee, (b) determine the lines of authority, (c) facilitate the performance appraisal and compensation program, (d) minimize employer liability under ADA and FLSA, and (e) make sure employees are assigned to the right job.

Q 8:   What is a skill-based pay plan?

A: Under a skill-based pay plan, employees are paid for the types of skills they are capable of using rather than for the skills they use to perform their current jobs. Also referred to as pay-for-knowledge plans, skill-based pay plans increase an employee's pay as new skills are mastered.

The employer with a skill-based pay plan defines a set of skills necessary to perform a family of jobs. Each level of skill is then assigned a pay level. New employees are paid at the entry-level skill level and receive training for the entry-level job. As employees acquire and master the skills at the current pay and skill level, they receive a base-pay increase and can then receive training for the next skill level. Some employers require employees to periodically demonstrate the skills previously acquired.

The primary objective and advantage of a skill-based pay plan is to cross-train employees because multiskilled employees are more valuable to the organization than employees with more limited sets of skills. A skill-based pay plan can also support other objectives such as the following:

- Improved product quality

- Increased productivity

- Increased teamwork

- Increased employee involvement and understanding of production processes

- Lower staffing requirements.

Although a skill-based pay plan can support many corporate objectives, there are potential disadvantages of using such plans:

- Increased compensation and training costs

- More employees reaching top-of-pay range

- More complicated compensation administration

- More frequent employee desire to change jobs

For additional information on this topic, please see the book *Strategic Pay: Aligning Organization Strategies and Pay Systems* by Edward E. Lawler III (1990).

Q 9:   What is *broadbanding*?

A: *Broadbanding* is an alternative to traditional salary-grade structures. Broadbanding is a structure in which several different job functions are clustered into one broad band. Broadbanding results in a flatter hierarchy and provides for more lateral movement within the company. Employees stay in the same band for a longer time but are encouraged to try other assignments within the same band, which creates a more versatile workforce. Broadbanding can also encourage an emphasis on teamwork and can reduce competition for promotions.

Q 10: What types of compensation plans are available for individuals who work in a sales capacity?

A: There are five basic compensation plans for sales employees: salary-only, commission-only, commission-plus-draw, salary-plus-commission, and salary-plus-bonus plans.

- **Salary-only plans**. In salary-only plans, income is derived entirely through a fixed salary. The company assumes all the risk because its cost remains the same whether the volume of sales is up or down. This plan could be used in situations where the sales cycle of a product or service is long or where it is difficult to measure individual sales results. It is important to provide other motivators as selling incentives.

- **Commission-only plans**. In commission-only plans, the sales employee assumes all the risk. Income is derived entirely through commissions. This plan might be appropriate in situations where the sales cycles of a product or service are short or where the employee has some influence over the sales volume.

- **Commission-plus-draw plans**. In commission-plus-draw plans, sales employees are provided with income in the form of a "draw," which is used as an advance. The advance is then charged against commissions or other incentive pay the employee earns. Recoverable draws carry forward until the employee earns enough in sales to repay the company. Nonrecoverable draws are forgiven if the employee is unable to repay it within a certain amount of time. The compensation plan may contain a provision that an employee will not continue to be employed if he or she is unable to repay the draw for a set number of months or sales periods.

- **Salary-plus-commission plans**. Salary-plus-commission plans are the most common type of sales compensation plan. They distribute the selling risk between the company and the employee. The salary component of the plan allows employees to focus their attention on other tasks that do not generate commission. The commission component of the plan rewards employees for sales.

- **Salary-plus-bonus plans**. Salary-plus-bonus plans are similar to salary-plus-commission plans in that they both provide a base salary plus incentive pay. Bonuses differ from commissions in that they typically reward sales employees for the achievement of specific, nonrecurring goals such as achieving a sales milestone.

Q 11: What is a *merit pay system*?

A: A merit pay system is a method of rewarding and motivating performance that results in employees in the same job receiving different pay rates; in other words, a merit system links pay to performance. There are two key ingredients in a merit pay system: (a) the merit increase delivery system and (b) the performance appraisal system. To succeed with the merit system, a company must conduct fair and consistent performance appraisals.

You must communicate the system clearly so that employees see the linkage and believe that improvement in performance will bring rewards in pay increases. The theory of a merit pay system is to view the salary range as a series of levels that relate to job performance. Reaching the top of the range is a matter of performance, not seniority. Table 5–1 illustrates the relationship of a salary grade to various performance levels.

The minimum rate represents the lowest pay level for a new employee who possesses the minimum qualifications. The midpoint level is pay to an employee who meets the expectations of the job, and the maximum level represents the most that a company is willing to pay someone to do the job.

Merit pay structures do not have a fixed rate at each step. Employees may receive any dollar amount within the range.

TABLE 5–1
SALARY GRADE—PERFORMANCE LEVEL RELATIONSHIP

Rate	Range Level	Performance Level
$20,000	Maximum	Highest performance level
18,000		Above expectations
16,000	Midpoint	Meets expectations
14,000		Below expectations
12,000	Minimum	New job

Q 12: What is a stock purchase plan?

A: An *employee stock purchase plan* (ESPP) is a plan in which an employer gives employees the option to obtain stock in the company at a future date for a predetermined price. Such options are often paid for through payroll deductions. Employees who acquire stock options receive preferential tax treatment when the stock is disposed of. For example, if employees purchase stock at a discounted rate, they do not have to recognize that income until they sell the stocks. Also, any gain in the stock is treated as regular income rather than a capital gain.

ESPPs differ from incentive stock options (ISOs) in that ESPPs are subject to nondiscrimination testing. Therefore, although ISOs are usually issued to executives and key employees, ESPPs are distributed more evenly throughout the company, which encourages broad-based employee ownership.

Q 13: What are some of the types of incentive plans available for compensating high-level executive employees?

A: Short-term incentives have significantly risen in popularity. Incentive plans often are performance based and tied to the organization's well-defined fiscal year objectives. To reinforce the pay-performance link, the executive should be able to exercise direct influence over the results. Payment is usually in the form of cash.

Long-term incentive plans cover compensation periods of more than 1 year. For many executives, long-term incentives make up the greatest portion of their total compensation because most organizations strive for long-term success. The plan often consists of a grant of stock options and restricted stock, as well as a long-term, cash-based performance plan. Long-term incentives can be divided into the following:

- **Investment plans**. Executives are granted rights or options to purchase the organization's common stock in the future.

    — Nonqualified Stock Options (NQSOs). NQSOs are the most frequently used investment plan and do not conform to Section 422A of the Internal Revenue Code. NQSOs allow the executive to purchase the organization's common stock at a specified grant price (usually the fair market value, or less, as of the date of the grant) over a given period of time, usually 10 years. The options can be exercised in any order and in any amount. At the time of exercise, the difference between the fair market value on the date of exercise and the grant price is taxed as ordinary income.

    — Incentive Stock Options (ISOs). ISOs conform to Section 422A of the Internal Revenue Code. They allow the executive to purchase the organization's common stock at a grant price that is at least equal to the fair market value as of the date of grant and is within 10 years of the grant date. The options can be exercised in any order up to a maximum of $100,000 in any year. Generally, there are no tax consequences to the executive at the time of exercise.

- **Appreciation plans**. Appreciation plans are payable in stock or cash. The executive receives the appreciation value of the stock over the period from stock grant to some future date. Appreciation plans are granted at no cost to the executive.

    — Stock Appreciation Rights (SARs). The executive can receive the appreciation value of the stock when the option is surrendered. SARs can be paid out in cash, stock, or a combination of the two. SARs are most often granted with NQSOs and ISOs. At the time of exercise, the appreciation value of the stock is taxed as ordinary income on the amount of the appreciation.

    — Phantom Stock. Phantom stock is a cash or stock award determined by the appreciation in stock price and based on book, fair market, or formula value at a fixed future date—usually from 5 to 10 years. At the time of exercise, the cash or stock award is taxed as ordinary income on the amount of the appreciation.

- **Full value plans**. The executive receives a specified value or the full value of the shares of common stock. As with appreciation plans, the executive is not required to make any investment.

    — Performance Share or Unit Plans. Such plans cover cash or stock award earned through achieving specific goals. Performance periods usually last from 3 to 5 years. The payment is taxed as ordinary income.

— Restricted Stock. This plan addresses a grant of stock at a reduced price with the condition that it may not be sold before a specified vesting period. The plan acts as a typical retention device because the executive usually forfeits the right to the stock if he or she leaves before the date that the restriction lapses. Excess over fair market value is taxed as ordinary income.

Recent innovations in stock options and long-term incentive plans should also be considered. These innovations include premium-priced options, reload options, dividend appreciation rights, performance vesting for stock options, stock options with a restricted stock "carrot," and time-accelerated restricted stock.

Q 14: How can we coordinate merit increases with our current performance appraisal system?

A: Correlating pay with performance requires two key elements: an effective performance appraisal system and a merit pay delivery system. If the merit pay plan is to be effective, the employees must find a connection between their merit increase and their performance evaluation. To have an effective performance evaluation system, an employer should train managers to be good evaluators.

Merit pay can be based solely on performance, or it can be tied to the position in the range. To set up a merit pay plan tied to the position in the range, first divide the pay range into quarters. Next develop a matrix based on the evaluation rating, as shown in Table 5–2.

Using this matrix, an employer can determine the amount of increase an employee should receive based on the current quartile of the employee's salary and on the rating of the employee's last review. For example, an employee's pay range is from $12,000 to $20,000 with a midpoint of $16,000. The employee's current salary is $13,500, and he or she received a commendable rating. First, determine the "compa-ratio" to find out where the salary falls in the range. You compare by dividing the actual salary by the range midpoint, that is $13,500/16,000 = .84 \times 100 = 84\%$. Use this calculation and look at the chart to find the percentage (%) column it falls into and follow down until you match it with the rating, in this case, commendable. The rate of the increase would be between 5% and 6%.

TABLE 5–2
EXAMPLE OF MATRIX BASED ON EVALUATION RATING

Quartile	1st Quarter	2nd Quarter	3rd Quarter	4th Quarter
Merit Pay	80% Minimum	90% Progress Point	100% Midpoint	110% Advanced Point	120% Maximum
Distinguished	7–8%	5.5–6.5%	5–6%	4–5%	0–2.5%
Commendable	5–6%	4.5–5.5%	4–5%	3–4%	0–1.5%
Fully Satisfactory	4–5%	3.5–4.5%	3–4%	2–3%	No increase
Adequate	3–4%	2.5–3.5%	2–3%	No increase	No increase
Needs Improvement	2–3%	No increase	No increase	No increase	No increase
Unsatisfactory	No increase	No increase	No increase	No increase	No increase

Q 15: Can we be sued by an agency temporary employee who is hurt at our workplace? Are temporary employees covered by our worker's compensation?

A: Yes, you could have some liability. Worker's compensation is one area where both the temporary agency and the client company have a joint employer relationship under several employment laws. When you hire a temporary worker who is employed by a temporary agency, that agency normally is covered by the Worker's Compensation Law, and you, as a client company, are not covered. The worker is not your employee. You can be sued by the injured party under your general liability policy. One way to avoid this situation is to make sure that the temporary agency you use has an Alternative Employer Agreement rider on its worker's compensation policy that will let the client company share protection under the temporary agency's worker's compensation policy. However, this rider would be more expensive for the temporary agency, and the agency would have to agree to such an arrangement in your contract with it. For more information, see the white paper *Temporary Staffing Agencies and Human Resources: Compliance Issues* (Schable, 1999) at <www.shrm.org/whitepapers>.

Fair Labor Standards Act

Q 16: What are employers required to do when they receive a wage garnishment notice for an employee?

A: Generally speaking, most garnishments have extensive instructions on the reverse side of the order. Often the instructions will (a) ask whether other garnishments on this employee already exist, (b) discuss the process of calculating disposable wages, and (c) almost always have specific instructions on replying to the court or third party that is designated to accept the garnishment.

Garnishments are regulated at both the state and federal levels. The federal laws supersede the state laws unless the state laws have greater protection for employees. Federal law establishes an upper limit on the amount that may be deducted from an employee's wages. Only disposable earnings are subject to garnishment. Disposable earnings include total compensation minus deductions required by federal and state law that include withholding for federal income, social security, and medicare taxes; state income and unemployment taxes; and any court costs for garnishment proceedings.

Different limits on the percentage of disposable earnings that may be deducted depend on the type of garnishment. Limits for garnishments range from 50% to 60% of disposable earnings for support orders and from 0% to 10% for unpaid student loans. No limit is set for court-ordered garnishments from bankruptcies. To be safe, check with your state's department of labor to get specific state regulations on garnishments.

Q 17: Are there any federal or state wage and hour restrictions on the employment of minors?

A: The Fair Labor Standards Act (FLSA) imposes restrictions on the employment of minors under age 18. State laws impose limits on employing minors. Employers must adhere to the state child labor laws if they are more protective than the FLSA provisions.

Minors who are ages 14 and 15 are permitted to work a limited number of hours but only outside school time and only in nonhazardous jobs. The Department of Labor (DOL) bars minors who are ages 14 and 15 from working in the following occupations:

- Manufacturing, mining, or processing

- Operation or tending of hoisting apparatus or power-driven machinery (other than office machines)

- Operation of motor vehicles or service as helpers on such vehicles

- Public messenger services

- Occupations that are hazardous for minors who are ages 16 and 17 or that are detrimental to their health or well-being

- Occupations in connection with any means of transportation, warehousing and storage, communications and public utilities, and construction work

- Minors who are ages 14 and 15 and who are permitted to work are subject to the following restrictions:

- All work must be performed outside school hours.

- A maximum 3-hour day and 18-hour week applies when school is in session.

- A maximum 8-hour day and 40-hour week applies when school is not in session.

- All work must be performed between 7 a.m. and 7 p.m. (9 p.m. from June 1 through Labor Day).

Minors who are ages 16 and 17 may be employed in any occupation other than an occupation declared hazardous by the Secretary of Labor. Minors of this age may be employed during school hours for any number of hours and during any period of time. Employers should check their state child labor law because it may provide minors who are ages 16 and 17 further protection.

Although the FLSA does not require employers to obtain age certificates for minors, employers may request unexpired age certificates to show proof that the minor is old enough to be lawfully employed. State laws may require additional documentation.

For additional information on child labor laws, check the DOL web site at <www.dol.gov>.

Q 18: Are employers required to pay a shift differential to employees who are working a second or third shift position?

A: Shift differentials or shift premiums are not required, but used by many employers to compensate employees who are scheduled to work less than desirable hours such as a second or third shift. Some employers also pay differentials for employees who work weekend shifts or perform undesirable tasks (dirty work premiums). Differential compensation is usually paid in addition to base hourly rates that are normally paid for jobs that do not require working a less-desirable schedule. Shift differentials can be paid by adding a specific flat rate of cents per hour to the regular base rate, or they can be computed on the basis of a percentage of the base hourly rate paid for the same kind of work being performed during normal working hours or under more desirable circumstances.

Extra compensation for working night or weekend shifts, as well as premiums paid for jobs that require performing undesirable tasks, is solely a matter of internal policy or may be part of an employment agreement. The FLSA does not require that an employer pay employees shift differentials or premium pay for working alternative shifts or for performing jobs with less than desirable tasks.

Although the FLSA does not require the payment of shift differentials or dirty work premiums, employers with shift operations need to be aware of how shift differentials affect overtime calculations for purposes of federal and state wage and hour laws. On a federal level, the overtime provisions of FLSA require employers to pay covered employees time and one-half of their regular rate for each hour or fraction of an hour worked in excess of 40 hours per week. An employee's regular rate is normally calculated by dividing the employee's total remuneration for the workweek by the number of hours worked during that period.

Shift differentials and dirty work premiums must be included as part of employees' total workweek remuneration when calculating their overtime pay rates under the law. However, if the differential or dirty work premium is at least time and one-half of the employee's regular rate and if it is paid to the employee pursuant to a collective bargaining agreement that specifies regular working hours, the differential may be excluded from the employee's regular rate and credited against overtime under the clock overtime rules of the FLSA.

In addition, certain state wage and hour laws provide employees with protections that are not covered under the federal FLSA laws. Therefore, employers should become familiar with both the federal and individual state requirements for calculation and payment of overtime rates.

Additional information on FLSA's overtime requirements can be obtained from DOL at <www.dol.gov>.

Q 19: What are the FLSA requirements for tipped employees?

A: The FLSA states that a tip is a gift or gratuity presented by a customer in recognition of some service performed by an individual. In absence of an agreement to the contrary, a tip becomes the property of the person to whom it was presented in recognition of that person's service. A tipped employee is any employee engaged in an occupation in which he or she customarily and regularly receives more than $30 a month in tips. According to the FLSA, the phrase "customarily and regularly" signifies a frequency that is greater than occasional but which may be less than constant.

Through several amendments to the FLSA, employers can pay tipped employees a salary of $2.13 per hour and credit tips received by the employee to make up the balance of the applicable minimum wage. For employers to claim this tip credit, they must explain the tip provision of FLSA to the employee. In addition, all tips received by the employee must be retained by the employee.

The burden of proof regarding the amount of tips is on the employer. The employer must determine that the amount is enough to credit against the applicable minimum wage, not simply an accounting of all tips received by each employee. If a discrepancy exists between the tip credit claimed by an employer and the amount of tips reported by the employee, there must be credible evidence to support the employer's claim. It is not sufficient to estimate the amount of tips on the basis of the business done at the tables served by the employee.

The employer will lose the tip credit if tipped employees are required to share their tips with employees who do not customarily and regularly receive tips. Tip pooling is permitted among employees who customarily and regularly receive tips.

When an employee performs a variety of different jobs, the employee's status as one who customarily and regularly receives tips is determined by the activities over the entire workweek. If the employee does not meet the requirements of a tipped employee, he or she must be paid the full applicable minimum wage.

Employers of tipped employees are required to record the following information:

- A symbol or letter on pay records identifying each employee who receives wages determined, in part, by tips

- The weekly or monthly amount reported by the employee to the employer about tips received (this record may consist of reports made on an IRS form)

- The amount by which the wages of each tipped employee have been deemed to be increased by tips as determined by the employer (not in excess of the statutory percentage of the applicable minimum wage)

- The hours worked each workday in any occupation in which the employee does not receive tips, along with total daily or weekly straight-time payment made by the employer for such hours

- The hours worked each workday in any occupation in which the employee does receive tips, along with total daily or weekly straight-time earnings made for such hours

Q 20: We have an employee who reported 48 hours on a time sheet but who worked only 40 hours for the week. Are we required to pay overtime for the additional 8 hours?

A: As required by the FLSA, overtime pay is required for hours in excess of 40 that are actually worked. In this instance, the employer asks why he or she put the additional hours on the time sheet. If it was recorded in error, the corrected time sheet should have the employee's signature to show that the employee agrees with the change. Although there is no requirement to pay an employee for hours that were not worked, a year or two from now the corrected time sheet will be evidence that the employee agreed that he or she worked only 40 hours rather than 48 hours.

Q 21: What must be included as *hours worked* when calculating weekly overtime?

A: Members often ask if overtime should be paid when part of the hours that an employee is paid are sick, vacation, or holiday pay. Employers are obligated to pay overtime only when the hours are actually worked. For example, an employee takes 8 hours of sick leave and then works 42 hours for a total of 50 hours in the work week. An employer would be obligated to pay for only 2 hours of overtime because the employee worked only 42 hours.

FLSA overtime rules require employers to pay nonexempt employees one and one-half times their regular rate of pay for each hour (or fraction thereof) worked in excess of 40 in a given workweek. *Hours worked* refers to actual hours worked during the workweek excluding vacation leave, holidays, and sick leave. Below are a few examples of employee activities and how those activities are regarded under the hours worked definition.

Travel time is not considered work time unless the following conditions are met:

Employees who drive vehicles that contain essential tools or equipment of the employer from their homes to work sites may be working while traveling.

Travel from home to a customer's site in response to an emergency call after the regular workday is work time.

When an employee who normally works at one location is sent out of town on a single-day trip, time that is spent traveling is work time.

An employee who travels away from home overnight is not working when he or she is a passenger on an airplane, train, boat, bus, or automobile outside his or her regular workhours. However, any time that the employee spends traveling as a passenger on a weekend will be counted as work time if the travel cuts across the hours that the employee would normally work during the week.

All travel that is compensable by contract, custom, or practice must be counted as work time, regardless of the previous limitations on counting travel as work time.

Training time is not considered work time when (a) attendance is outside of regular workhours, (b) attendance is voluntary, (c) no productive work is performed during the training, and (d) the training is not directed toward making the employee more proficient in his or her present job.

On-call time is not considered work time if the employee can use the time spent on call primarily for his or her own benefit. If, however, an employee is required to wait at the employer's premises or at a particular location other than the employee's home, all waiting time must be counted as work time.

Time not worked, whether or not it is paid time off, does not count toward the 40-hour threshold used to calculate overtime pay.

For more information about the FLSA, the DOL's Employment Standards Administration has a *Handy Reference Guide to the FLSA* on the Internet at <www.dol.gov/esa/public/regs/compliance/whd/hrg.htm>.

Q 22: Do we have to give unused vacation pay to employees who leave our company?

A: Accrued vacation is normally paid to employees who are leaving the company regardless of the reason for separation. Some companies may also pay terminating employees prorated vacation pay for any vacation time that they would have earned during the next year, provided they have met all necessary eligibility requirements under the employer's policy.

Although employers may place certain restrictions on vacation pay rights, in states such as California, Illinois, and Massachusetts, the state law provisions require an employer to pay any accrued vacation pay on termination of employment with the company. In many other states, vacation pay is included in the definition of *wages* in the state's wage and hour laws, which also requires employers to pay terminating employees for this time. It is always advisable to check individual state laws on payment of final wages to ensure compliance, and to avoid any penalties and fines. A state law guide such as the *State-by-State Guide to Human Resources Law* (Buckley & Onen, 1998) can serve as a very practical resource, and it is available through the SHRMStore by calling (800) 444-5006 or at the SHRM web site at <www.shrm.org>.

Q 23: What are the requirements for meals and breaks under FLSA?

A: The FLSA makes no requirements to provide breaks or meal times for employees. The obligation to provide meal time and rest periods to employees defers to state law. Approximately half of the states require some time for meal time or rest periods or both. Those states include California, Colorado, Connecticut, Delaware, Hawaii, Illinois, Kentucky, Maine, Massachusetts, Minnesota, Nebraska, Nevada, New Hampshire, New Mexico, New York, North Dakota, Oregon, Pennsylvania, Puerto Rico, Rhode Island, Tennessee, Utah, Washington, West Virginia, and Wisconsin. Some states' provisions apply only to specific industries. For those states without provisions for meal time or rest period, reason should regulate the employer's policy. Requiring employees to work all day without time to eat or rest would most certainly have an adverse effect on morale and productivity.

Q 24: Are employers obligated to pay for meal and break times?

A: Such pay depends on the length and location of the meal or break. A break for 20 minutes or less is considered compensable time. A meal time is typically 30 minutes or longer and is, therefore, not considered compensable time according to the FLSA. If work is being performed and if the employee is not relieved of duties during a meal time, then the time would be considered compensable. For example, receptionists who are required to answer the telephones while eating lunch should be compensated for this time because they have not been relieved of their duties. The employer does not have to allow the employee to leave the premises, but unless the employee has been relieved of duties, the meal time is compensable.

Q 25: What if an employee doesn't want to take a break? Our employee would like to work through lunch and breaks and then leave early.

A: In states where employees are required to have break and meal periods, employers must ensure that individuals take them. If the employee works through those periods, the employer is violating the state code. Furthermore, if the employer doesn't compensate the employee when he or she works through those times and does not take a break, the employer is violating wage payment requirements for hours worked. Remember, when the employee is actually performing work, he or she must be paid for that time. The employer cannot make deductions for meal or break periods to imply compliance with state laws about meal and rest time. Employers in those states that require a meal or rest period should ensure that their employees are in compliance.

Q 26: We just received a request for jury duty leave from an employee. Do we have to pay the employee during this leave?

A: Maybe. Although there is no federal requirement under the Jury Systems Improvement Act to provide paid leave, the law does provide protection for employees from retaliation for serving on a federal jury. Most states provide similar, or even broader, protections. However, only a handful of states (Alabama, Colorado, Connecticut, District of Columbia, Louisiana, Massachusetts, Nebraska, New York, and Tennessee) currently require private sector employees to be compensated for such leave. Most of those states require only that such compensation be granted for a few days.

Public sector employees receive greater protection; employees who work for the state or local government are much more likely to receive compensation during periods of jury leave. About half of the states also include provisions specifically protecting employees from discharge or discrimination when subpoenaed to serve as a witness.

Payment for exempt employees called for jury duty is a different matter. By definition, employees who are properly classified as exempt from overtime under FLSA must be paid on a salary basis and cannot have their pay reduced for absences of less than a week for jury duty or attendance as a witness. Exempt employees, however, do not need to be paid during any week in which they perform no work.

As a result of the above provisions, private sector employers will most likely be able to develop a policy on jury and witness leave that is consistent with the organization's HR philosophies and resources. A survey conducted by the Bureau of Labor Statistics in 1993 indicates that 86% of medium to large employers have a policy or practice of paying workers for absences caused by jury duty. Organizations interested in establishing competitive policies may want to consider providing some form of compensation for jury and witness leave.

Because of the varied circumstances that can arise with regard to jury duty (e.g., short versus long periods of leave, part-time versus full-time employee status, etc.), it is a good idea to develop a clear policy that is consistent with federal and state requirements and that addresses these and other issues. Once the policy is in place, administer it consistently and be certain that employees are not in any way coerced, discriminated against, or retaliated against for exercising their civic responsibilities.

Q 27: How many hours does an employee have to work each week to receive benefits?

A: It is up to the company, for the most part, to decide how many weekly hours constitute a full-time or part-time week and what the weekly hour requirement is for an employee to earn benefits. There are basically two categories of benefits: (a) those that an employer chooses to give its employees such as vacation pay, health insurance, retirement plans, and life insurance; and (b) those that an employer is required to provide such as worker's compensation and unemployment compensation. When an employer provides the first category, the weekly hour requirement for eligibility is affected only by the following:

- An employee who is covered by the FLSA must be paid overtime when he or she works more than 40 hours in a workweek. This act is where the workweek standard of 40 hours originated. It is perfectly legal, and quite common, to define the full-time workweek and the eligibility cut-off for benefits as 37.5 hours, or 35 hours, or any other number of hours as long as this FLSA obligation is met.

  Several states have wage and hour requirements that require overtime to be paid when the workday exceeds 8 hours. In those states, this obligation must also be met when constructing the workweek.

- Under the Employee Retirement and Income Security Act (ERISA), employees who have completed 1,000 hours of service within a period of 12 consecutive months must earn a year of participation and vesting in the organization's pension and profit-sharing plans—if the organization offers such plans. This regulation applies even if the person is defined as part-time by the company's policy and, because of that definition, he or she is not eligible for benefits.

Companies should be aware of the possibility of an adverse impact when deciding which employees will receive benefits. For example, if your office and administrative employees receive certain benefits that your manufacturing plant employees do not receive, make sure there is no adverse effect for any protected employees. If your manufacturing plant employees are mostly women or minorities, you may be guilty of adverse impact discrimination, even though this discrimination was not your intent.

As with all other company policies, the decision for benefit eligibility should be fair and consistent. An accountant in department X should receive the same benefits as an accountant in department Y. If some employees will receive more benefits than others, there should be a clear distinction between the two. For example, only executives are eligible to receive supplemental life insurance, or only employees who are at the director level or higher start at 3 weeks of vacation leave. Most employees today value benefits as highly as, if not more than, they value their salaries. Organizations should give such decisions plenty of forethought.

Q 28: Are employers required to use time clocks?

A: No. Although federal wage and hour laws do require employers to maintain accurate records of time worked, they are not required to use time clocks, timecards, or any other specific system of recording time. If employees are required to punch a time clock, employers can disregard voluntary early arrivals or late departures provided that employees are not performing any work during those hours. However, employers must compensate employees for additional time worked that is not recorded on their timecards.

Employers can use the following two rules for treatment of small amounts of scheduled or unscheduled time worked or missed by employees:

- *Rounding-off practices* means employers may round off employees' starting or stopping time to the nearest 5 minutes or one-tenth or one quarter of an hour (employers' choice) provided that those rounded-off hours average out over time and that employees are properly compensated for all time actually worked.

- *De minimus rule* means an employer may also disregard insubstantial or insignificant amounts of time if, as a practical administrative matter, he or she cannot precisely record the small portion of time involved. The *de minimus* rule may be applied only where the periods of time worked are uncertain, are indefinite, and involve merely a few minutes. However, employers cannot fail to count as hours worked any part of fixed or regular working time or ascertainable periods of time worked that employees are required to spend on assigned duties.

Companies requiring employees to punch a time clock cite several advantages, including (a) easier and more certain recordkeeping in the event of a challenge or Labor Department inspection; (b) accuracy of payroll records; (c) clear records of late arrivals, early departures, and overtime worked; and (d) time clocks make dishonesty difficult.

Increasingly, employers are allowing employees to keep written time records of time worked rather than punching a time clock. Major reasons for such practices are (a) to increase employee morale, (b) to eliminate excess payroll and administrative work caused by incorrect punching of cards by employees or by malfunctioning time clocks, and (c) to correct the record because time clocks fail to measure actual time worked.

Whether employees are required to punch a time clock or to keep written records of time worked, employers should have a policy that clearly defines employees' responsibilities and duties with respect to maintaining records of time worked. Such policies should also address guidelines for performing overtime work and penalties for failure to comply.

Q 29: What is the difference between exempt and nonexempt employees?

A: The terms *exempt* and *nonexempt* come from FLSA. The FLSA requires that employees be paid at least the minimum wage and overtime for hours worked over 40 a week. *Nonexempt* employees are covered by the FLSA, and the provisions of the law apply to them. Some employees are *exempt* from (not covered by) the law and do not have to be paid the minimum wage or overtime if certain requirements are met.

The most common exemption is for white-collar employees. For you to meet this exemption, your white-collar employees generally must meet the DOL definition of an executive, administrative, or professional position; of a highly skilled computer-related occupation; or of work in outside sales. In addition, white-collar employees must be paid on a salary basis.

To be paid on a *salary basis* generally means that the employee is paid the same, predetermined amount for each week that he or she performs any work. The theory is that a white-collar employee is paid for the work done, not for the number of hours worked. Nonexempt employees can also be paid a salary, but must be paid overtime for any hours they work over 40 a week.

The DOL has a short and long test for executives, administrative employees, and professionals. Those short tests and the test for outside-sales employees and employees in computer-related occupations are summarized below. If you have a specific question about whether a given employee meets the test, you should contact the DOL.

- **Executive exemption**

    — The employee must have a weekly salary of at least $250 (annualizes to $13,000). (For employees who make $155 or more but less than $250 per week, you must use the long test.)

    — In addition, the employee (a) has as his or her primary duty managing an enterprise, department, or subsidiary, and (b) regularly directs or supervises the work of at least two full-time employees.

- **Administrative exemption**

  — The employee must have a weekly salary of at least $250 (annualizes to $13,000). (For employees who make $170 or more but less than $250 per week, you must use the long test.)

  — In addition, the employee (a) has as his or her primary duty performing office or other nonmanual work that deals with management policies or general business operations and (b) regularly exercises discretion and independent judgment.

- **Professional exemption**

  — The employee must have a weekly salary of at least $250 (annualizes to $13,000). (For employees who make $155 or more but less than $250 per week, you must use the long test.)

  — In addition, the employee has as his or her primary duty work that (a) requires advanced scientific knowledge or learning and the regular use of independent judgment; (b) is artistic, original, and creative; or (c) teaches or instructs.

- **Computer-related exemption**

  — The employee must earn more than $27.30 an hour.

  — In addition, the employee has as his or her primary duties (a) the application of systems analysis techniques and procedure, including consulting with users on hardware and software specifications; (b) the design of computer systems that are based on user specifications; (c) the modification or creation of computer programs that are based on system design specifications; (d) the modification or creation of computer programs related to machine operating systems; or (e) a combination of the above responsibilities.

- **Outside-sales exemption**

  — The employee works no more than 20% of any workweek in nonexempt activities.

  — The employee regularly works away from the employer's workplace when making sales.

Q 30: Our company is developing a policy on company uniforms. What issues should we be aware of, and can an employer require that employees pay for their own uniforms?

A: Although some employers choose to provide employees with uniforms, there is no legal requirement to do so, even when uniforms are deemed a condition of employment.

Because the employer decides who will actually pay for uniforms, certain issues need to be considered when designing internal policies: Who will be responsible for purchasing uniforms? Will the cleaning or laundering services be provided by the employer? Will employees be solely responsible for all uniform-related costs? In addition, any relevant tax information associated with uniform allowances or purchases should be addressed.

Employers who choose to provide uniforms have the option of purchasing them directly, reimbursing employees for purchase costs, or offering a clothing allowance. Although for employers the cost of employee uniforms are deductible as a necessary business expense, the allowance can be excluded from an employee's wages and be exempt from employment taxes only under certain conditions: (a) The uniform is specifically required as a condition of employment, (b) the uniform cannot be adapted for general use as regular clothing, and (c) allowances are made under a defined fringe benefit plan that is separate from wages.

Employers who require that employees purchase their own uniforms must exercise a measure of caution to ensure that uniform-related costs do not reduce employee wages below minimum wage requirements set forth by FLSA or by local and state laws. The purchase cost of uniforms may qualify as a miscellaneous itemized deduction and be exempt from an employee's income, provided the following requirements are met: (a) The uniforms are a condition of employment, and (b) the uniforms cannot be adapted for general use as regular clothing. The allowance can be taken only by employees whose total itemized deductions exceed at least 2% of their adjusted gross income.

Q 31: An employee we fired for misconduct has company-owned equipment at his home. Can we refuse to issue his final paycheck until he returns it, or can we deduct the equipment's cost from his pay?

A: We would not recommend either action. Most states require prompt payment of final wages after an involuntary termination. The majority of states also specify that final checks must cover all compensation owed the employee, including earned bonuses and unused vacation. Employers should be cautious in making pay deductions. In most cases, deductions not mandated by law or court order are permitted only if there is a voluntary, written agreement with the employee and if the deductions do not reduce pay below minimum wage. Check with your legal counsel when considering such arrangements.

Q 32: Once applicants have verbally accepted a job offer, we ask them to sign an at-will employment agreement. When we cover their moving costs, can we include a clause in the agreement requiring them to reimburse us for relocation expenses if they resign within a year of their hire date?

A: Yes. According to the management consulting firm Runzheimer International, an increasing number of organizations are asking employees to sign payback agreements. Used most frequently with international relocations, such contracts help protect an employer's investment and discourage employees from leaving. The amount owed is usually prorated according to how much of the contract term has elapsed.

Although payback agreements are becoming more common, they are not always enforced. In their 1995 survey, Runzheimer found that 66% of companies using payback contracts actually sued to recover relocation expenses, and most of the cases were settled out of court. We recommend getting assistance from an attorney when drafting a payback agreement to ensure that it will be enforceable.

For more information on the relocation practices survey, please contact Runzheimer International at (800) 558-1702.

Q 33: An employee just provided us with a 2-week notice of resignation. Can we decline the notice and inform the employee that today will be the last day of employment?

A: Generally employers are not required to accept a 2-week notice, providing there is no existing employment contract between the parties to honor such notice of a resignation.

If employers decline to accept the 2-week notice, they are, in effect, terminating their employee. Therefore, the former employee has the right to claim unemployment insurance if his or her employment plans should, for some reason, be eliminated.

Employers generally expect professionalism from employees, including the expectation that departing employees will provide a 2-week notice before termination. In fact, some employee handbooks specifically state that employers expect such notice. Some states view the employee handbook as a binding document. If employers terminate employees upon receiving notice of resignation, future departing employees may be reluctant to provide such notice for fear that they will be terminated immediately and will not receive compensation for their last 2 weeks of employment.

If you feel strongly that any resigning employees should leave immediately for any reason, we suggest that you tactfully inform them that they will be compensated for the final 2 weeks and that it is not necessary that they remain on the premises after close of business.

Q 34: We would like to provide our employees with a bonus for time spent on call. Will this bonus affect their pay?

A: We would like to provide a bonus to those employees who are on call. How will this affect their pay?

Employers can provide exempt employees with a bonus without worrying about additional pay issues. When providing a bonus to nonexempt employees, employers need to consider whether the amount should be included in the employees' regular rate for overtime purposes. When an employer provides a bonus to employees expressly for being on call and not because they performed work while they are on call, then those employees are being compensated when it is not allocatable to specific hours of work. Even though the amount is not allocatable to specific hours of work, it is paid compensation for performing a duty involved in the employee's job. It is thus not excludable and is similar to bonuses paid for safety or attendance.

Therefore, if a nonexempt employee works only 40 hours per week, the on-call bonus is simply added to the paycheck. If the employee incurs overtime hours during the course of the week and if the bonus is part of an employer agreement, then the bonus amount must be added to the normal hourly rate of pay and divided by the total number of hours worked as you compute the correct hourly rate of pay. This newly computed rate will be used to calculate any overtime compensation due to that employee.

Q 35: Is it OK to give exempt employees overtime or extra pay for hours worked in excess of a predetermined amount?

A: Generally speaking, the courts have ruled that additional compensation paid to exempt employees is permissible and will not destroy the salary basis of payment that is required for exempt status. The basic reason that the Department of Labor seems to consistently support this opinion may be that the employee will continue to receive a predetermined amount of pay for performing a job not subject to a reduction that is based on quality or quantity of the work. This being said, when employers begin to watch the actual hours of work for an exempt employee, they may be endangering his or her exempt status. The safest route is to provide some sort of a bonus or compensatory day if the extra effort is so extraordinary that you feel the need provide a reward.

Q 36: Can an employer make partial-day deductions in pay from an exempt employee's paycheck for leaving work early?

A: No. An exempt employee must receive the full salary for any week in which he or she works. According to the FLSA salary-basis test, an employer can make deductions from an exempt employee's salary under the following circumstances:

- The employee is absent for a full day or more for personal reasons.

- The employee is in violation of safety rules of major significance.

If an employer has a bona fide vacation, sick, or personal leave policy in place, it is permissible for the employer to substitute the accrued paid leave for the time the employee is absent from work, even if it is less than a full day. However, note that when the employee is absent for less than a full day and does not have any time accrued or has a negative balance, the employee will need to be paid the entire salary for that workweek. In addition, if an employee works any hours during the week in which he or she is required to be on jury duty, witness duty, or military duty leave, you are required to pay the full salary for the entire week. If an employee is absent from work for an entire workweek, no compensation is required.

Q 37: How do we calculate overtime pay for our nonexempt employees who are paid at more than one hourly rate during the workweek?

A: Employees who are covered by the overtime payment requirements of the FLSA are entitled to be compensated for any hours worked over 40 in a workweek at the rate of time and one-half of the employee's regular rate of pay. However, some employees are paid different rates for performing different jobs during the same workweek. Others receive differential pay for working less-desirable shifts such as night shifts or weekend work. In those situations, calculating overtime pay according to the regular rate of pay may be more complicated for employers.

In situations where an employee has worked at more than one rate during the workweek, the regular rate of pay is figured by calculating the weighted average rate of pay for the week. For example: An employee worked 35 hours during the workweek at a rate of $5.50 per hour as a checker at the grocery store. She also worked 7 additional hours as an office clerk doing filing in the store's business office and was paid at a rate of $7.00 per hour for performing those duties. The regular rate of pay for this employee is $5.76 per hour.

To calculate, you should do the following:

1. Multiply the number of hours worked by the rate at which the hours were worked. (Do this calculation for all rates at which work was performed.)

2. Total all the figures from the above calculations.

3. Divide the total sum by the total number of hours worked during that week.

To calculate weekly pay, you should do the following:

1. Multiply the regular rate by the number of hours that should be compensated at the regular rate.

2. Multiply the regular rate by 1.5 (time and one-half).

3. Multiply the sum by the number of overtime hours worked during the week.

4. Add the total sums together to obtain the weekly rate of compensation.

It is important to note that the regular rate of pay must be calculated each workweek separately, even if the employee is paid biweekly. Also keep in mind that different states and different industries have regulations and legislation that affect what hours should be paid at overtime rates.

References

Chapter 5. Compensation

Buckley, J. F., & Onen, R. M. (1998). State by state guide to human resources law. Available: SHRMStore, (800) 444-5006 or <www.shrm.org/ shrmstore>.

Department of Labor (DOL). (19xx). Handy reference guide to the FLSA. Washington, DC: Employment Standards Administration, DOL. [On-line]. Available: <www.dol.gov/ esa/public/regs/compliance/whd/hrg.htm>.

Lawler, E. E. III. (1990). Strategic pay: Aligning organization strategies and pay systems. San Francisco: Jossey-Bass.

Schable, S. R. (1999). Temporary staffing agencies and human resources: Compliance issues. (White paper). [On-line]. Available: <www.shrm.org/whitepapers>.

Society for Human Resource Management (SHRM). (Annually). Consultants forum directory. [On-line]. Available: <www.shrm.org>.

Society for Human Resource Management (SHRM). (1996). Performance appraisal forms: A collection of samples. 2nd ed. Available: SHRMStore, (800) 444-5006 or <www.shrm.org/shrmstore>.

Schoonover, S. (1998). HR competencies for the year 2000: A professional's toolkit for performance development. Available: SHRMStore, (800) 444-5006 or <www.shrm.org/shrmstore>.

Schoonover, S. (1998). HR competencies for the year 2000: Take the wake up call. Available: SHRMStore, (800) 444-5006 or <www.shrm.org/shrmstore>.

William M. Mercer & Society for Human Resource Management (SHRM). (Annually). HR management compensation survey. Louisville, KY: William M. Mercer and SHRM.

CHAPTER 6

BENEFITS

General

Q 1: How can we compare our organization's benefits to those offered by other companies?

> **A:** Organizations are frequently interested in "benchmarking," or comparing, their benefit costs and benefits offered with those offered by other organizations. Here are a few sources:
>
> - Bureau of Labor Statistics at <www.bls.gov/ebshome.htm>
>
> - U.S. Chamber of Commerce at (202) 659-6000 or <www.uschamber. org>
>
> - Employee Benefits Research Institute at (202) 659-0670 or <www. ebri.org>
>
> - International Foundation of Employee Benefit Plans at (414) 786-6700 or <www.ifebp.org>
>
> The SHRM Online HRLinks have a variety of benefit-related sources that will lead you to additional sources of information. SHRM produces an annual benefits survey and the Information Center may be able to offer additional assistance and to answer questions about specific types of benefits.

Q 2: Is there a benchmark for percentage of payroll costs for employee benefits?

> **A:** Benefit costs vary according to geography, benefit offerings, size of employer, and industry. According to a 1997 U.S. Chamber of Commerce survey, the average cost of employee benefits as a percentage of payroll is approximately 41.3%.
>
> The Chamber offers this advice to help you compile benefits cost data for your organization:
>
> 1. Determine the total payments for benefits:

- Company's share of mandated benefits (such as social security)

- Retirement plan contributions

- Life insurance premiums

- Medical benefits claims or premiums

- Leave benefits paid

- Miscellaneous benefits (such as tuition reimbursement, parking, meals, or child care)

- Employee deductions for benefits, including mandated benefits

2. Calculate the number of full-time equivalent employees by dividing the hours for all employees by the hours for a full-time employee.

3. Determine the benefit payments according to the following:

- The benefit costs as a percentage of payroll are calculated by using the total derived from 1 above, divided by the total gross payroll.

- The benefit costs as cents per payroll hour, or the cost per hour per employee, are calculated by using the total derived in 1 above, divided by the total hours worked, including overtime.

- The benefit dollars per year per employee are calculated by using the total derived from 1 above, divided by the total from 2 above.

Other resources for employee-benefit cost data include the Employee Benefit Research Institute at (202) 659-0670 and <www.ebri.org>, or the International Foundation of Employee Benefit Plans at (414) 786-6700 and <www.ifebp.org>.

Q 3: What law governs the operation of employee benefit plans?

A: The Employee Retirement Income Security Act (ERISA) provides uniform guidelines for employee benefit plans. ERISA was enacted in 1974 and protects the interest of participants and their beneficiaries. Employee benefit plans encompass welfare benefit plans and employee pension plans. According to ERISA, a welfare plan is defined as any plan, fund, or program that is established or maintained by an employer or by an employee organization or both for the purpose of providing a benefit to its participants or their beneficiaries through the purchase of the following:

- Insurance

- Medical, surgical, or hospital care or benefits

- Benefits in the event of sickness, accident, disability, death, or unemployment

- Vacation benefits

- Apprenticeship or other training programs

- Daycare centers

- Scholarship funds

- Prepaid legal services

- Severance

- Any benefit described in Section 302(c) of the Labor Management Relations Act, 1947

ERISA was created to (a) ensure that participants and beneficiaries receive pertinent information regarding their benefit plan, (b) provide standards for managing the benefit plan and its funding, (c) ensure that funds are set aside to pay promised benefits, (d) ensure that participants receive pension benefits after meeting specified requirements, and (e) provide protection to participants whose pension plans have been terminated.

ERISA is enforced by the Department of Labor (DOL) and the Internal Revenue Service (IRS). They may be contacted for additional information on ERISA requirements.

Q 4: We're thinking of outsourcing our benefits administration. What should we consider?

A: Generally speaking, you should outsource an HR function such as benefits administration if it provides an opportunity to shift HR efforts toward value-added applications. By eliminating this type of administrative and labor-intensive function, HR can focus on things that add profit and value to the organization such as strategic planning and succession planning. The decision to outsource involves analyzing its effect on the organization. You must weigh the trade-off between cost, efficiency, quality, and HR's strategic objectives.

To make an informed decision about outsourcing benefits administration, you should conduct a needs assessment and you should form an assessment team to conduct the analysis. This team should consist of members from HR, legal, finance, accounting, and information technology (IT). The team should consider a number of questions such as these:

- How can outsourcing enhance the quality of benefit services?

- Will benefit-services processing be streamlined?

- What effect will outsourcing have in helping HR and the organization achieve strategic goals?

- Who performs the benefits administration?

- What are the administrative tasks involved and their associated costs?

- Will outsourcing reduce benefits administration costs?

- How will those employees displaced by outsourcing be accommodated?

- What technological support is required, and is it available through the vendor (e.g., voice-integrated response)?

- How will relations and communications with active and retired employees be affected by outsourcing—for better or worse?

- Will the vendor customize its services to accommodate your organization's specific needs and culture?

- Will the vendor put its fee at risk if service quality diminishes?

- Will the vendor ensure that any legal requirements are addressed?

The contract with the vendor should be a written company or site-specific contract rather than a standard vendor contract. A standard contract does not account for the specific needs of your organization and usually requires only that the vendor provide the same level of service that your organization currently provides. Customize the contract to ensure that your organization gets what it pays for. The contract should specify a number of important items: (a) designation of responsibilities, (b) performance benchmarks, (c) service accountability, (d) reporting system, (e) procedures and penalties for undelivered services, (f) protection against vendor negligence or misconduct, (g) pricing schedule, and (h) method of renewal and termination.

Successful outsourcing of benefits administration depends on finding a qualified service provider, monitoring the vendor's service quality, and managing the relationship as your organization's needs change.

Q 5: At what point does an employee become classified as a full-time employee (and thus eligible for company benefits)?

A: Surprisingly, the classification of part-time and full-time status is a matter of individual company policy. No federal requirements specify that full-time status will be achieved upon completion of a specific minimum number of hours of work per week or per year. In practice, a company's classifications often depend on the requirements of the company's health plan.

However, two federal laws affect benefit eligibility for part-time employees: ERISA and FMLA. ERISA (Employee Retirement Income Security

Act) requires, in general, that employees become eligible for pension benefits (if the company offers them) upon reaching age 21 and completing 1 year of service. Service of 1 year is defined as any 12-month period in which an employee completes 1,000 hours of service. Thus, part-time employees who regularly work 20 hours a week and have done so for more than 1 year would be eligible for pension plan benefits.

The FMLA (Family and Medical Leave Act) has a similar requirement. Employees are eligible for unpaid leave, restoration to their job upon completion of leave, and continued health benefits during leave (if available before the leave) if they have been employed for at least 12 months (which need not be consecutive) and have completed at least 1,250 hours of service during the 12 months just before the start of leave.

ERISA and FMLA both have other requirements that are beyond the scope of this answer. However, minimum service periods are important to remember for organizations that regularly employ part-time people.

Q 6: What types of expenses can an employee be reimbursed for under a medical flexible-spending account?

A: Expenses that can be reimbursed through a medical flexible-spending account include (a) co-insurance payments, (b) deductible payments, (c) eyeglasses, (d) hearing devices, (e) dental care not provided through another health insurance plan, (f) prescription drugs, (g) psychiatric care, (h) psychologists' fees, and (i) emergency ambulance service.

Q 7: When can employees make changes in elections under a Section 125 plan?

A: When employers offer a cafeteria plan, they are using Section 125 of the Internal Revenue Code (IRC), which allows certain benefits to be provided on a pretax basis under a single plan. To comply with IRC 125, employers must meet several standards. There are rules regarding (a) who can participate, (b) flexible spending accounts, (c) nondiscrimination requirements, and (d) how and when employees must make benefit elections; there are also definitions of unqualified and qualified plans.

Cafeteria plan elections must be made before the beginning of the plan year. The elections must state the benefit chosen plus the corresponding salary reduction, and the election must be for a 12-month period. Once elected, the benefit must be used or lost. The subject of making elections and subsequent changes has been covered in the IRS temporary regulations. The temporary regulations were issued in November 1997 and expire 3 years after the date of issuance.

Generally speaking, in accordance with Temporary IRS Regulation 1.125-4T, the employee, the spouse, or a dependent must experience a change in status to qualify for an election change. Changes in status include a legal change in marital status (to include legal separation) or a change in the number of dependents by birth, adoption, or death. Changes in status also occur when the employee, the spouse, or a dependent experiences a change in employment status or a substantial change in work schedule. If a change makes a dependent newly qualified or newly disqualified from a benefit plan, such as becoming a full-time student or quitting school, the situation will meet the requirement of a change in status. Changes in residence or work location of a dependent, the employee, or the spouse also qualify as reasons to change elections.

Finally, if an independent, third-party provider makes significant increases or decreases in the cost or coverage, a cafeteria plan may allow a participant to revoke an existing election.

Q 8:   How can we use our intranet to assist us with benefits communication and administration?

A: Your intranet can allow you to provide cost-effective, self-service components throughout your organization. Use of the intranet for benefits communication and administration is particularly efficient in multilocation organizations. (For information on international intranets, please see the May 1998 *HRMagazine* "Focus" article titled "International Intranets.") Whether you're a multinational organization or a single-location employer, there are many ways you can put your intranet to work for you.

Some potential intranet applications related to health and welfare plans include the following:

- View summary plan description (SPD) (DOL has approved an electronic-only SPD for health plans.)
- Open enrollment
- Statements of benefits enrollment confirmation
- Personalized benefit statements
- Primary care physician directory and selection
- Administration of change of family status
- Vendor-customer service numbers
- Enrollment, change, claim forms
- Dependent and beneficiary information
- Employee and benefits handbook

- Claims processing

- Links to provider and related web sites

Some potential intranet applications related to pension and retirement plans include the following:

- View SPD (currently must still be available in hard copy)

- Account balance access

- Asset allocation changes

- Contribution percentage and amount changes

- Retirement education literature

- View fund performance and prospectuses

- Defined contribution plan enrollment

- Investment modeling

- Links to provider and related web sites

- View and post frequently asked questions

The International Foundation of Employee Benefit Plans (1998) offers "Communicating Employee Benefits via the Web," a survey of 1,625 corporate members. A total of 433 individuals (27%) responded to the survey. Of those, nearly one-third of the members (125) use the Web for communicating employee benefits. Of those already using Internet or intranet technology for employee benefits communications, 95% anticipate transferring more functions to the Internet or intranet. Two-thirds (66%) of those not using the Internet or intranet do plan to use Internet technology in the future. To receive a free copy of the survey, call the Public Relations Department at (888) 33-IFEBP (334-3327), e-mail <pr@ifebp.org>, or at the web site <www.ifebp.org/pdf/commonweb.pdf> with your name and mailing address.

Q 9:   What is a health insurance opt out?

A: A health insurance opt out means an employer can offer—under a cafeteria plan—cash, extra benefits, or additional credits in return for an employee's decision to reduce the level of benefits selected under certain benefit options or to "opt out" of a benefit altogether. The refunded cash, benefits, or credits allow the employee to spend the money on other benefits. Employers consider an opt-out provision when there are costly benefit options. Ideally, the cost of the cash or other benefits generally is cheaper than paying for the rejected benefit.

The opt-out provision does not eliminate all cost concerns. Employers who offer the opt-out provision have to be careful that the option does not cause an adverse selection. Employees may perceive that they are losing their benefit dollars if they do not receive a payment equal to the value of their forfeited benefit. The employer should ensure that the savings for rejecting the benefit is greater than the cost of rejecting the benefit. The savings accumulated from the opt out can be used toward administrative costs or to help subsidize other benefits.

The opt-out provision should be offered only when it is financially beneficial to the employer. Before implementing an opt-out feature, the employer needs to determine the two costs involved in providing an opt-out payment: (a) the cost of the payment and (b) the savings by not providing the rejected benefit.

Q 10: Is there a household maximum on participation in a flexible-spending account for dependent care?

A: A *dependent care flexible-spending account* is a type of dependent care assistance program. The flexible-spending account for dependent care allows an employee to set aside pretax dollars for use in reimbursing qualified costs for dependent care. If the dependent care assistance program meets the requirements of IRC Section 129, the maximum amount that can be contributed is $5,000 or $2,500 per year for married taxpayers filing separately. Under Section 129, the contributions are not subject to federal income tax withholding or to Federal Insurance Contribution Act (FICA) or Federal Unemployment Tax (FUTA) taxes.

Information pertaining to the *income tax credit for dependent care* must be made available to employees if the employer is sponsoring a dependent care assistance program. The employer must provide a description of the income tax credit for dependent care, as well as the conditions for which the tax credit provides the employee with a greater advantage than receiving benefits under the employer's plan.

Individuals who are working or attending school and who have a need for dependent care services can use the income tax credit for dependent care. The individual can receive a federal income tax credit of 20–30% of employment-related expenses for dependent care. The maximum amount that can be credited each year is $2,400 for taxpayers with one qualified dependent and $4,800 for those with two or more qualified dependents.

Employees offered the opportunity to participate in a dependent care assistance program should assess whether the income tax credit is more advantageous to them than the $5,000 maximum allowed by the assistance program. It is permissible to use both the tax credit and the assistance program; however, the eligible expenses that are applied to either method will reduce the expenses available to the other method dollar for dollar.

Q 11: We want to offer employees the opportunity to obtain a graduate degree but understand that we cannot offer graduate programs on a tax-free basis under Section 127. Is there any way we can provide this type of tuition assistance?

A: Although the provision for tax exemption for tuition assistance for graduate courses under Section 127 was discontinued on June 30, 1996, there is still a possibility that graduate courses are not taxable. The cost of graduate courses could possibly be deductible as a working condition fringe benefit (commonly called *educational reimbursement plans*). Educational reimbursement plans are designed as pay-as-you-go plans and provide employers with more freedom as to the structure of the plan. However, certain guidelines must be met for educational payments to be considered as a working condition fringe. A *working condition fringe* is defined by IRC Section 132(d) as any property or services provided by an employer to an employee to the extent that if the employee paid for such property or services, such payment would be deductible under IRC Section 162.

For educational payments to fulfill the requirements of deductibility as a trade or business expense, they must meet three tests:

- The education obtained must maintain or improve the skills required by the individual's employment, trade, or business; or the education must meet the express requirements of the employer or of an applicable law or regulation for the individual to retain employment status or rate of compensation.

- The education should not qualify the individual for a new trade or business.

- The expense must not be incurred on education that satisfies the minimum educational requirements for the taxpayer's present trade or business.

Finally, you should make sure the expenses meet the definition of educational expenses; otherwise they are taxable. Educational expenses include (a) tuition, books, laboratory fees, and supplies; (b) refresher or continuing education courses; (c) reasonable expenses for typing a paper and conducting research in connection with the education; (d) expenses for tutorial instruction or correspondence courses; and (e) certain transportation costs. Because of the complexity of this exception, we strongly recommended that you seek the advice of your tax advisor or legal counsel before providing educational reimbursements for graduate course work.

Q 12: What is *imputed income,* and what does it have to do with our life insurance benefit?

A: Group term life insurance coverage that is less than $50,000 ($2,000 for spouse and dependent coverage) and that is provided by the employer is not included in an employee's taxable gross income. Coverage that is over $50,000 (greater than $2,000 for spouse and dependent coverage) may need to be included in the employee's taxable gross income. The amount of coverage that is included in an employee's taxable gross income is considered to be the employee's *imputed income.*

To determine the cost of the amount of coverage exceeding $50,000, you must use the Uniform Premium Table, not the actual premiums paid by the employer. The Uniform Premium Table is published by the IRS. (Note: The IRS has released the proposed changes to the Uniform Premium Table effective July 1, 1999.)

Table 6–1 shows the Uniform Premium Table that determines the amount that must be included in the employee's gross income if the employer-provided group life insurance exceeds $50,000. You compute the cost for each month by multiplying the number of thousands of taxable insurance (dollar amount exceeding $50,000) by the monthly cost factor provided in the table.

TABLE 6–1
UNIFORM PREMIUM TABLE EFFECTIVE JULY 1, 1999

Age	Monthly Cost per $1,000
Under 25	$0.05
25 to 29	0.06
30 to 34	0.08
35 to 39	0.09
40 to 44	0.10
45 to 49	0.15
50 to 54	0.23
55 to 59	0.43
60 to 64	0.66
65 to 69	1.27
70 and above	2.06

The following example illustrates use of the Uniform Premium Table:

Mary, a 45-year-old employee with Company X, receives a $200,000 group life insurance policy from X. The group life insurance coverage is 100% company paid. The first $50,000 is tax free for Mary. However, the cost for the additional $150,000 is included in Mary's taxable gross income. According to the Uniform Premium Table, the cost (monthly) for the additional coverage is $.29 per $1,000 of coverage. Therefore, the amount to be included in Mary's gross income will be $522 (150 × .29 × 12 months) for the taxable year.

Consolidated Omnibus Budget Reconciliation Act (COBRA)

Q 13: What happens when a person experiences another qualifying event while on COBRA?

A: Under COBRA, if a beneficiary is entitled to 18 months of coverage and that person experiences a second qualifying event, the beneficiary would be entitled to a total of 36 months of coverage beginning at the date of the original qualifying event. For example, if an employee is laid off, the employee and his or her dependents would be entitled to 18 months of coverage. If that employee then died, his or her dependents would be entitled to a total of 36 months of coverage beginning at the date of the employee's termination.

Q 14: What are the COBRA notification requirements, and where can we get sample notifications?

A: The COBRA notification requirements fall into four general categories: (a) notice on entering the plan; (b) notice to a third-party administrator, if applicable; (c) notice to participants from an administrator; and (d) notice to an administrator from participants and dependents.

- **Notice on entering the plan.** Participants who enroll in a health plan should receive written notice of their COBRA rights when they enroll in the plan. The DOL will recognize good-faith compliance if the employer mails the notice first class to the employee's and the dependent's last known addresses. In addition to the written notice, an explanation of COBRA rights should be included in an employer's summary plan description.

- **Notice to a third-party administrator.** When an employer uses a third-party administrator, the employer is responsible for notifying the third-party administrator of qualifying events. The employer has 30 days from (a) the date of the covered employee's death, (b) the date of the covered employee's termination (for reasons other than gross misconduct), (c) the date of covered employee's Medicare eligibility, and (d) the date of the employer's bankruptcy.

- **Notice to participants from an administrator.** When a qualifying event occurs, the administrator of the health plan is responsible for notifying all qualified beneficiaries of their COBRA rights. This notice must be provided within 14 days of the plan administrator's knowledge of the qualifying event.

- **Notice to an administrator from participants and dependents.** Spouses and other dependents who lose their eligibility status (because of divorce, college graduation, etc.) under the employer's plan must notify the plan administrator of the qualifying event. If the plan administrator does not receive the notification within 60 days of the event or of the date the dependent would have lost coverage because of the qualifying event (whichever is later), the administrator is not required to offer COBRA.

There are special notification provisions for qualified individuals who have a disability at any time during the first 60 days of COBRA coverage. The provision allows such an individual an additional 11 months of COBRA coverage—for a total of 29 months of continuation coverage—if the individual notifies the plan administrator of the disability within 60 days of the disability determination by the Social Security Administration. If there is then a determination that the individual is no longer disabled, the individual has 30 days to notify the plan administrator. COBRA coverage may be terminated at the beginning of the month following the determination that the individual is no longer disabled.

Q 15: What is HIPAA, and how does it relate to COBRA?

A: The Health Insurance Portability and Accountability Act (HIPAA) became effective on July 1, 1997, with staggered effective dates for certain provisions of the law, depending on a particular plan's plan year. Under the new HIPAA regulations, certain requirements are imposed on group health insurance plans to make health benefits more portable for employees moving from one employer to another. The law also requires that any individual who had coverage under a group health plan must be provided with a certificate of credible coverage that states the actual length of the coverage period. HIPAA also prohibits denying an individual's coverage because of that particular individual's health status. In addition to the above, certain limitations are now placed on the pre-existing condition exclusions in health insurance plans.

HIPAA imposed certain additional changes to COBRA effective July 1, 1997. Under the former COBRA regulations, the disability extension—from 18 months of coverage to 29 months of coverage—applied only to individuals who were actually disabled at the time of the qualifying event. Under new HIPAA regulations, the disability extension is now applicable to any individual who became disabled within the first 60 days of COBRA continuation benefits. Another amendment provides that employers can no longer cancel an individual's COBRA continuation benefits because that individual has obtained new coverage under another plan. Last but not least, pre-existing conditions can be satisfied by providing a certificate of credible coverage under COBRA continuation benefits.

Q 16: Are employers always required to extend COBRA coverage?

A: An employer should send a COBRA notice to any qualified beneficiary who experiences a qualifying event that results in a loss of coverage under the group health plan. A qualified beneficiary is an individual who is covered under the health plan on the day before a qualifying event occurs. Qualifying events include the following:

- Termination of employment

- Reduction in hours

- Death of a covered employee

- Divorce or legal separation

- Covered dependent child's ceasing to be a dependent child under the terms of the plan

- Covered employee's enrollment in Medicare

- Employer's commencement of bankruptcy proceedings

The only time an employer is not required to extend COBRA rights to the employee and other qualified beneficiaries is when the employee is terminated for gross misconduct. This exemption is to be used only in extreme and outrageous cases of employee misconduct. The gross misconduct standard is a difficult standard to meet, and the COBRA rules do not provide clear guidance regarding this issue.

Q 17: If an employee is terminated for gross misconduct, is the employer required to provide COBRA coverage to the employee's spouse and dependent children?

A: Because termination for gross misconduct is not deemed to be a qualifying event under COBRA, employers are generally not required to extend COBRA continuation benefits to any employee whose termination is a result of gross misconduct. Whether the employee's spouse and dependent children should also be denied entitlement to COBRA continuation benefits has become an issue for the courts.

In certain cases, district courts have rejected an employer's argument that when an employee is terminated for gross misconduct, the employer's duty to provide qualified beneficiaries with COBRA notification is eliminated. Because the term *gross misconduct* is not readily defined in the COBRA regulations and because the IRS has decided not to provide guidance on what constitutes gross misconduct, the burden of making such decisions falls primarily on the employer.

Without guidance from the DOL or the IRS on this issue, employers should exercise extreme caution in asserting gross misconduct for COBRA purposes, unless the employee's conduct was extremely flagrant. If an employer plans to deny coverage to beneficiaries on the basis of the gross misconduct exception, it would be advisable to seek the guidance of legal counsel before making such a determination.

Q 18: **One of our employees, who is also covered under the spouse's insurance plan, has resigned. Does this spousal coverage constitute *other coverage* under the COBRA regulations, thus making the employee ineligible for COBRA continuation coverage?**

> **A:** IRS regulations that became effective February 3, 1999, when they were published in the *Federal Register*, clarify that an employee who has other coverage *before* the COBRA election is still entitled to elect COBRA coverage. The employer no longer must determine if denying COBRA coverage to someone who already has other coverage would cause a significant gap in coverage, thus resulting in a qualifying event. Under the new regulations, an employer may deny the employee COBRA continuation coverage—because of other group health plan coverage or entitlement to Medicare benefits—only if the qualified beneficiary first becomes covered under the other health plan or Medicare *after* the date of the COBRA election.
>
> An employer may not terminate coverage just because an individual is merely eligible for coverage under another group health plan; the former employee must actually be enrolled in the plan. Moreover, the individual could be eligible for COBRA continuation coverage because of a preexisting condition or exclusion that, even with HIPAA protections, would create a gap in coverage.

Family and Medical Leave Act (FMLA)

Q 19: Are employees entitled to continuation of benefits while on FMLA leave?

A: Yes. The *Final Regulations* of DOL (1993) specify that "an employer must maintain the employee's coverage under any group health plan on the same conditions as coverage would have been provided if the employee had been continuously employed during the entire leave period." Therefore, employees who have family medical coverage before taking FMLA leave are entitled to family medical coverage while taking FMLA leave just as if they are working. Such coverage would include any benefits provided through the company's group health plan, including dental, vision, and so forth, as well as any new benefits that are provided during the course of the employee's leave—as long as such benefits are part of the group health plan. This inclusion is also the case if group health plan benefits are provided through a cafeteria plan or flexible spending account.

The employees are responsible for premium contributions at the same level as if they are taking no leave. If the employee is taking paid leave (such as short-term disability, vacation, or sick leave) substituted for unpaid FMLA leave, premium contributions must be made in the same manner as they are customarily made (for instance, payroll deduction). If the FMLA leave is unpaid, the employer can require one of several payment alternatives. On the employee's return to work, the employee's premium contributions will revert to the procedure in place before the leave.

Nothing in FMLA requires that employees continue to accrue seniority or other benefits (such as vacation or sick leave) during periods of FMLA leave. Employee entitlement to other types of benefits (such as life insurance or holiday pay) depends on the employer's policy for employees on other types of paid or unpaid leave. However, when they return from FMLA leave, employees are entitled to be reinstated to the same position held when the leave began, or to "an equivalent position with equivalent pay, benefits and terms and conditions of employment" (DOL, 1993). Benefits in this case include all benefits provided to employees (such as vacation leave, sick leave, life insurance, or pension) not just the group health plan benefits required to be continued during FMLA leave. The intention is to return the employee to the same status as when the leave began.

If employees choose not to continue health coverage during FMLA leave, they must still be reinstated to the group health plan without penalty immediately following the end of the leave. The requirement to continue such benefits ceases if and when the employment relationship terminates (such as leave extends beyond 12 weeks, position is eliminated, or employees inform employer that they choose not to return to work). In limited cases, employers may be able to recover costs paid for health insurance during FMLA leave.

Q 20: We have concerns about whether an employee is fit to return to work after a medical leave. Are there rules regarding fitness-for-duty certifications?

A: Yes. If we assume that the employee was on a medical leave for which he or she was protected by FMLA, the FMLA regulations include the following stipulations regarding fitness-for-duty certifications:

- The certification can address only the specific condition for which the leave was used.

- The physician needs to provide only a "simple statement of the employee's ability to return to work" (DOL, 1993).

- The employer cannot request a second or third opinion—as is allowable for other medical certifications—but can only have the employer's physician contact the employee's physician for "clarification" of the simple statement (DOL, 1993).

- Both in the employee handbook and at the time leave is requested, the employer must provide notice that such certifications will be required.

- State and local laws, as well as provisions in a collective bargaining agreement, may affect interpretation of these regulations, particularly where the outcome is more beneficial to the employee (Sect. 825.310, DOL *Final Regulations*, 1993).

Q 21: We have an employee who is receiving worker's compensation. Is this employee also eligible for FMLA leave?

A: As long as the on-the job injury qualifies as a serious health condition under FMLA, the employee is eligible for worker's compensation and FMLA leave concurrently. To qualify for FMLA leave, the employee must have "a serious health condition that makes the employee unable to perform the functions of the position of such employee" (DOL, 1993). FMLA leave is still subject to proper notification and designation by the employer. The following conditions apply if the employer designates time off under worker's compensation as being FMLA leave:

- The employee or employer cannot substitute any paid vacation or sick leave during the time the employee is receiving payments from worker's compensation.

- Once an employee's worker's compensation payment ends, the employer may require that the employee substitute accrued paid leave for the remaining time on FMLA leave. The employee can also elect this substitution as an option.

- The employee has the right to continue his or her health insurance. The employer may require that payments be made by the employee but cannot charge any additional fees for any administrative expenses.

- The worker's compensation statute allows the employer or the employer's representative to have direct contact with the employee's worker's compensation health care provider.

- If, at the end of the FMLA leave entitlement, the employee is still unable to return to work, he or she will lose the right for reinstatement under FMLA. However, the employer must look to the worker's compensation statute or ADA for any relief or protections. In addition, if the employee does not reinstate at the end of the 12-week entitlement, all benefits under FMLA cease. The last day of FMLA leave would then trigger a qualifying event under COBRA.

Worker's compensation allows a medical provider to certify that the employee is able to return to work under a "light or modified duty" capacity. If the employer chooses to provide the employee with a modified- or light-duty position, the employee does have the right to accept or deny the position. If the employee denies the position, it is likely that he or she will no longer be eligible for worker's compensation payments. However, employees will still be eligible to continue FMLA leave until the time that they are able to return to work or until their 12-week entitlement expires.

Q 22: We have an employee who is almost at the end of the 12 weeks of FMLA leave. Can we terminate the employee?

A: Before you terminate an employee at the expiration of 12 weeks of FMLA leave, you should consider the following guidelines:

- If the employee is not able to return to work because of a serious health condition, is the condition considered a disability under ADA or under state or local law? If so, then allowing additional leave may be considered reasonable accommodation.

- Is the serious health condition a result of a work-related injury or illness? If so, then the state worker's compensation laws may come into play. Employers should check with their worker's compensation carrier for the laws particular to their state.

- Does the company have a long-term disability program? If so, will the employee be eligible to receive benefits if terminated at the end of 12 weeks of FMLA leave?

- Did you evaluate the situation by examining past practices? Again, if there have not been similar situations in the past, how you handle this situation may set a precedent for the future.

- If the employee is terminated because he or she is unable to return to work, does the company have a rehire policy or preferential hiring list? Should the employee be able to return at a later date?

Q 23: We have an employee who is pregnant and will be delivering her baby shortly. She is not eligible for FMLA leave. How do we handle this situation?

A: Under Title VII of the Civil Rights Act, an employer may not discriminate against a woman because she is pregnant. Pregnancy and childbirth must be treated the same as any other temporary disability under an employer's leave, insurance, and fringe benefit plans.

Although employers are not required to have disability policies or leave programs, if they do, and if other employees who take temporary disability leave are permitted to return to their jobs when they are able, pregnant women must be afforded the same opportunity.

Additionally, pregnancy is not a protected disability under ADA because it is not a permanent condition that affects one or more major life activities. Any accommodations an employer is required to make for a pregnant employee stem from Title VII and from the employer's own policies and practices concerning other temporary disabilities.

Consider the following when an employee is not eligible for leave under FMLA:

- Does the company have a short-term disability program?

- Does the company provide any other unpaid leaves of absence?

- How are other individuals treated who have had a temporary disability (such as heart attack or stroke)?

- Did you evaluate the situation by examining past practices? If there have not been similar situations in the past, how you handle this situation may set a precedent for the future.

Q 24: Is an employee still protected by FMLA if a parent, spouse, or child for whom he or she is caring passes away during the leave?

A: This is a very sensitive question, but the answer is no. The employee is no longer covered under FMLA if the family member for whom the employee is caring passes away. However, the eligible employee may be re-certified under FMLA for some other reason if he or she has not used the entire 12 weeks of entitlement.

Some confusion has been expressed about the situation when a mother miscarries or a child passes away shortly after birth. At what point can an employer request the mother to return to work? FMLA covers the mother until she is able (as certified by her physician) to return to work. This leave is limited to the 12 weeks allowed under FMLA. Be sure to refer to your state's provisions. Some states have family and medical leave laws that may be more generous.

An issue may also arise when an elderly parent passes away during family leave and the employee requests additional time off to finalize the estate, which may require personal time for activities such as travel outside the state. Although FMLA allows employees to request leave to assist with "activities of daily living" or "instrumental activities of daily living" (DOL, 1993), this allowance is not the case after a death occurs. FMLA was not intended for this purpose.

The company should review its bereavement policy or practice to determine if the employee would be eligible for any additional time off. Be sure to refer to your state law for any additional requirements in this area. Keep in mind that a death in the family is a private and emotional issue that should be handled as sensitively as possible.

Q 25: One of our male employees wants to take leave on a part-time basis to care for his mother, who has a chronic health condition. Must we permit this arrangement under FMLA?

A: Yes, provided his mother's condition qualifies as a serious health condition under FMLA. This "intermittent- or reduced-leave schedule" may be taken so that the employee may provide actual care for his mother or may provide emotional and psychological support. If a parent is "incapable of self-care" under FMLA in three or more "activities of daily living" such as bathing, dressing, or eating; or in "instrumental activities of daily living" such as cooking, cleaning, or paying bills, the employee may take leave to provide those services for his mother. The employee requesting the intermittent-leave or reduced-leave schedule should work with you in planning a schedule that will not create a hardship on business operations (DOL, 1993).

If it is difficult to accommodate an intermittent-leave or a reduced-leave schedule in the position your employee currently holds, he may be reassigned to an alternate position. However, he must receive the same pay and benefits, and the reassignment may be only for the period of FMLA leave. At the end of the leave, he must be placed in the same position or a position equivalent to the one he held at the time he went on FMLA leave. (Note that the pay and benefits of the alternate position may be changed to create the needed equality between the original and the alternate positions). Although the duties of the alternate position for the leave period do not have to be comparable to those of the original position, they must be such that they are not viewed as punitive or retaliatory or that they create a hardship on the employee. The *Final Regulations* of DOL (1993) cite the following as some examples of unacceptable alternative positions:

- A white-collar employee assigned to perform a laborer's work

- A day-shift employee assigned to the graveyard shift

- An employee's transfer to a branch a significant distance from his or her normal job location

Calculate the amount of leave for an intermittent-leave or a reduced-leave schedule on the basis of the amount of leave actually taken. If the employee's reduced-leave schedule is 2 hours per day, only those 2 hours each day or one-fourth of the 8-hour workday are counted toward the 12-week entitlement. Deductions for portions of a day do not affect an employee's status under the Fair Labor Standards Act.

Note that special rules pertain to an intermittent-leave or a reduced-leave schedule for instructional employees. Also, you may choose whether to permit an intermittent-leave or a reduced-leave schedule for the birth of a child or for the placement of a child for adoption or foster care. Your attempt to accommodate an employee who needs this kind of leave can foster a good working relationship that can have a very positive, long-lasting effect.

Q 26: How are the FMLA rights of employees handled when the employer undergoes a merger or an acquisition?

A: Employees will generally maintain their rights under FMLA even if their current employer merges with or is acquired by another company. The original company must be a *covered employer* under FMLA for the employee to have the right to take up to 12 weeks of leave (a) for the birth or adoption of a child, (b) for the employee's own serious illness, or (c) for the illness of a dependent who requires care. A covered employer employs 50 or more employees within 75 miles of the work site during at least 20 workweeks in the current or preceding year. If a company that falls under this definition merges or is acquired, the newly formed company will usually be considered a *successor-in-interest* and, therefore, the rights will most likely transfer.

The conditions that must be met for the new company to be considered a successor-in-interest are the same conditions that were established under Title VII of the Civil Rights Act and under the Vietnam Era Veterans Readjustment and Assistance Act of 1974. No single factor can determine whether a company is a successor-in-interest. Instead, the circumstances are always considered in their entirety. Those conditions, as stipulated in the *Final Regulations* of the DOL (1993), are as follows:

- Substantial continuity of the same business operations

- Use of the same plant

- Continuity of the workforce

- Similarity of jobs and working conditions

- Similarity of supervisory personnel

- Similarity in machinery, equipment, and production methods

- Similarity of products and services

- Ability of the predecessor to provide relief

If the new company is determined to be a successor-in-interest, the employees from the previous employer cannot be deprived of their FMLA rights, even if the new company is not considered a covered employer. If the successor employer is covered under FMLA, the time the employees worked for the previous employer must also be counted when FMLA eligibility is computed. For example, an employee who worked 10 months and 1,200 hours with the original employer would have to work only 2 more consecutive months and 50 more hours with the new employer in order to meet the 12 months and 1,250 hours eligibility requirement for FMLA leave.

An employee who was eligible to take leave and had notified the previous employer of that intention may not be denied leave by the successor employer. By the same token, any employees who began their FMLA leave with the preceding employer must be allowed by the successor employer to continue the leave. In addition, all other requirements that apply to covered employers would still apply to the successor-in-interest with regard to those FMLA leaves earned before the merger or acquisition, even if the successor employer is not covered. Those aspects include (a) continuing required benefits, (b) reserving the employee's original or a substantially equivalent position, and (c) refraining from discriminating in any way against employees who have exercised their rights under FMLA.

Retirement

Q 27: What are the IRS limits on benefits and contributions for qualified retirement plans?

A: The 2000 IRS dollar limits on benefits and contributions for qualified retirement plans are on Table 6–2 as follows:

TABLE 6–2
2000 LIMITS ON BENEFITS[a]

Benefit	Contribution
Maximum annual pay out from a defined benefit plan at the Social Security normal retirement age (Section 415(b))	$135,000
Maximum annual contribution to an individual's defined contribution account (Section 415(c))	30,000
Maximum elective Section 401(k) and Section 403(b) deferrals	10,500
Section 457 deferral limit	8,000
Maximum amount of annual compensation that can be taken into account for determining benefits or contributions under a qualified plan	170,000
Test to identify highly compensated employees	85,000
Savings Incentive Match Plan for Employees (SIMPLE) plan elective contributions	6,000
Compensation threshold to participate in simplified employee pensions	450
Employee Stock Option Plan (ESOP) 5-year distribution limit	755,000
ESOP 5-year distribution-lengthening threshold	150,000

[a]   Every year, the IRS issues new limits to reflect the cost of living.

Q 28: What are the participant communication (disclosure) requirements for our 401(k) plan?

A: A number of reports and documents must be either kept "on hand" or sent directly to the plan participants or beneficiaries. The following items must be disclosed:

401(k) Plan Reports and Documentation

Summary plan description. A summary plan description (SPD) summarizes participant rights and obligations under the plan and is designed to be easily understood. The SPD must be distributed on several occasions. It must be given to each new participant within 90 days of enrollment. If there are changes to the plan, participants and beneficiaries must be given a copy every 5 years. If there are no changes, copies of the plan must be distributed every 10 years.

Summary of material modifications. A summary of material modifications (SMM) must be furnished if a change affects the information that is included in the SPD but that has not yet been incorporated into the SPD. The SMM must be furnished no later than 210 days after the end of the plan year in which the change was made. The SMM also must accompany all distributions of the SPD that have not yet been modified.

Annual report. The annual report must include a statement of plan assets and liabilities, of changes in the balance of the fund, and of changes in financial position. The annual report must be made available to any participant or beneficiary who requests a copy.

Summary annual report. The summary annual report consolidates the major changes that are discussed in the annual report. Within 9 months after the end of the plan year, the plan administrator must furnish each beneficiary and participant with a summary annual report.

Plan documents. The plan administrator should have copies of all related materials available for participants and beneficiaries. Relevant documents must include contracts, trust agreements, and collective bargaining agreements.

Statement of benefits. Any participant who makes a request in writing should receive a statement of the total benefits that have accrued under the plan and of the nonforfeitable benefits that have accrued.

Q 29: Can we have a mandatory retirement age in our retirement plan provisions?

A: The Age Discrimination in Employment Act (ADEA) and the IRC generally prohibit a qualified plan from discriminating against a participant because of age. Such discrimination includes stipulating a mandatory retirement age for employees. A qualified plan must allow all employees to participate, regardless of age, when they meet the plan's eligibility requirements. A qualified plan may not reduce or stop the accrual of benefits under the plan simply because the participant has reached a certain age. Qualified plans may put in place certain benefit caps. For instance, the plan can set a maximum number of years of service that may be counted under its benefits formula or can provide for a maximum benefit that may be earned. The plan may provide for a reduced benefits accrual rate after a prescribed period of time. Plans may set a normal retirement age, which is the lowest age specified in the plan at which the employee may retire and still receive full benefits under the plan.

Q 30: What is a cash balance retirement plan?

A: A *cash balance plan* is a defined benefit plan in which employees are provided a hypothetical account that represents the amount of money that has been contributed by the employer. Cash balance plans are seen as dependable and secure income because the account values can never decrease. Similar to all defined benefit plans, cash balance plans require employers to promise an amount to be paid to the employee on retirement. In contrast, the cash balance plans are not related to an employee's age. Because the contributions are not related to a participant's age, cash balance plans provide a more generous benefit to younger employees and employees who terminate before retirement.

An employee will have a cash balance account established once he or she is eligible to be a plan participant. Each month the employee's cash balance account will receive additional company funds or credits. These credits are a predetermined flat percentage of pay (commonly 4% or 5%) with another formula measuring social security integration. Employee balances grow according to a predetermined annual interest rate (usually related to the consumer price index (CPI) or the yield on a 1-year Treasury bill). This interest rate needs to be communicated to plan participants at the beginning of each plan year.

The vesting schedule of a cash balance plan must be in accordance with the IRS code. Thus the 5-year and the 3- to 7-year vesting schedules apply. However, to make the plan more attractive, employers usually speed up the vesting schedule. When an employee ends employment, he or she has the option (a) to receive the account balances in a lump-sum payment, (b) to have the account balances rolled over to an Individual Retirement Account (IRA), or (c) to have the account balances remain in the plan to earn the determined interest rate until retirement.

Cash balance plans are not withdrawable during the course of employment. However, the cash balances can be used as collateral to plan loans. When making withdrawals from the cash balance account after retirement, the plan participant has the option to receive a lump-sum payment or an annuity payment.

References

Chapter 6. Benefits

Department of Labor (DOL). (1993). *Family and Medical Leave Act final regulations.* [On-line]. Available: <www.dol.gov/dol/esa/fmla.htm>.

Meade, J. (1998). International intranets. In *Focus on HR technology, HRMagazine*, 43 (Supplement): 10–14.

CHAPTER 7

EMPLOYEE AND LABOR RELATIONS

Q 1:   What is the function of the National Labor Relations Act (NLRA)?

A: The NLRA grants employees two basic rights: (a) the right to form, join, or assist a union and (b) the right to engage in concerted activities for mutual aid or protection, which is any effort by two or more employees to improve pay, benefits, or working conditions. The NLRA of 1935 is commonly referred to as the Wagner Act. Senator Robert Wagner was the principal author of the initial statute. The Wagner Act also did the following:

- Allowed employees the right to organize

- Required employers to bargain with employees collectively

- Gave employees the right to engage in concerted activities

- Created the National Labor Relations Board (NLRB) as the regulatory agency

Under the NLRA, an employer cannot legally take any adverse employment action against employees who engage in union activities.

Q 2:   What are employers required to do under the Labor Management Relations Act?

A: The Labor Management Relations Act (LMRA), commonly referred to as the Taft-Hartley Act, had two primary purposes: (a) to lessen industrial disputes and (b) to place employers in a more equal position with the unions in bargaining and labor relations procedures. The LMRA shifted the emphasis in federal labor law from an attitude of federal protection for the rights of employees to a more balanced statutory scheme that added restrictions on unions, while guaranteeing certain freedoms of speech and conduct to employers and individual employees.

The purpose and policy of the LMRA is as follows:

- To prescribe the legitimate rights of both employees and employers in their relations affecting commerce

- To provide orderly and peaceful procedures for preventing employees and employers from interfering with each other's legitimate rights

- To protect the rights of individual employees in their relations with labor organizations whose activities affect commerce

- To define and proscribe the labor and management practices that affect commerce

- To protect the public's rights in connection with labor disputes affecting commerce

Congress amended the Wagner Act in 1947 with the passage of the LMRA. Problems with the Wagner Act included (a) violent strikes and picketing, (b) secondary boycotts that injured third parties, (c) the NLRB's manner of determining appropriate bargaining units, (d) union corruption, and (e) frequent work-assignment disputes among unions.

Q 3: What are employers required to do under the Norris-LaGuardia Act?

A: The Norris–LaGuardia Act of 1932 restricts federal courts' intervention in labor disputes by limiting the courts' ability to issue restraining orders and injunctions. For a federal court to issue an injunction in a labor dispute, an employer must prove the following:

- Unlawful acts, usually of a violent or fraudulent nature, have been threatened and will be committed, or they have taken place and will continue.

- The employer will suffer irreparable damage unless these acts are prevented or halted.

- Continued picketing would cause the employer more harm than the union would suffer if the picketing were halted.

- The employer has no legal remedy other than to seek an injunction.

- Local police authorities and officials are either unable or unwilling to protect the company's property.

- The employer comes to court having satisfied every legal obligation imposed on it in connection with the labor dispute.

A federal court can issue a temporary restraining order for a period of up to 5 days if the employer does the following:

- Claims that picketing will cause the employer to suffer irreparable damage if the picketing is not stopped

- Posts security in an amount fixed by the court in case the employer's claims later are proven false

Q 4:   How are union campaigns initiated?

A: Union campaigns can be initiated by an employee or by a union organizer. Unions sometimes target specific industries or companies. The logic is that if a union is successful at targeting a portion of an industry or one company, then more employees may be willing to unionize. When an employee approaches a union, the union usually will look at what size the employee population is, how much it will cost to unionize, and whether the complaints made by the employee are shared by other employees before the union decides to approach the company.

Several steps may occur when unionization takes place.

1. The union and employees will make contact to see what the possibility of unionizing is. This contact can take place by having group meetings outside the place of employment, through individual meetings, and by mailing materials to employees' homes. The main purpose of this initial contact is for union officials to gather information on the employees' grievances, needs, and concerns and to seek the employer's financial information, policies, and practices. In addition to obtaining this information, this is the union's first opportunity to win employee support and to build a case against the employer.

2. Union officials and the employees schedule an initial meeting. This meeting is the union's opportunity to gauge how much employee support it has and to explain how the union can help employees. It also gives the union an opportunity to see which employees can be counted on to provide the leadership that will be needed during the union campaign.

3. The union seeks employee support by forming an employee committee to gain additional support. Another method of gaining support is by handbilling whereby union organizers distribute literature to employees. The handbills discuss the reasons to join the union. Such handbills are usually distributed to employees as they leave work, or the handbills are mailed to their homes. It is extremely important for the union to gain momentum at this point. For an election to occur, the union will need 30% of the employees to sign authorization cards that indicate their willingness to be represented by a union.

Q 5:   What percentage of employees who have signed authorization cards is required under the NLRB to proceed with a union election? What percentage of employees must vote for the union to win?

A: During an organizing campaign, union representatives seek employee interest by having the employees sign authorization cards to indicate that the employees want union representation. At least 30% of the eligible employees in a prospective bargaining unit must sign authorization cards before the NLRB will order an election. A simple majority of 50% plus one person must vote in favor of union representation in order to win the election.

Q 6:   What is the difference between a *consent election* and a *directed election*?

A: An election conducted by the NLRB is one of the ways that employees can select or reject a particular labor union to bargain on their behalf with their employer. Elections serve various purposes: some are purely representational, some are procedural, and some are based on certain statutory requirements.

Once an appropriate bargaining unit has been designated, an NLRB regional director will order an election. The regional director will then hold a prehearing conference to attempt to resolve bargaining unit issues and questions of voter eligibility without having to resort to a full hearing. This election is known as a *consent election*. This type of election eliminates the need for a formal hearing.

If all parties voluntarily reach an agreement, the parties will enter into and sign a written agreement ("Agreement for Consent Election") that will set forth the details of the election. The "Agreement for Consent Election" form is then presented to the NLRB for approval. Under this type of agreement, the parties agree to the following:

- The employer is engaged in commerce.

- An appropriate bargaining unit exists.

- An election will be conducted.

- A specific payroll will be used to determine eligibility.

- The rights to hearings at any stage are waived.

- The rulings of the regional director on all questions relating to the election will be final and binding.

- The NLRB regional director will conduct investigations and rule on any challenged ballots if they are sufficient enough to affect the results.

- The regional director will rule on any objections to the conduct of the election. If it is found that they have merit, the director may set aside the election and conduct a new election.

- The regional director will issue to the parties involved (a) a certificate of the results if the employees voted against representation or (b) a certification of representation if the union received a majority vote.

The regional director will make all of the necessary arrangements to conduct an election. In the absence of a consent election agreement, the regional director will proceed to a hearing. When the parties are unable to reach an agreement regarding basic election issues such as (a) the appropriateness of a bargaining unit, (b) an eligibility date, and (c) the time and place for elections, the result is a *contested election*.

If evidence presented at a hearing establishes the existence of questions regarding representation and appropriateness of the bargaining unit sought by the petitioning party, the regional director will issue a "Decision and Direction of Election," which is also known as a *directed election*. *Directed elections* are simply another name for *contested elections*. This type of election is expressed in terms of agency personnel participating rather than the parties' choice of consenting to or contesting certain details. Directed elections may also be conducted by an NLRB regional director in accordance with an NLRB-directed election, or they may be issued by a regional director after a formal hearing.

Q 7:   What employee categories are excluded from the bargaining unit?

A: Employees excluded from coverage under the NLRA include supervisors, managers, confidential employees, and others. Under NLRA,

- A *supervisor* is defined as someone who uses independent judgment to make personnel decisions or to recommend personnel decisions. Personnel decisions include hiring, promoting, transferring, rewarding, and terminating employees.

- A *managerial employee* is defined as someone who makes, executes, and exercises independent judgment about management policies. Managerial employees normally do not manage people.

- A *confidential employee* is defined as someone who assists and acts in a confidential capacity to the management personnel who make and implement labor relations policies, or as someone who has regular access to confidential information about future bargaining strategy or changes that the employer anticipates may result from collective bargaining.

- Other employees who are excluded from the bargaining unit include independent contractors, agricultural laborers, domestic servants, people employed by a parent or a spouse, and public employees.

Q 8:   What can management do during a union campaign?

A: During a union campaign, employers are permitted to engage in activities that will not interfere with an employee's ability to make a free choice in a union election. If threats of reprisal, promises of benefits, or other actions would serve to coerce employees, an unfair labor practice charge will be brought against the employer. If the NLRB finds violations, the union essentially wins without the election.

Here are some important guidelines (Collier, 1998) that a supervisor may legally follow:

- Tell employees that the supervisors and the company are opposed to unionization.

- Tell employees that the employees do not have to sign union cards and that the law says that they have the absolute right to refrain from joining a union.

- Tell employees that they do not have to speak to union organizers or to admit organizers into their homes.

- Tell employees about the benefits that they enjoy, and compare those benefits with those in unionized companies.

- Tell employees that with a union they may have to bring their problems to a shop steward instead of dealing with their supervisor.

- Tell employees of the disadvantages of belonging to a union, such as the payment of dues and initiation fees and the possibility of fines and assessments.

- Tell employees that, if they engage in an economic strike, they may be permanently replaced and will be reinstated only if an opening occurs.

- Tell employees that they may be required to picket other employers, even when they are not on strike.

- Tell employees that a union can always out-promise an employer, but the union can guarantee nothing.

- Tell employees about any arrest records of union officials.

- Urge employees to vote against the union; suggest that they encourage others to do the same.

- Tell employees that merely signing a union authorization card or application for membership does not mean they must vote for the union in an election.

- Tell employees about any untrue or misleading statements made through an organizer, by handbill, or through any union propaganda.

A supervisor should not legally (Collier, 1998) do the following:

- Promise employees pay increases, promotions, improved working conditions, additional benefits, or special favors on the condition that the employees vote against or refuse to join the union.

- Threaten employees with loss of job or reduction in wages, or use threatening or intimidating language calculated to influence employees in the exercise of their right to support a union.

- Tell employees that they would have received a wage increase except for the start of the union campaign.

- Tell employees that the union will have to strike to obtain concessions from the employer.

- Discriminate against employees who are taking part in union activities by separating them from other employees and by transferring them to undesirable tasks in retaliation for their union activities.

- Ask employees to inform a supervisor if, while working, they are pressured to sign an authorization card while the supervisor is not enforcing a valid no-solicitation rule.

- Solicit employees to request the return of their authorization cards.

- Visit employees at their homes to urge them to vote against the union.

- Prohibit the wearing of union buttons or insignia.

Q 9: What are employees' rights during a union campaign?

A: The NLRA provides employees the right to organize and to engage in concerted activities. Therefore, solicitation to join the union, distribution of union material, and attendance at meetings held at nonwork places or during nonwork hours are all permissible. However, to be covered under NLRA, the employees' activity must be a *protected activity*. A protected activity must be reasonably seen as affecting the terms and conditions of employment.

Q 10: What is the *excelsior list*?

A: Excelsior Underwear, Inc., was the first company that the NLRB required to provide a list of the names and addresses of all the employees who were eligible to vote in a consent election. Now all employers are required to provide this list to the NLRB within 7 days after a consent election is ordered. The NLRB then provides the list to the union. In this manner, the union is given access to employees who will be the voters in the upcoming election. The NLRB views this as a way to ensure that employees are informed about the arguments both for and against electing a particular bargaining representative.

Q 11: What are mandatory bargaining subjects? Which subjects are optional? Can management refuse to bargain the optional subjects?

A: The NLRB has categorized subjects of bargaining into three categories: mandatory, permissive, and illegal.

- **Mandatory**. Topics subject to mandatory bargaining are generally defined as those that address wages, benefits, hours, and other terms and conditions of employment. Some examples of mandatory bargaining subjects areas follows:

  — Bonuses

  — Drug and alcohol testing

  — Grievance procedures

  — Health and welfare plans

  — Major business changes

  — Management rights

  — No-strike clauses

  — Partial closure or sale

  — Pension plans

  — Plant rules and discipline

  — Safety and health

  — Seniority and promotions

  — Stock purchase plans

  — Union security

  — Wages and increases

  — Work assignments

- **Permissive**. Topics that may be legally proposed by either side for collective bargaining are called *permissive* and also *voluntary* or *nonmandatory*. Neither side may compel the other to bargain on these subjects. Some examples of permissive bargaining topics are as follows:

  — Administrative expense funds

  — Bargaining unit definition

  — Employees excluded from coverage of the NLRA

  — Industry promotion funds

  — Internal union affairs

  — Performance bonds and indemnifications

  — Personal service contracts (PSC)

  — Selection of bargaining representative

  — Settlement of unfair labor practices

  — Transcript of negotiations

  — Union label

  — Union recognition clauses

- **Illegal**. Topics that neither the employer nor the union may insist that the other party agree to are called *illegal* or *unlawful* provisions. Such insistence is in violation of the duty to bargain in good faith provisions of the NLRA. Some examples of illegal bargaining subjects are as follows:

— Closed-shop clauses

— Practices in conflict with the NLRA or any federal antitrust statutes

— Practices in conflict with the union's duty of fair representation

— Preferential treatment by a hiring hall

Q 12: What is the process to decertify a union?

A: The process to decertify a union starts with filing a petition at the regional NLRB office. The petitioners for decertification can be any employee or group of employees, except supervisors; any nonemployee, except the employer; or any labor organization.

If 30% of the employees sign the petition, the NLRB may hold a hearing and authorize an election to decertify the union. A *decertification election* is an election held following the filing of a petition by employees who allege that the union previously certified or currently recognized by the employer as the bargaining representative no longer represents a majority of the unit employees. A union that wins a decertification election will be certified by the NLRB as a bargaining agent, just as if the union had won a certification election. A recognized or certified union that loses will be decertified. Decertification occurs if a majority of the employees votes against the union. A tie vote will result in decertification because the union has received less than a majority of the votes cast.

Employers need to be careful if employees inquire about the decertification of a union. An employer's initiating or even encouraging a petition for decertification can be considered interference and an unfair labor practice. Decertification is a matter between the employees and the union—any impetus for decertification must come from the workers rather than the employer. An employer can lawfully provide accurate information to its employees regarding the decertification procedures, as long as the company does so without threatening its employees or promising them benefits. The safest course of action for an employer is simply to provide the employees with accurate factual information regarding the decertification procedure.

Q 13: What types of strikes are protected by the NLRA?

A: The NLRA protects the following types of strikes:

- A *primary strike* is protected by the NLRA. A primary strike is a planned work stoppage to force a demand on the workers' employer.

- An *economic strike* is designed to enforce employees' economic demands (e.g., wages, hours, terms and conditions of employment) on the employer. If a contractual agreement does not waive the right to engage in an economic strike, the strike is protected by NLRA. The employer can hire *permanent* replacements. Employers are under no obligation to reinstate a striker until his or her former job becomes available.

- An *unfair labor practice strike* is protected by NLRA. Employees engage in an unfair labor practice strike if they feel that their employer has committed unfair labor practices as defined by the NLRA. The employer can hire replacements but cannot hire permanent replacements. Strikers are guaranteed reinstatement.

The NLRA protects certain related activities including the following:

- *Picketing* in the form of walking or standing near the entrance to a business to inform the public about a labor dispute is protected.

- *Area standards picketing* to inform the public that an employer offers lower wages and fewer benefits than union employers in the area is protected.

- *Common-situs picketing* is picketing an employer at a site shared by other employers and is protected if it falls within the guidelines established by *Sailors Union of the Pacific v. Moore Dry Dock Co.* in 1950.

- *Handbilling* is posting or handing out printed materials that inform the public of a labor dispute and is protected.

- *Consumer boycotting* that requests the public to refrain from the purchase of an employer's products because of a labor dispute is protected. However, picketing related to the boycott is not protected.

Q 14: What are the steps of the arbitration process?

A: Arbitration is a binding agreement determined by a third party. The main advantage of arbitration from the employer's perspective is that it is faster and less expensive than going to court. However, employees have complained that arbitration (a) allows no way to challenge an unpopular decision, (b) favors employers, and (c) does not offer the same remedies that a court may offer.

There are three main components of an arbitration process:

1. **Prehearing briefs**. At this point, management and union representatives have the chance to present their views and describe their evidence to the arbitrator. The briefs are used to assist the arbitrator and the two parties to focus on the issue at hand.

2. **Arbitration hearing**. This hearing is when both parties have the chance to present their case and evidence. During this hearing, it is very common to call witnesses who have observed particular events. Important evidence that may be presented by the employee or management could help prove past practices. Some examples of evidence that could be used are time cards, performance appraisals, customer or co-worker complaints, and warnings. It is possible that closing statements could take place at this hearing. This hearing is an opportunity for both parties to summarize key aspects. However, closing statements are normally skipped if both parties plan to submit posthearing briefs.

3. **Arbitrator's decision**. It is common for labor contracts to require that a decision be made within a certain time period. However, if no clause is in the contract, the arbitrator can make the decision within 30 minutes of the close of the hearing, or he or she could take a few months. When making a decision, an arbitrator will discuss (a) the issue presented, (b) the statement of facts, (c) the positions of the parties, (d) the analysis or discussion, and (e) the award.

For more information on arbitration, contact the American Arbitration Association at (212) 484-4000 or at <www.adr.org> and <www.arb-forum.com>.

Q 15: What is an unfair labor practice by management?

A: The NLRB has created an extensive listing of employer actions that it considers would unduly interfere with an individual employee's labor rights. The NLRA has defined five categories of unfair labor practices that are prohibited for employers. Below is a summary of the five categories of unfair labor practices, along with a brief explanation of each category.

1. **Interference, restraint, or coercion**. An employer cannot interfere with, restrain, or coerce employees in the exercise of their rights. Most violations of this section include supervisors who (a) make threatening statements, (b) question employees who assert their labor rights, or (c) make false statements to workers seeking unionization.

2. **Employer domination or support of a labor organization**. An employer may not try to dominate or interfere with the formation or

administration of any labor organization, or to contribute financial or other support to such an organization.

3. **Discrimination on the basis of labor activity**. An employer may not discriminate against an employee in hiring, or tenure of employment, or any term or condition of employment in order to encourage or to discourage membership in any labor organization.

4. **Discrimination in retaliation for going to the NLRB**. An employer may not discharge or otherwise discriminate against an employee in terms and conditions of employment because he or she has filed charges or given testimony.

5. **Refusal to bargain**. An employer will be in violation of the NLRA if the company (a) refuses to bargain collectively with the representatives of the employees, (b) refuses to recognize a majority union, (c) takes unilateral actions, (d) refuses to provide necessary information to union representatives, (e) refuses to sign a written contract once an agreement is reached, (e) or imposes conditions on its willingness to bargain.

As the federal agency charged with the enforcement of the NLRA, the NLRB has procedures in place for investigating, hearing, and remedying unfair labor practices once a charge is received. Employers who are unionized or in the process of unionization are advised to familiarize themselves with the various NLRA labor laws in place if they are to avoid unfair labor practice charges. Additional information regarding labor laws can be obtained from the NLRB at <www.nlrb.gov>.

Q 16: What is an unfair labor practice by the union?

A: The NLRA outlaws several union activities. Examples of union unfair labor practices (ULP) follow:

- Coercing the employer
- Coercing the employees
- Causing the employer to discriminate against employees
- Refusing to bargain in good faith
- Inducing strikes for forbidden reasons such as secondary boycotts
- Forcing the employer to make certain work assignments
- Forcing the employer to bargain with an uncertified union
- Charging excessive initiation fees

- Forcing or attempting to force employers to pay for workers the employer does not need

- Forcing or attempting to force employers to pay for work that is not or will not be done

Q 17: What is the procedure for filing an unfair labor practice?

A: A violation of any of the provisions of the NLRA is called an *unfair labor practice* (ULP). Any individual or organization may file a charge with the NLRB if he or she feels a ULP has been committed. Charges are to be filed with the regional director for the region in which the ULP has occurred or is alleged to have occurred. A charge that alleges a ULP in two or more regions may be filed with the regional director for any of the involved regions.

The ULP charge is submitted on a standard form that is available from the NLRB regional offices. The charge must contain the name and address of both the charging party and the charged party, as well as a statement of the facts central to the alleged ULP. Charges may be filed in person at the regional office or by mail (preferably registered or certified mail).

A ULP charge must be filed and served on the charged party within 6 months of when the alleged ULP was committed. If the ULP is a continuing violation, the charge is considered timely if filed within 6 months of the last occurrence.

Q 18: What is the *yellow dog contract*?

A: The *yellow dog contract* was an agreement that an employee was required to sign before receiving a job, stating that he or she would not join or support the union. The Norris–La Guardia Act of 1932 declared yellow dog contracts unenforceable in the federal courts. Such contracts are also illegal under the Railway Labor Act, the NLRA, and currently under the laws of 34 states.

Q 19: Can employers form employee participation committees without violating the NLRA? What kinds of issues can such committees discuss?

A: While not every employee involvement committee formed by an employer will be considered to be a labor organization as defined by the NLRA, employers should be cautious when forming such employee involvement groups. The definition of a labor organization as defined by the NLRA is any organization, agency, or employee representation committee or plan in which employees participate and that exists for the purpose, in whole or in part, of "dealing with employers concerning grievances, labor disputes, wages, rates of pay, hours of employment, or conditions of work." The NLRB will then evaluate the amount of employer domination and support given to the committee so it can determine if the employer is superseding any of the functions of a union and, therefore, is engaging in unfair labor practices. Two notable court cases have addressed this issue.

The first case to test the legality of employee participation committees was the Electromation case in 1988. Electromation Inc. created "action" committees composed of selected employees to address issues such as absenteeism, pay progressions, and attendance policies. The committees were disbanded before the Teamsters Union election at the Electromation Plant. The Teamsters still filed an unfair labor practice stating that the committees were actually labor organizations in violation of the NLRA.

The NLRB's final determination agreed with the Teamsters that the sole purpose of the participation committees was to address employee's dissatisfaction with conditions of employment. The NLRB did clearly state that it was not totally banning participation committees and could see circumstances in which such committees would not violate the NLRA.

The second notable case, which was the first to address labor management participation committees in a union environment, was against E. I. du Pont. In this particular case, management set up seven committees to address issues such as recreation, safety, and fitness matters. A manager was assigned to each committee to develop an agenda and to facilitate the meeting. The NLRB found that the committees were, in fact, discussing mandatory bargaining subjects and were primarily dominated by management. Therefore, they were in violation of the NLRA.

Learning from these two cases, employers find some guidelines that they can follow when forming employee participation committees. First, they should make sure that issues typically discussed at the collective bargaining table are not topics addressed by employee committees. Second, management should not have a majority of the members nor dominate the committee.

Safe issues for employee committees to address include social and athletic activities. Those topics are not typically viewed as mandatory bargaining subjects. There have been other instances where committees have addressed various other subjects with varying committee structures, and those instances have not been viewed as violations of the NLRA. The safest route when contemplating the formation of such employee involvement committees is to discuss the details with a knowledgeable employment law attorney who can provide sound legal advice.

References

Chapter 7. Employee and Labor Relations

Collier, T. O. Jr. (1998). *Supervisor's guide to labor relations*. Alexandria, VA: Society for Human Resource Management.

CHAPTER 8

HEALTH, SAFETY, AND SECURITY

Q 1: **Does the Occupational Safety and Health Act (OSHA) cover all employers? What about telecommuters?**

> **A:** Virtually all employers are obliged by law to provide their employees with safe and healthful working conditions. All employers must provide a workplace free of recognized hazards. The Occupational Safety and health Act of 1970 applies to any "person engaged in a business affecting commerce, including an individual, partnership, association, corporation, business trust, legal representative, and any organized group of persons with employees." Employers covered by OSHA must follow the standards, regulations, and guidelines applicable to their particular industry.
>
> Even when no OSHA standard covers a particular situation, employers still have a general duty under the Act to provide their employees with a safe and healthy place to work. In accordance with this standard, employers need to be careful in approving home offices. For both OSHA and worker's compensation-related reasons, employers should inspect the workers' home workstation to ensure the environment is safe. Further, telecommuting agreements should include language on the boundaries within which the employee will be deemed to be "at work" and those areas that will be excluded from the office environment.

Q 2: **What are OSHA's recordkeeping requirements?**

> **A:** Recordkeeping is important because it helps to identify high-hazard industries and to advise employees of the status of their employer's history. OSHA requires employers with 11 or more employees (with certain exceptions[*]) to maintain records at each of their locations. Those employers must do the following:

---

[*] Employers with 10 or fewer employees are *exempted* from recordkeeping requirements unless asked by the Bureau of Labor Statistics to participate in a study. OSHA recordkeeping is *not required* of employers in certain industries (although the employers are still covered by the act) including finance, retail trade, real estate, and service industries with Standard Industrial Classification (SIC) 52–89. However, the following service industries *are required* to maintain records: building materials and garden supplies (SIC 52), general merchandise and food stores

- Record all occupational injuries and illnesses. Each injury or occupational illness must be recorded within 6 working days after receiving the information. The "Annual Log and Summary of Occupational Injuries and Illness" (OSHA Form No. 200) and the "Supplementary Record of Occupational Injuries and Illness" (OSHA Form No. 101) were created to help employers comply with the recording requirement. These forms do not have to be used as long as the required information is recorded properly.

  The following information from OSHA Form No. 200 must be recorded and maintained at the location of the injury or occupational injury:

  — Case or file number (company has assigned for tracking)

  — Date of injury or onset of illness

  — Employee's name, occupation or job title, and department

  — Description of the injury or illness

  — Number of days away from work, number of days of restricted work activity, or both

  — Date of death or fatalities

- The OSHA Form No. 101 for each occupational injury or illness must include these:

  — Identifying information for the injured or ill employee

  — Location of the injury or illness

  — Description of the injury or illness

  — Date of occurrence

  — Parts of the body affected

- The employer must record these:

  — Fatalities, regardless of the time between injury and death

  — Cases, other than fatalities, where occupational injury or illness has caused the employee to miss work

  — Cases, other than fatalities, *without* lost workdays, that (a) result in transfer to another job or termination, (b) require medical treatment beyond first aid, (c) involve loss of consciousness or restriction of work or motion, or (d) are diagnosed illnesses reported to the employer but not classified as fatalities or lost workday cases

---

(SIC 53 and 54), hotels and other lodging places (SIC 70), repair services (SIC 75 and 76), amusement and recreation services (SIC 79), and health services (SIC 80).

- Maintain records on a calendar-year basis (January 1–December 31) for a 5-year period. In addition, if employee medical records are maintained, they must be kept for the duration of employee's tenure with the employer, plus 30 years. Employee exposure records, if the employer maintains them, must be kept for a minimum of 30 years.

- Post annual totals for injuries and illnesses from data on OSHA Form No. 200. The information must be posted from February 1 through March 1 of each year and must cover the previous year's data. The report must be posted in an area frequented by employees such as break room, a time clock location, or the HR office.

OSHA also has recordkeeping requirements for specific standards such as exposure monitoring (e.g., asbestos) and medical monitoring records. Employers should familiarize themselves with OSHA's recording requirements relevant to their industry.

Although *not all* employers are required to maintain injury and occupational illness records, *all* employers must comply with OSHA standards, display the OSHA poster, and report to OSHA within 8 hours following the work-related death of any employee or the in-patient hospitalization of three or more employees as a result of a work-related incident.

Q 3: What are OSHA's reporting requirements?

A: The Department of Labor (DOL) requires employers to notify OSHA within 8 hours of an incident that involves a fatality or the hospitalization of three or more employees. (Note: State laws may require notification to a state agency within a shorter period of time.) Although a fatality or the hospitalization of three or more employees does not mean a violation has occurred, OSHA is required to inspect for hazardous work conditions. All employers are subject to the 8-hour notification rule.

For an employer to provide an oral report to OSHA on a fatality or multiple hospitalizations, the company must call an OSHA area office that is nearest to the accident site; notify, in person, an OSHA area office nearest to the accident site; or call the OSHA central phone number, (800) 321-OSHA (6742). Because OSHA requires prompt notification, these three methods are the only methods that are acceptable and that comply with the regulations. In addition to an employer providing an oral notification, the company can fax, mail, or hand deliver the required information as a back-up measure.

When an employer makes a report of a fatality or multiple hospitalizations, the following information must be included:

- Name of the establishment

- Location of the incident

- Time of the incident

- Number of fatalities or hospitalized employees

- Contact person

- Telephone number

- Brief description of the incident

If an incident occurs and a fatality or the hospitalization of three or more employees occurs within 30 days of the incident, the employer is required to provide the same notification within 8 hours of learning of the fatality or hospitalization.

For more information on OSHA reporting requirements, visit the web site at <www.osha.gov>.

Q 4: What is the best way to prepare for an OSHA inspection?

A: The best way to prepare for an OSHA inspection is to conduct an internal audit of health and safety conditions. This audit will alert you to problems that exist and will allow you the opportunity to correct them. Your internal audit should include a review of the following:

- Compliance with OSHA notice-posting requirements

- Proper use and condition of protective equipment

- Proper use and condition of work equipment

- Proper use of safety procedures

- Accident and injury patterns in the company's history

- Employee input about job hazards

- Noise levels in various work areas

- Employee exposure to toxic substances

- Walkways cleared of tripping or slipping hazards

- Lighting levels

- Bookcases, shelves, and cabinets secured from tipping

- Safety training procedures in place

- Safety rules and procedures provided in written format

- Availability of first aid

- Evacuation routes identified

- Alarms tested

- "Material Data Safety Sheets" available

- Air quality monitored

- Fire extinguishers present and operational

- Storage of flammable materials

Q 5: What are the penalties for an OSHA violation?

A: The Consolidated Omnibus Budget Reconciliation Act of 1990 (COBRA) has increased OSHA civil penalties since the law was enacted in 1970. Penalties for failing to post required notices or keep accurate records may go as high as $10,000 each, depending on the gravity of the violation, the size of the company, and the employer's "good faith." Violations of safety standards or rules may subject the employer to a penalty of up to $7,000 each. For repeated and willful violations, OSHA may impose penalties of up to $70,000 each. No company that commits a willful violation can receive a fine less than $25,000.

OSHA also sets forth criminal penalties that can be imposed only by the courts after a trial. For a willful violation resulting in death, the maximum penalty is $250,000 per violation for an individual employer and $500,000 per violation for a corporation. Convicted company officials also can be imprisoned for up to 6 months. Employers that willfully make false statements may be subject to criminal penalties, including up to 6 months imprisonment. For assaulting or intimidating an OSHA inspector or for resisting, opposing, or interfering with an inspection, the maximum penalty is $5,000, imprisonment for up to 3 years, or both.

Q 6: What are the recommended steps for an accident investigation?

A: Investigating accidents as they occur is important to aid in preventing future accidents. When conducting an accident investigation, an employer should first appoint someone to investigate the incident. This responsibility is quite often assigned to the immediate supervisor of the employee involved in the accident. Then management will review the results. The appointed individual should take photographs or make drawings of the accident scene before anything is moved or removed so the scene can be reviewed at a later date. All involved individuals should be interviewed as soon as possible so they will be more likely to remember details. Witnesses should be interviewed separately so as not to influence one another.

The supervisor should then use the information to fill out a report similar to the sample accident report that follows as Table 8–1:

TABLE 8–1
SAMPLE ACCIDENT REPORT

Name of employee: _____

Date: _____

Time: _____

Department: _____

Descriptions of the accident:

- By supervisor: _____

  _____

  _____

- By witnesses: _____

  _____

  _____

- By employee involved: _____

  _____

  _____

What was (were) the potential cause(s) of the accident?

- Unsafe actions (e.g., not wearing safety equipment): _____

  _____

  _____

- Unsafe environment (e.g., equipment, weather, wet floor, etc.): _____

  _____

  _____

- Corrective action suggested to prevent recurrence: _____

  _____

  _____

Date action taken: _____

Signatures: Manager: _____

                 Supervisor:_____

                 Employee:_____

Q 7:   What are the elements of a safety promotion program?

A: Undoubtedly, an effective safety program can have an extremely positive effect on an organization in numerous ways. With a good safety program in place, employee morale, health, and safety can certainly increase, and the costs involved with worker's compensation claims, absenteeism, turnover, and OSHA violation citations and fines can potentially decrease.

In addition, accidents often result in distractions that can have a major effect on organizational productivity.

Some organizations may experience so few accidents that a formal safety program to protect their employees may not be necessary. In such ideal circumstances, it may be sufficient for managers and supervisors to simply watch over their employees to ensure that they are following safe work practices. However, it should go without saying that those organizations are probably few and far between and that they are, generally speaking, the exception to the rule.

An effective health and safety program should contain the following four basic elements:

- A strong management commitment to safety as expressed through policy, financial support, active involvement in program implementation, and demonstration of concern for workers' well-being

- Efficient hazard identification, engineering controls, job-safety training, and safety evaluation programs that are designed to anticipate and manage potential hazards

- An effective employee communication and involvement program that is designed to motivate employees and management to deal with safety problems and with each other in a positive and proactive way

- A safety and health training program that will be integrated with management systems to deal with safety as an important part of plant operations

Besides these basic elements, many companies try to make safety a way of life for their employees by establishing safety programs that may include certain incentives such as contests, safety performance awards, or safety suggestion programs to encourage employees to cultivate safe practices and to promote safety awareness and adherence to safety rules on the job. For a safety program to be truly successful in reducing injuries, it should be as comprehensive as possible and should be based on the underlying principle that most injuries are preventable.

Additional guidance on OSHA health and safety requirements, as well as for writing a health and safety plan, can be obtained from OSHA at <www.osha.gov> or by calling (202) 523-6091.

Q 8: What resources are available that provide ergonomic advice or recommendations for workplace modification and design?

A: Information to facilitate the design, modification, or management of work processes is part of an ergonomics guideline developed by the

American Society for Testing and Materials, which can be contacted at (610) 832-9585 or on the web site at <www.astm.org>.

OSHA maintains an Internet site that is devoted to ergonomics issues and that provides information on workplace measures to reduce the possibility of repetitive stress injuries. The address is <www.osha-slc.gov/SLTC/ ergonomics/>.

Some additional resources for workplace ergonomic information include the following:

- Human Factors and Ergonomics Society (HFES) can be reached at (310) 394-1811.

- Advanced Ergonomics, Inc., can be reached at (800) 682-0169 or at <www.advancedergonomics.com>. It furnishes a variety of ergonomic services and publishes *The Advanced Ergonomics Manual*.

- Clayton ErgoTech can be reached at (800) 374-6967. It offers ergonomic consulting, training materials, and videos.

- ErgoCare Ergonomic Specialists can be reached at (408) 253-2170. It provides workstation evaluation and ergonomic workstation products.

- Humanics ErgoSystems can be reached at (818) 345-3746. It conducts workplace assessments, ergonomics training, product research and evaluation, and more.

- National Coalition on Ergonomics can be reached at (202) 293-3384 or <www.ncergo.org>.

- Center for Office Technology can be reached at (703) 684-7760 or <www.cot.org>.

- ErgoWeb can be reached at <www.ergoweb.com>.

- Center for Workplace Health Information can be reached at <www.ctdnews.com>. It publishes a newsletter plus books on ergonomics and on the prevention and treatment of cumulative trauma disorders.

- NC Ergonomics Resource Center can be reached at (919) 515-2052. It has programs and services in occupational ergonomics, including compliance-based ergonomics programming, education and training, and workplace and job analysis.

Please note that these resources are suggestions only. They have not been tested by SHRM and are not recommended over other companies or organizations.

Q 9:   What are the essential elements of an effective safety and health program?

A: The elements of an effective safety and health program include the following:

- The active support of senior management, including the provision of required resources and access to qualified and competent professional personnel

- Written safety responsibilities for line managers and supervisors, plus a commitment on their part to be accountable for workplace safety and health (Staff management must play an active supporting role.)

- The active involvement of employees in program design and operation

- Written program goals, objectives, policies, procedures, implementation plans, and review processes that are communicated to employees (Those written statements should be signed by the Chief Executive Officer (CEO) or location manager to demonstrate management's commitment to the program. Information should be communicated to employees by bulletin board announcements, newsletters, and meetings.)

- A plan for dealing with hazards (The plan should be part of the program and should include hazard anticipation, recognition, evaluation, and abatement. To facilitate its use, the plan should provide for materials inventory, regular internal inspections and environmental monitoring, complaint investigations, and emergency procedures.)

- Education and training focusing on the relevant and present hazards and on the responsibilities of management and employees in dealing with those hazards (Training in the use of relevant personal protective and response equipment should also be included.)

- The review of OSHA's general duty clause and specific standards to ensure the proper monitoring and assessment of hazards and of record maintenance

- OSHA's requirements and state laws regarding the communication of hazards to employees and employee access to hazard data

- The use of technologically feasible and cost-effective engineering controls, or the availability of personal protective equipment where such controls are not available

Q 10: What are some building security protocols a company can establish?

A: Some commonly used and routine building security measures include the following:

- Hiring security staff members

- Installing security hardware such as locks, fences, and safes

- Educating employees and managers on security procedures

- Preparing an investigation plan for following up on security incidents

- Making sure that the exterior of the building is well lit

- Installing a security alarm or access control system

- Installing surveillance equipment

- Establishing a visitor sign-in policy

Q 11: What are the warning signs for workplace violence?

A: An employee exhibiting the following indicators is not necessarily an individual who is prone to violence. However, violence is always a possibility when these warning signs are evident:

- Excessive tardiness or absences

- Increased need for supervision

- Reduced productivity

- Inconsistency

- Strained workplace relationships

- Inability to concentrate

- Violation of safety procedures

- Changes in health or hygiene

- Unusual behavior

- Fascination with weapons

- Substance abuse

- Stress

- Excuses and blaming

- Depression

Members seeking additional information or resources related to workplace violence should avail themselves of the resources on the SHRM web site, particularly the white papers section, or you can contact the Information Center for further assistance.

Q 12: What should an HR professional do when he or she suspects an employee may be potentially violent?

A: Perhaps the most important step is to establish a workplace violence policy before a problem ever exists. The policy should express the company's efforts to provide a safe environment for its employees. A list of prohibited conduct (not to be all inclusive) should establish the basic activities that will not be tolerated. The policy should include a discussion of the process and of the need to report dangerous situations, along with a description of how problems will be addressed. An excellent example of such a policy exists at our web site in the white papers section under the heading "Health/Safety/Security."

Although disciplinary action and the possibility of termination are viable options, the primary goal is to get the employee back on track. When an employee begins to act erratically, you want to have the ability to maintain the safety of your workers. It will be important to reserve the right to disarm a security guard or to restrict the activities of an employee who handles potentially dangerous equipment.

Before an event occurs, the HR staff members should have a prepared a list of sources for help. The list should include referral to the Employee Assistance Program (EAP) and a referral to your own medical plan (most health plans have some counseling or psychological aid). You should look into aid that is available for various problems, and is generally free of charge, within your city, county, and state.

When an employer suspects that a problematic situation may develop, it is time to intervene in a uniform and fair manner. The employer should carefully prepare for the confrontation. Each situation is different and demands different actions. Common sense generally dictates the most appropriate course of action. Remove any obvious safety threats to include any weapons or objects that can be used as weapons. Remain calm and use an even tone of voice. Assess whether the individual can be reasoned with, and then decide how you will proceed. Have help available in the event of an altercation or violent response by the employee. Some situations will lend themselves to discussion while others will require possible assistance and support from outside authorities. You should be prepared with completed paperwork to document the decision, and you should anticipate likely questions.

The very best preparation is rehearsal with a previously selected intervention team. A great deal of comfort and confidence can be acquired through repetition and role-playing. The comfort and confidence aids the intervention team's ability to discharge a potentially volatile situation.

For further information, several white papers that address violence in the workplace are available under "Health/Safety/Security" on the SHRM web site.

Q 13: What are the employer's responsibilities and liabilities regarding negligent hiring or retention?

A: The possibility of a claim of negligent hiring is a reason to ensure that recruiting and selection methods include background and reference checking. Under a claim of negligent hiring, an employer can be held liable for someone who is injured by an employee who has committed some wrong on the job. The person who is injured, whether another employee or a customer, can contend that the employer's negligence put the employee in a position to hurt someone.

Generally, employers have always been held responsible for the behavior of their employees as they perform their jobs. Under negligent hiring, the employer is responsible when the employee, acting outside the scope of his or her job, commits an act of violence. The theory is that the employer knew or should have known that the employee had a background that would preclude his or her hire into the job.

Negligent retention is based on an employer's failure to be aware of an employee's unfitness for a particular position and on the employer's subsequent failure to take any corrective action such as training, reassignment, or discharge to remedy the problem. The principal difference between negligent hiring and negligent retention is based on the time at which the employer is charged with knowledge of an employee's unfitness.

Negligent hiring focuses on the adequacy of the employer's pre-employment investigation of the applicant's background. Negligent retention occurs during the course of employment when the employer becomes aware or should have been aware of an employee's unfitness for a position and then the employer fails to take any further actions such as investigation, reassignment, or discharge.

Employers should understand the theory of negligent hiring or retention and should balance this understanding with equal employment opportunity mandates and privacy concerns to develop effective pre-employment and employment policies.

Q 14: What are OSHA's requirements for health care workers under the Bloodborne Pathogens Standard?

A: OSHA implemented the Bloodborne Pathogens Standard (BPS) in 1992. The standard protects all employees in positions where it is "reasonably anticipated" that the employee will be exposed to blood or other potentially infected bodily fluids. Although the vast majority of protected workers are in the health care industry, the standard also covers employees in linen services, medical equipment repair, emergency technicians, funeral services, and other industries.

The BPS can be divided into two categories: risk management and recordkeeping. Under the risk management requirements, an employer must do the following:

- Implement universal precautions.

- Have a written exposure control plan.

- Have exposure control procedures.

- Provide personal protective equipment.

- Provide training and hazard communication.

- Provide free Hepatitis B vaccinations.

- Provide free postexposure incident medical evaluations, lab tests, treatment, and counseling.

Under the recordkeeping requirements, an employer must take these steps:

- Maintain exposure records for the duration of the exposed employee's employment plus 30 years.

- Record needle sticks (if medical treatment is necessary) on OSHA Form No. 200.

- Maintain training records for 3 years.

For additional information on OSHA's BPS, please see the SHRM white paper titled *The Bloodborne Pathogens Standard and Applications for Human Resource Professionals* (Froelich & Cullen, 1999) at <www.shrm. org/whitepapers/documents/ 61820.asp>. OSHA (1996) has issued a booklet called *Occupational Exposure to Bloodborne Pathogens* to help employers comply with the BPS. For a free copy, please send a self-addressed mailing label to OSHA Publications Office; 200 Constitution Ave., NW, Room N3101; Washington, DC 20210.

Q 15: Is there any worker's compensation liability to our company if employees injure themselves playing a pick-up game of basketball during lunch?

A: It is quite likely that there will be worker's compensation liability found on the employer. What makes this a tough question is that each state has its own worker's compensation laws, its own courts, and its own interpretation of what is and what is not a compensable injury. Generally speaking, if the injury occurs on the premises during a lunch or break period, or if the employer directly or indirectly implied that participation was required, or if the employer derived some benefit from the employee engaging in the activity that caused the injury, the injured party is likely to be eligible for worker's compensation benefits.

When an injury occurs during work-related recreational, social, or athletic activities, the main question is whether there is a link between the injury and the person's employment responsibilities. To help avoid liability, always maintain evidence that participation or attendance at any recreational activity was communicated as being completely voluntary.

Save copies of any postings with your statement that participation is not required. Be sure supervisors do not encourage employees to participate. Get the employees' acknowledgment in writing. Although a release will not necessarily remove all liability, it can serve as excellent evidence that the employees were fully informed and not coerced into participating in or attending an activity.

Q 16: We have employees who drive as part of their job. Are we required to drug test them?

A: Not necessarily. Just because you have drivers does not mean that you are required to test them for alcohol and drugs, although it would be in the employer's best interest to test employees who drive for that employer. An employee who is in an accident while working for the employer can create a big financial liability, as well as a negative public image for that employer. Employers who are recipients of federal transportation funds and contractors, operators, or subrecipients who provide mass transportation or safety-sensitive services for employers who receive federal transportation funds are covered by the drug- and alcohol-testing regulations of the Department of Transportation (DOT).

Covered employees in safety-sensitive positions usually include commercial truckers, air carrier flight and support personnel, and railroad employees. Though the DOT is split into six different agencies, employees who are covered by the testing regulations generally fall into the following categories:

- Commercial vehicle operators
- Operators of nonrevenue service vehicles, if the job requires a commercial driver's license
- Dispatchers and anyone who controls the dispatch or movement of revenue service vehicles or equipment used in revenue service
- Maintenance personnel for revenue service vehicles (except cleaning crews)
- Security guards who carry firearms

For more information on DOT's drug- and alcohol-testing regulations, visit the DOT web site at <www.dot.gov>.

Q 17: **We suspect that an employee in the warehouse is under the influence of drugs. May we send him for drug testing even though we do not currently have a drug-testing policy?**

A: No. It is unwise to drug test employees without having a written policy on drug testing. When you single an employee out for drug testing and you do not have a policy, your action violates many state provisions and can be perceived as a discriminatory practice. Furthermore, the employer should not accuse an employee of substance abuse. An employer should focus instead on the employee's performance problems. Substance abusers quite often have problems with attendance, high accident rates, and overall low productivity and accuracy. Start by addressing such performance issues through the company's regular disciplinary provisions or its performance management program.

The employee may admit to the substance-abuse problem during this process. The employer should then adhere to the company policy on substance abuse. If the company does not have a policy, management should decide how it wishes to address the issue now and in the future. Quite often companies will refer their employees to an Employee Assistance Program at this stage. The employer should also make the employee aware of what benefits, if any, are provided by the medical insurance plan, as well as inform the employee of his or her rights for time off under the Family and Medical Leave Act, if the employee and employer meet all the eligibility requirements.

Many employers have a concern about how the Americans with Disabilities Act (ADA) relates to employees with substance-abuse problems. The ADA covers only those individuals who have been or are currently in rehabilitation and are no longer substance abusers. The ADA does not offer coverage to employees who are current abusers, who come to work under the influence of drugs or alcohol, or both, even if they are currently in rehabilitation. An employer cannot discriminate against an individual because he or she is in rehabilitation.

In cases where an employee admits to a substance-abuse problem but fails to get assistance, the employer should continue to discipline the individual for any performance-related problems. In safety-sensitive environments, such as when operating machinery or driving vehicles, we strongly recommend that the company put a *for cause* or postaccident drug-testing policy in place. Otherwise, it is very difficult to address the substance-abuse problem if you do not have a way to confirm the suspicion.

Q 18: Our company's president would like to implement a drug-testing program. What are some guidelines?

A: Employers adopt drug-use and drug-testing policies to comply with state and federal laws and to combat the high costs and risks associated with workplace drug abuse.

Many employers adopt policies that not only cover drug use but also cover substance abuse issues such as the abuse of alcohol and both illegal and legal drugs. Employers adopt such policies because abuse of alcohol or legally prescribed drugs poses the same risks to workplace safety and employee productivity as does the abuse of illegal drugs. Testing an employee for illegal drug use without screening for alcohol is of little value in determining whether the employee is fit to work.

An employer establishing a drug- and alcohol-abuse policy must (a) take the ADA into account, (b) be aware of federal antidrug initiatives that affect contractors and employers in safety-sensitive industries, and (c) be familiar with applicable state law.

The ADA does not prevent an employer from taking steps to combat the use of drugs and alcohol in the workplace. It specifically provides for an employer to prohibit the use of drugs and alcohol in the workplace and to prohibit employees from being under the influence of drugs or alcohol in the workplace. An employer can discharge or deny employment to current users of illegal drugs without fear of being held liable for disability discrimination.

Current users of illegal drugs are not protected under the ADA. However, people who are addicted to drugs but who are no longer using drugs illegally and who are receiving treatment for drug addiction or who have been rehabilitated successfully are protected from discrimination under the ADA. Individuals who are not illegally using drugs are also protected under the ADA.

The ADA sets limits on employment-related medical examinations. An employer is prohibited from requiring a job applicant to undergo medical testing before the employer has made a conditional offer of employment. However, drug testing is not considered a medical test. Therefore, an employer can require applicants to take pre-employment drug tests and can require employees to take drug tests whether or not the tests are job related.

Under the ADA, employers are required to keep the results of medical tests strictly confidential. Although drug tests are not confidential medical records under the ADA, there are several reasons for an employer to safeguard the confidentiality of all drug test results:

- Drug tests can reveal information about lawfully prescribed drugs, which are subject to the ADA's confidentiality protections.

- Drug tests can reveal information about a disability, which is subject to ADA's confidentiality provisions.

- Some states have medical record confidentiality provisions that are more protective than the ADA.

- Inadvertent disclosures of drug test results can lead to liability for defamation, invasion of privacy, or negligence.

An employer setting up a drug-testing program should be aware of federal antidrug initiatives. The Drug-Free Workplace Act covers federal government agencies, federal contractors with contracts or purchase orders totaling $25,000 or more, recipients of federal grants, and any individuals awarded federal contracts. Under the Act, employers must (a) establish an employee drug awareness and education program, (b) publish and provide workers with an antidrug policy statement, and (c) meet other requirements. The DOT's Drug Testing Rules cover employers in the air, rail, trucking, and mass transit industries and employers with operations otherwise covered by DOT. Those rules require the testing of employees in safety-sensitive positions for alcohol and illegal drug use.

Most states have laws that address workplace drug use and drug testing. Many states specifically authorize or regulate employee drug testing. For instance, some states require employers to put their testing program in writing. Other states prohibit disciplinary actions against employees who test positive without a second confirming test, or they require that testing be performed only in state-approved labs. Because states have their own approach to drug-testing issues, employers should carefully review the law in the states in which they operate before they adopt a drug-testing policy.

Q 19: What kind of first-aid equipment do we need to provide in an office environment? Are there any OSHA requirements?

A: OSHA does not currently have specific guidelines on emergency medical care and first aid for office environments. Overall, OSHA requires only that employers ensure medical personnel be readily available for advice and consultation on matters of workplace health. If, however, no medical facility is close to the workplace, then the employer must train persons to perform first-aid functions and must provide necessary first-aid supplies within the workplace. Most employers call emergency medical technicians (EMT) or paramedics for major medical emergencies as they occur, and most provide first-aid supplies for smaller incidents. Another good practice is for employers to provide training opportunities on cardiopulmonary resuscitation (CPR) and first aid for their employees.

Q 20: Should we provide aspirin and other over-the-counter medication in our first-aid supplies or through the HR Department?

A: It is probably better to provide medication through a self-service arrangement. Employers should not prescribe or force medication on employees but simply provide employees with access to medication. Employers should not make any recommendations regarding medication unless they have trained medical personnel to do so. Otherwise, employers who do not know about the interactions of the different medications that an individual may be taking could make a lethal suggestion. Also, it is probably a good practice to have individual dose packages available to inhibit tampering and to advise employees to dispose of any opened packages.

References

Chapter 8. Health, Safety, and Security

Froelich, W., & Cullen, E. (1999). *The Bloodborne Pathogens Standard and applications for human resource professionals.* (White paper no. 61820). [On-line]. Available: <www.shrm.org/whitepapers/documents/61820.asp>. Accessed 5/99.

Occupational Safety and Health Administration (OSHA). (1996). *Occupational exposure to bloodborne pathogens.* Available: OSHA Publications Office; 200 Constitution Avenue, NW, Room N3101; Washington, DC 20210.

CHAPTER 9

INTERNATIONAL HUMAN RESOURCES

Q 1: **Our company is opening an office abroad. What are some good resources for employment laws for different countries?**

> **A:** The following are good resources for information about employment laws in foreign countries.
>
> - **Background notes**. The U.S. Department of State provides country background notes. Those notes list information on geographic entities and international organizations and are updated periodically. Although background notes are not available for all countries, the existing ones are posted free on the Department of State's web site at <www.state.gov/www/background_notes/index.html>.
>
> - **Country profiles**. *Country Profiles* are comprehensive reports from Employment Conditions Abroad (ECA) International for HR managers and expatriates. They contain in-depth background information about the country, including its history, political landscape, and economic background, as well as practical relocation information such as cost and availability of housing, education, and goods and services. The reports are updated annually and are available for 77 countries on a purchase basis. For additional information, contact ECA-Windham, 55 Fifth Avenue, New York, NY 10003; telephone (212) 647-0555; fax (212) 647-0494; or the web site at <www.windhamworld.com>.
>
> - **Doing business in**.... PriceWaterhouseCoopers publishes a series of books on doing business in various countries. You may purchase the publication about just a few countries, or you may purchase the whole series. For additional information contact Publications Department, PriceWaterhouseCoopers, telephone (800) 579-1646 or (212) 596-8000, fax (212) 790-6621, or the web site at <www.pricewaterhousecoopers.com>.
>
> - **Employment law**. *International Labor and Employment Laws*. This publication, by the American Bar Association, Timothy J. Darby and William L. Keller (1997), is available in the SHRMStore at <www.shrm.org/shrmstore> or by calling (800) 444-5006.
>
> - **Web sites**. The following web sites also provide information on the employment laws for different countries:

— <www.shrmglobal.org> (for members of SHRM Global only)

— <www.shrm.org/hrlinks/intl.htm>

— <www.embassyworld.com>

Q 2:   What are the differences among a *local national,* an *expatriate,* a *third-country national,* and an *inpatriate*?

A: The following explains the differences:

- **Local nationals**. Also known as host-country nationals, these employees are hired for jobs in their own country. For example, a United Kingdom citizen who is employed at Coca Cola's U.K. subsidiary is a local national.

- **Expatriates**. U.S. companies have historically defined expatriates as employees who are asked to work outside their home countries for a period of time with the intent of eventually returning to their home countries. Expatriates who are from the country where the company is headquartered are referred to as headquarters expatriates. An expatriate may also be referred to as a parent-country national.

- **Third-country nationals (TCNs)**. These employees are not from the home country or the host country. TCNs have traditionally been technical or professional employees hired for short-term employment and are often considered as international freelance employees.

- **Inpatriates**. These foreign national employees have been transferred to the United States for a lengthy work assignment.

Q 3:   How should we compensate an employee on a foreign assignment?

A: The most common approaches taken by organizations are the *balance sheet* (or buildup system), *negotiation, localization, lump sum,* and *cafeteria* plans. Each plan is best suited to certain situations, and each plan has its advantages and disadvantages:

- **Balance sheet**. This approach is most common. The main emphasis of the balance sheet is to pay an expatriate comparably to incumbents in same or similar positions in the home country. Thus, the expatriate neither gains nor loses from a financial perspective.

  A home-country salary (base salary plus incentives) is determined for the expatriate. Frequently, this salary is determined in the same manner as that for a domestic position, such as by a job evaluation or a competency-based plan, market surveys, merit, and incentives. This salary is then broken into four categories. The categories are taxes, housing, goods and services, and reserve (e.g., savings and discretionary payments).

The employee is required to use his or her salary to pay the typical amount toward each of these four categories. The typical amount reflects consumption patterns in the home country as determined by surveys from various consulting firms. The employer retains any amount under the typical amount and pays for any amount over the typical amount for each of the categories. Organizations often provide a relocation incentive in addition to the salary because certain assignments and locations require more than comparable pay to motivate an employee to take the foreign assignment.

The balance sheet approach is most appropriate for experienced mid- to senior-level expatriates. Its advantages include keeping the expatriate whole with respect to incumbents in the same or similar positions in their home country. In addition, this approach allows for ease of movement between foreign assignments and back to the home country (*repatriation*). Conversely, the balance sheet approach is complex to administer and intrudes into the expatriate's finances.

- **Negotiation**. The advantage of the negotiation approach is that it is conceptually simple. The employer and the expatriate simply find a mutually agreeable package. However, this approach tends to be relatively costly, and it creates comparability problems when an increasing number of expatriates are compensated with the method. Negotiation is most often used for special situations or in organizations with few expatriates.

- **Localization**. This approach involves basing the expatriate's salary on the local (host country's) salaries. It is easy to see that the same position in different countries can have quite different salaries. This approach contrasts to the balance sheet approach. The localization approach also provides for cost-of-living allowances, which can be applied to taxes, housing, and dependents and which is similar to the balance sheet method.

Some advantages of the localization approach include ease of administration and equity with local nationals. Some disadvantages include the usual need for negotiated supplements and pay based on host country economics versus performance and job responsibilities.

- **Lump sum**. This approach uses the home country's system for determining base salary. In addition to the salary, the expatriate is offered a lump sum of money to apply to items that he or she values versus a specific amount for taxes, housing, and so forth. This approach is advantageous because it does not intrude into the expatriate's finances, and the employer does not pay for things the expatriate does not want. A disadvantage to the lump sum approach is the calculation of the lump sum. It can involve a complex and time-consuming analysis. This approach is most often used for 1- to 3-year assignments.

- **Cafeteria**. Senior-level expatriates and those with high total incomes relative to base salary are often compensated by the *cafeteria* method. This approach can be more cost-effective than other methods. The cafeteria method is similar to the lump sum plan, but instead of being provided a single sum of money, the expatriate is offered a selection of options to choose from. Options might include a company car or company-paid tuition for the expatriate's children. There is, however, a limit to choices and amounts.

Q 4:   What are the selection criteria for an international assignment?

A: When filling a position for an overseas assignment, consider using a team approach. The interview team consists of at least three individuals: a manager from the home country, a manager from the host country, and an HR representative. The manager from the home country will be able to act as a sponsor to the individual. The host-country manager will be able to give a perspective of what is required to get the job done and will be aware of what challenges the expatriate may encounter. The HR representative should help the managers through the selection process by educating them about the selection tools available, as well as making sure that they comply with state and federal regulations.

The selection team should follow a couple of steps before the interviews:

- **Define the assignment goals**. If you have broad strategic goals, you will help the expatriate, as well as help the company to get maximum results from the assignment.

- **Evaluate the culture**. Culture shock is one of the main reasons for a failed assignment. By evaluating the culture's demands, differences, and barriers, you will help to determine what the training needs are. In addition, by having this information available, you may cause candidates to withdraw themselves from the selection process.

Once a selection team is in place and it has determined the strategic goals and cultural issues, it can begin the selection process. Because of the extraordinary challenges that an expatriate can encounter, the selection criteria for a successful candidate are more extensive than for a home-country position.

As with any position, job knowledge and personality traits are major factors for a successful assignment. However, experts say that it is impossible to concentrate on one or the other. Because such assignments present a wide variety of challenges, it is impossible to say that one candidate will be more or less successful according to his or her job knowledge or personality. One method to determine the potential success of an expatriate was developed by Michael Tucker of Tucker International (see <www.tuckerintl.com>). According to his Overseas Assignment Inventory, there are 14 predictors of a successful expatriate:

• Expectations	• Patience
• Open-mindedness	• Social adaptability
• Respect for other beliefs	• Initiative
• Trust	• Risk-taking
• Tolerance	• Sense of humor
• Control	• Interpersonal interest
• Flexibility	• Spousal communication

If employees accept an overseas assignment, their family will also be affected. It is essential to assess the family's readiness and willingness to live overseas. It has become a common practice to interview the spouse and children to determine their ability to adapt to a different culture. Here are some issues to consider:

- Is the marriage stable?

- Do the children have any learning disabilities that would affect their ability to adapt to a new culture?

- Does the family have any responsibilities for taking care of other family members?

- Are the children attached to any specific sport or activity that may not be available in the host country?

Although these are very private issues for an employee and an employee's family to reveal to the employer, it is essential that these topics are discussed, because the number one reason for the failure of an assignment is discontent within the family.

Q 5:   What are some resources for cross-cultural training?

A: The following are some resources for cross-cultural training:

Advance International Ltd. (312) 477-1590	Center for Global Assignments (801) 375-1402
Berlitz International, Inc. (800) 528-8908	Clarke Consulting Group, Inc. (415) 591-8100

Cultural Awareness
International
(214) 559-2742

D.C. Associates
(312) 915-6612

The David Eaton Group
(617) 338-8883

Delphi International
(202) 898-0950

Development Dimensional
International
(800) 933-4463

Global Dynamics
(973) 927-9135

Global Leadership Institute
(602) 992-2868

Global Management
(608) 836-0088

Global Management
Development Services
(203) 373-1673

Global Training Associates
(703) 757-0060

Griggs Productions, Inc.
(415) 668-4200

inLingua/Accuworld
(312) 641-0488

The Intercultural
Communication Institute
(509) 297-4622

Intercultural Management
Training & Consulting
(703) 727-0909

Intercultural Training
Resources Inc.
(415) 749-2920

International Counseling
Institute
(212) 265-8480

Japan Intercultural Consulting
(312) 528-1376

The Language Center, Inc.
(412) 261-1101

Language Enterprise
(212) 243-4280

Lawrence Reynolds Associates
(817) 848-4545

Lloyd, Thomas & Ball, Inc.
(202) 244-9445

Martha K. Nelson and
Associates
(901) 754-3155

Multinational Related
Services, Inc.
(313) 354-4080

N.W. Currie & Company
(908) 725-2297

The Odenwald Connection
(972) 496-3902

Options Resource and Career
Center, Inc.
(713) 465-1118

Overseas Training and
Orientation Program
(415) 337-8393

Pacific Area Communicator of Intercultural Affairs (714) 840-3688

Peter Muniz & Company (908) 545-8269

Prudential Relocation Intercultural Services (303) 546-1011

Rapport International (410) 647-5071

Sietar International (202) 466-7883

Terra Cognita (212) 262-5789

Training Management Corporation (609) 951-0525

Transnational Management Associates Ltd. (UK) 44-171-917-2784

Note that inclusion on this list does not imply endorsement by the Society for Human Resource Management.

Q 6: How can a company manage an expatriate employee's performance?

A: Failed international assignments can be extremely costly to an organization. Companies should place great emphasis on the importance of selecting appropriate staff members for international assignments. A consistent and detailed assessment of an expatriate employee's performance, as well as appraisal of the operation as a whole, is critical to the success of an international assignment. Issues such as the criteria and timing of performance reviews, raises, and bonuses should be discussed and agreed on before the employees are selected and placed on international assignments.

Although appraising the performance of an expatriate employee is just as important as appraising the performance of employees hired for domestic assignments, each international assignment is different and unique unto itself. A general rule in appraising expatriate employees is that each international office should use a different appraisal system. Employers should not take a performance appraisal system that was designed for appraising domestic employees and try to modify it for use with expatriate employees because many variables (e.g., environment, task criteria, and personality factors) need to be understood and taken into consideration when assessing an expatriate employee's performance.

Before an expatriate employee departs from the home-base country, the HR Department should work with the managers responsible for expatriate employees to develop a critical professional profile for each employee who is placed on an international assignment. This profile should clearly outline what the company's expectations and productivity standards are in areas such as profitability and operation efficiency.

Although establishing performance criteria is a difficult task because of the many differences in international environments, equitable productivity standards that are applicable to manufacturing and service industries will need to be determined within each foreign subsidiary. Performance criteria and goals are best established by combining the values and norms of each local environment with the home-office's performance standards. An individual country profile should be developed and should take into account the foreign subsidiary's environment. This profile should be used to review any factors that may have an effect on the expatriate employee's performance. Such factors include language, culture, politics, labor relations, economy, government, control, and communication.

Once any underlying factors that may affect an expatriate employee's performance have been determined, the information should be used to group together the organization's multinational subsidiaries into country clusters on the basis of similarities among each country's environmental factors. Critical professional profiles for each expatriate employee should be compared against others within that country cluster to ensure that proper performance measurement criteria are, in fact, being used when appraising individual employees who have been placed on international assignments.

Additional information about managing expatriate performance, as well as other issues involved in international assignments, is available through an organization called the Integrated Resources Group (IRG). This organization has compiled a report titled *Expatriate Adjustment and Performance* (Scott, 1997) that details the anonymous views of 81 experienced American expatriate business managers and executives. The presentations in this report provide unique access to the perceptions of business managers and executives who have served with distinction in expatriate assignments. For additional information on this study, as well as the many other services that IRG provides, visit the web site at <www.expat-repat.com>, or call (915) 676-2290.

Q 7:   How do we handle taxes for expatriates?

A: Companies generally take one of four approaches to handling taxes for their expatriate workers:

- **Laissez-faire**. In this approach, the company is not actively involved in managing U.S. and foreign taxes. Essentially, the employee is responsible for any taxes incurred. However, often the employer increases the expatriate's compensation to cover the additional tax expense.

- **Ad hoc**. In an ad hoc approach, the employer determines tax reimbursement on a case-by-case basis. Essentially, each expatriate employee negotiates his or her own deal with the company. This approach may work when a company's international workforce is small, but as the international program grows, the negotiation process can become cumbersome.

- **Tax protection**. In the tax protection approach, the company figures the expatriate's hypothetical U.S. income tax and compares it with actual taxes paid. At the end of a year, the company reimburses any disparity. If the expatriate pays less in taxes than he or she would have paid in the United States, the expatriate keeps the difference. A disadvantage of this program is that it can create inequities between expatriates in low-tax-cost countries and those in high-tax-cost countries.

- **Tax equalization**. In a tax equalization program, the expatriate's tax situation is neither better nor worse than it would have been in the United States. A hypothetical U.S. tax is withheld from each paycheck. Foreign taxes are either paid by the employer or reimbursed. Although this program ensures equity among expatriates, it requires more administrative resources than the other methods.

Q 8:   Do expatriates receive the same benefits as they would have in their home country?

A: Expatriate benefits usually are not exactly the same as those of U.S. workers. Furthermore, expatriates in different countries usually receive different benefits because of several factors, including different legal requirements, the effect of exchange rates and inflation in different countries, and differences in the quality of benefit coverage available.

Employers should create a written policy that clearly states the goals of the company's expatriate benefit plan. A corporate expatriate benefit policy should include guidelines to aid in developing benefits packages. The benefits level should be determined through a collaboration with local management according to the guidelines set out in the policy.

Q 9:   Do other countries have associations like SHRM?

A: Other countries do have associations similar to SHRM. See resources to assist you in locating those organizations at <www.shrm.org/hrlinks/intl.htm>.

Q 10: How do we find out what visas are required for an expatriate assignment?

A: Entry visa requirements may vary by country. Anyone who intends to enter a foreign county should contact the country's consulate or embassy to receive information on visa requirements. The following is a list of visas that may be required, depending on the nature of business to be conducted in a particular country:

- A work permit authorizes paid employment in a county.

- A work visa authorizes entry into a country to take up paid employment.

- A dependent visa permits a family to accompany or to join an employee in a country of assignment.

- A multiple entry visa permits multiple entries into a country.

To locate information on embassies and consulates from around the world, contact <www.embassyworld.com>.

Q 11: What is typically included in an expatiate relocation package?

A: Employment tax rules do not require employers to withhold federal income taxes or to apply special social security or unemployment taxes to relocation assistance payments. Therefore, the employee reaps the full benefit of covered expenses. A multitude of factors that need to be considered are included in relocation packages.

- The employee's possessions need to be shipped both to the new location and back home at the conclusion of the assignment. Employers need to define the limits of what will be transported—personal boats, automobiles, pianos, pool tables, and so forth. A stance on moving the employee's car, providing assistance in purchasing or leasing another vehicle, or providing a company car will need to be addressed. Once all items have been addressed, the company may need to make arrangements for storage of items that are not shipped.

- When an assignment will run in excess of 5 years or housing may be difficult to locate, companies may provide funding for trips to the new location to locate housing—expenses will include airfare, lodging, meals, and car rental. Often the trip may be combined with a required business trip.

- When the employee is unable to move directly into the new residence, the company, to a reasonable degree, will generally provide for temporary accommodations and meals. Employers should be careful to define what reasonable living expenses will include and to what limit per day.

- The employee will often be leaving a home behind. Where this is the case, employers will frequently provide the option of either guaranteeing the purchase of the employee's home or providing rental management. When the home is going to be sold, the employer should set out the method of assessing the home's value, paying the closing costs, and setting a time frame for the employee to accept the agreement.

Employers generally reimburse expenses affiliated with securing a new place of residence—be it buying or leasing. Again, the employer generally covers the closing costs.

Q 12: What is done to repatriate an employee who is returning from an assignment abroad?

A: Ideally, the repatriation process begins before the expatriate leaves his or her home country and continues throughout the international assignment by addressing the following issues:

- **Career planning.** Many managers are responsible for resolving difficult problems abroad and expect that a well-done job will result in promotion on return, regardless of whether the employer had made such a promise. According to a 1996 Conference Board survey titled *Managing Expatriates' Return* (Gates, 1996), 87% of companies indicated that most international assignments do not result in a promotion on repatriation, though only 49% of respondents said that the potential for promotion was discussed before they accepted the international assignment. This misconception can be avoided by straightforward career planning that should occur in advance of the employee's accepting the international assignment. Employees need to know what impact the expatriate assignment will have on their overall advancement in the home office and that the international assignment logically fits in their career path.

- **Mentoring.** The expatriate should be assigned a home-office mentor. Mentors are responsible for keeping expatriates informed on developments within the company, for keeping the expatriates' names in circulation in the office (to help avoid the "out of sight, out of mind" phenomenon), and for seeing that expatriates are included in important meetings. Mentors can also assist the expatriate in identifying how his or her overseas experience can best be used on return. The best results are achieved when the mentor role is part of the mentor's formal job duties.

- **Communications.** An effective global communication plan will help expatriates feel connected to the home office and will alert them to changes that occur while they are away. The Internet, e-mail, and

Intranets are inexpensive and easy ways to bring expatriates into the loop. In addition to formal e-mail communications, home-office employees should be encouraged to keep in touch with peers on overseas assignments. Employee newsletters that feature global news and expatriate assignments are also encouraged.

- **Home visits**. Most companies provide expatriates with trips home. Although those trips are meant predominantly for personal reasons, scheduling time for the expatriate to visit the home office is an effective method of increasing the expatriate's visibility. Having the expatriate attend a few important meetings or make a presentation on his or her international assignment is also a good way to keep the expatriate informed.

- **Preparation to return home**. The expatriate should receive plenty of advance notice (some experts recommend up to 1 year) of when the international assignment will end. This notice will allow the employee time to prepare the family and to prepare for a new position in the home office. Once the employee is notified of the assignment's end, the HR Department should begin working with the expatriate to identify suitable positions in the home office. The expatriate should provide the HR Department with an updated resumé that reflects the duties of the overseas assignment. The employee's overall career plan should be included in discussions with the HR professional.

- In addition to home leave, it may be necessary for a company to provide trips for the employee to interview with prospective managers. The face-to-face interview will allow the expatriate to elaborate on skills and responsibilities he or she obtained while overseas and will help the prospective manager determine if the employee is a good fit. Finding the right position for the expatriate is crucial to retaining the employee. Repatriates who feel that their new skills and knowledge are underutilized may grow frustrated and leave the employer.

- Ongoing Recognition of Contributions. There are several ways an employer can let the repatriate know that his or her efforts are appreciated, including the following:

  — Hosting a reception for the employee to help him or her reconnect and meet new personnel

  — Soliciting the repatriate's help in preparing other employees for expatriation

  — Asking the repatriate to make a presentation or to prepare a report on his or her overseas assignment

— Including the repatriate on a global task force and asking him or her for a global perspective on business issues

For more information on this topic, consider the following resources:

- *The Art of Coming Home* by Craig Storti (1997). This publication is available at <www.amazon.com> or by calling the Intercultural Press at (800) 370-2665.

- *Managing Expatriates' Return* by Stephen Gates (1996). This resource is available at <www.conference-board.org> or by calling the Conference Board at (800) 872-6273.

- *So You're Coming Home* by J. Stewart Black and Hal Gregersen (1999). This book is available in the SHRMStore at <www.shrm.org/shrmstore> or by calling (800) 444-5006.

Q 13: How much time do employers offer expatriates for home leave? Do employees pay for their plane tickets?

A: According to the RIA Group (1999), companies usually pay for at least one economy class, round-trip airfare per year so that expatriates and their families can return to their home country. Although many companies favor from 4 to 6 weeks of home leave for the expatriate every 2 years, some companies prefer annual or triennial home leaves. Some companies are experimenting to allow expatriates to take home-leave vacation in the destination of their choice instead of requiring that they return to the corporate headquarters or to the expatriate's home country.

Q 14: Can spouses work abroad? What kind of benefits are provided for spouses?

A: One of the deciding factors for expatriate assignees to accept foreign assignments is often the ability of their spouses to find employment abroad. Not all countries allow spouses of immigrants to work in their countries. It is definitely an important issue to discuss and plan with the employee when a career interruption for the spouse might be likely. It is not uncommon for companies to offer the spouse a lump-sum payment for the inconvenience of having his or her career interrupted. If work is allowable, employers often offer assistance in finding positions, although it is quite often difficult to find a position that fits the individual skills and desires of the spouse. Companies are realizing that if they want their employees to be more mobile, more creative and innovative practices for spouse employment will have to be created and used.

Q 15: How should companies prepare employees and their families for assignments abroad?

A: A successful overseas assignment is based on how well employees and their families are prepared for the experience of living overseas. For you to help prepare families for an assignment in a foreign country, here are some issues to consider:

- Before the assignment starts, offer training on the culture of the host country. Include information on the factors that will affect the daily lives of the families.

  — What can they expect to find when they need health care?

  — What sort of housing is available, and how will the company arrange for the moving process?

  — What is the educational system like, and will the children attend local or special schools?

  — What sort of retail establishments are there, and how will fundamental items like groceries be purchased?

  — Is the host country considered a safe place to live, and what security arrangements are made for safety?

The family will feel more comfortable if it knows what to expect on the basics of daily living. Language training would be a great help, and it would also help to build the confidence of family members so that they will be able to function well in the host country.

For spouses who work, decide what, if any, assistance your company can offer to help the spouse adjust to the changes. You could (a) offer education or training, (b) help in finding employment overseas, or (c) help in finding volunteer opportunities. The full support of the employee's spouse is crucial to a successful overseas assignment.

During the assignment, be sure that the employee and family have a mentor or a support system to help them with all of the questions they'll have in the host country. This person should be knowledgeable about the culture of the country and should be willing to offer assistance, as needed. The mentor or support system should be located nearby and is often a function of the HR manager in the host country.

Near the end of the assignment, discuss when repatriation will occur. Offer repatriation counseling, as needed.

References

Chapter 9. International Human Resources

American Bar Association, Darby, T. J., & Keller, W. L. (1997). *International labor and employment laws.* Available: SHRMStore, (800) 444-5006 or <www.shrm.org/shrmstore>.

Black, J. S., & Gregersen, H. (1999). *So you're coming home.* Available: SHRMStore, (800) 444-5006 or <www.shrm.org/shrmstore>.

Gates, S. (1996). *Managing expatriates' return.* Available: The Conference Board, (800) 872-6273 or <www.conference-board.org>.

Price Waterhouse Coopers. (Various). *Doing Business in....* [Series of books for various countries with varied dates]. Available: Publications Department, Price Waterhouse Coopers, (800) 579-1646, (212) 596-8000, fax (212) 790-6621, or <www.pricewaterhousecoopers.com>.

Scott, R. E. (1997). *Expatriate adjustment and performance.* Available: Integrated Resources Group (IRG), (915) 676-2290 or e-mail <irg@expat-repat.com>.

Storti, C. (1997). *The art of coming home.* Available: Intercultural Press, (800) 370-2665 or <www.amazon.com>.